Management Science in Practice

Management Science in Practice

Terry Williams

John Wiley & Sons, Ltd

Copyright © 2008   John Wiley & Sons, Ltd
                     The Atrium, Southern Gate, Chichester,
                     West Sussex PO19 8SQ, England
                     Telephone +44 (0) 1243 779777

Email (for orders and customer service enquiries): cs-books@wiley.co.uk
Visit our Home Page on www.wiley.com

Other Wiley Editorial Offices

John Wiley & Sons Inc., 111 River Street, Hoboken, NJ 07030, USA

Jossey-Bass, 989 Market Street, San Francisco, CA 94103-1741, USA

Wiley-VCH Verlag GmbH, Boschstr. 12, D-69469 Weinheim, Germany

John Wiley & Sons Australia Ltd, 42 McDougall Street, Milton, Queensland 4064, Australia

John Wiley & Sons (Asia) Pte Ltd, 2 Clementi Loop #02-01, Jin Xing Distripark, Singapore
129809

John Wiley & Sons Canada Ltd, 6045 Freemont Blvd, Mississauga, ONT, L5R 4J3

Wiley also publishes its books in a variety of electronic formats. Some content that appears in
print may not be available in electronic books.

Library of Congress Cataloging-in-Publication Data

Williams, Terry.
    Management science in practice / Terry Williams.
        p. cm.
    Includes bibliographical references and index.
    ISBN 978-0-470-02664-9 (pbk.)
    1. Operations research. 2. Management science. I. Title.
    T57.6.W639 2008
    658.4′034 – dc22

                                    2008011003

A catalogue record for this book is available from the British Library

ISBN: 978-0-470-02664-9

Typeset by SNP Best-set Typesetter Ltd., Hong Kong
Printed and bound in Great Britain by TJ International, Padstow, Cornwall

Contents

Part IV: Practice

About This Book

This book is about what it means to be a professional Management Scientist. It is written for those studying Management Science, for those practising Management Science, or simply for those who are interested and want to know more about the subject – what it means and how it is practised. ("Operational Research" – also called "Operations Research" outside Europe – as we'll see in the book refers to roughly the same subject.)

The book is divided into four parts. The first part looks at just what *is* Management Science. That's not an easy question to answer, although both the Operational Research Society in the UK and the equivalent US society, INFORMS, make a start by having the following statement on their websites: "In a nutshell, operational research (O.R.) is the discipline of applying advanced analytical methods to help make better decisions" (www.orsoc.org.uk and www.scienceofbetter.org./). Much of Chapter 1 will therefore be spent looking at what Management Science is, and at the sort of problems that Management Scientists try to tackle. These are rather different now to the sort of problems the discipline tackled when it started over half a century ago – we're now having to look at more "messy" problems and having to take more account of the social, organizational and political "soft" issues as well as the more easily quantifiable "hard" physical issues. Because of the changing nature of the problems we investigate, and the changing nature of our role in advising management, modern Management Science requires particular styles of interventions into problems by Management Scientists. Chapter 2 will therefore look at different styles of how Management Science approaches clients and problems. These two chapters form Part I.

Part II of the book looks at the toolbox of techniques we might use – not describing the individual techniques (as that would require a small textbook on each technique, and no doubt we'd miss many out), but rather describing a framework for how problems are structured and how solution techniques are selected, so that you can feel equipped with the knowledge of what tools are available. Following on from our discussion in Part I of the "messiness" of real-life problem situations, Chapter 3 first discusses how you can approach practical problems and bring structure to them. Management Scientists will often need to adopt a multi-methodology approach because real-life problems are complicated and "messy", so some of these approaches are described in the next chapter. Then the following chapter gives a taxonomy of techniques to enable the reader to understand what the techniques are about, how they relate to each other, and when they might be used. The book won't tell you everything you need to know about these techniques, but will hopefully give you an idea of what is in the Management Scientist's toolbox.

There is almost no mathematical content in the book, even though much of it is describing work that we do that does use mathematics. This isn't to downplay the need for the well-rounded Management Scientist to be able to express his or her models in mathematical terms and manipulate those models – it is simply that, if we gave examples of all of this work, the book would be twice as long. It does, however, try to give a little of the flavour. The book aims to complement the "techniques" that are often taught, and aims to describe what you need to become a well-rounded, professional Management Scientist. Besides, the Management Scientist doesn't need to be an expert mathematician anyway – the key to this aspect of Management Science is conceptual: it is to be able to take a structured description of a real-world problem and express it in mathematical terms.

Part III is a pragmatic part, and describes some practical skills necessary as part of the practice of Management Science as we approach these newer problems. Chapters cover the proposal stage of an intervention, issues about data, what is "appropriate" modelling, creativity in modelling, and a number of other practical skills. These are not individual chapters with separate points, but they flow from the idea of Management Science praxis that we started building up in Chapter 1 and continue to develop in the later chapters. They try to begin to describe the making of a well-rounded Management Science professional.

Part IV then takes this further by taking a broader look at the profession and what it means to be a professional Management Scientist. We look at Management Science Groups in practice and what makes them "successful" (or not!), and then look at how we practise: what an ethical practice is and the idea of "Reflective Practice", which we shall see follows on from the issues we started discussing in Part I of the book.

Thus we'll have gone full circle, with a line of argument that flows from the complexity of the problems with which we, as professional Management Scientists, are faced today. This means that the book does have a definitive viewpoint, which is set out initially during the first few pages of Chapter 1 and then expounded throughout the book, trying to present practical Management Science, grounded in the real world rather than the imaginary "play" models that are sometimes presented as Operational Research. The book is written from the UK – and this is perhaps a particularly UK stance on Management Science – but it appears to the author to be the type of Management Science that can be particularly effective in making a difference to its client groups universally, and the book tries to make the presentation applicable internationally.

I hope you find this book instructive and entertaining. Above all, I hope it helps you to reflect on your work as a Management Scientist, or Operational Researcher, and develop your work to make a better contribution to practice.

Terry Williams

Part I
Management Science

1

What Is Management Science?

1.1 Introduction to Management Science

What is Management Science (or a closely linked term, as we said at the start, "Operational Research" – or "Operations Research" outside Europe)? Well, that is a difficult question, and one that we'll spend this chapter investigating. As we said in our introduction, we can start with the beginning of the definition that appears both on the website of the Operational Research Society in the UK (www.orsoc.org.uk) and on the website set up by the American Operational Research/Management Science organization INFORMS, which is devoted to looking at what OR is and how it can help (www.scienceofbetter.org./). This says: "In a nutshell, operations research (O.R.) is the discipline of applying advanced analytical methods to help make better decisions" (INFORMS, 2006). So, Management Science/Operational Research is aimed at those who have to make decisions, or understand situations better, in industry, commerce, government, defence – in a whole multitude of arenas. And it uses a panoply of analytical methods to better understand those decisions or situations in order to help those decision-makers.

Operational Research, as it was originally known, has been around under that name for over 60 years. An excellent history of the field by Kirby and

Capey (later extended into a major work (Kirby, 2002)) begins: "At the end of the Second World War, operational researchers could congratulate themselves on their substantial and, on occasion, decisive contributions to the allied war effort in a number of theatres. In the North Atlantic, for example, they had assisted in the defeat of the U-boat weapon by devising, inter alia, optimal convoy tactics, the most effective settings for depth charges, and efficient servicing schedules for long-range aircraft . . ." (Kirby & Capey, 1998). These successes led to OR (as it became abbreviated) being taken up enthusiastically by many organizations, most notably in the UK by the National Coal Board and organizations within the iron and steel industry, where it scored major successes in its ability to analyse complicated problems and both facilitate rational decision-making and enable increases in efficiency to be made. This era saw the birth of the subject as a postgraduate degree in various universities, and a gradual move thereafter into undergraduate education.

As management in the 1970s looked to put their organizations on a more "scientific" footing (Locke, 1981) and the abilities of scientific computing (which Operational Research could build upon to substantially increase its power) increased exponentially, the scope for Operational Research could have been expected to have increased dramatically. But the subject faced a dilemma, and to some extent a division, the effects of which can still be seen today. The field of Operational Research, as originally interpreted – using mathematical and analytical techniques to solve well-defined problems, based on concrete measurable entities – continued, and is alive and well, particularly in the US (as "Operations Research"). But many practitioners saw that the real problems that they wanted to solve were less well-defined, and included variables and entities that could not be easily defined and measured unambiguously, and issues that needed wider exploration. That is not to say the subject split, but there were clearly different directions for the subject. (Some would call the latter practitioners "Management Scientists", considering that "Operational Research" tends to have a more mathematical flavour than "Management Science". However, as is often the case in these types of issues, there is no agreement on these labels, and many commentators would not recognize this distinction. INFORMS, to which we have referred previously, was actually formed from a merger between the Operations Research Society of America (ORSA) and The Institute for Management Sciences (TIMS) (also based in the US), but the motivation for setting up TIMS, although partly founded on the subject areas that might not flourish within ORSA, was also based on the perceived predominance of military work and membership policies of ORSA (Lathrop, 1957).)

The problems with the Operational Research approach were most famously espoused in two papers by Russ Ackoff. In the first (Ackoff, 1979a), he declared that the underlying paradigm of current Operational Research, which he termed "predict and prepare", was not suitable for modern organizations, which do not simply passively respond to the environment but actively engage with it – and this is a topic we'll return to over the first two chapters of this book. But the attempt by mathematicians to model these messy situations was "equated by managers to mathematical masturbation and to the absence of any substantive knowledge or understanding of organizations, institutions or their management". In his second paper (Ackoff, 1979b), he gave his proposals for the future of OR. He talked about making Operational Research participative and "based on planning with people, not for them" (taken from Pidd's (2001) summary, where he explains how this echoes Mintzberg's later analysis of big corporate planning exercises that are left unimplemented, and also a major critique of what came to be called in the mid-twentieth century "scientific management" or "Taylorism", that of separating planning from action). Again, we'll come back to this, particularly in Chapter 2. But Ackoff also explained how this would require a change in Operational Research practice and education, from applying mathematical techniques in a vacuum to a practice in which "understanding how people worked in organizations was fundamental. Thus mathematics becomes the servant rather than the master."

This led to a reawakening of Operational Research, particularly in the UK, as it came to grapple with the nature of the situations within which it was now being asked to intervene. One of the important influences in the UK was Eden, who a few years after Ackoff's paper explained that "although our heritage is the 'application of science', it is a narrow vision of science which has dominated the profession . . . it has largely been the application of applied mathematics, statistics, and computer sciences. Thus, while the definition of OR in the UK is not narrow, the practice has proven to be so" (Eden, 1982). Repeating Ackoff's quote above, he continues: "The emphasis on this particular sort of science has meant that the profession has recruited predominantly from disciplines that characteristically attract convergent, rather than divergent, thinkers. A reinforcement of the profession is thus made up of those who believe in a form of objectivity that is a poor match for the realities of organizational life" (Eden, 1982). A defining moment of this reawakening came as the UK Operational Research Society set up a Commission to look into the practice and future of Operational Research (reported in Mitchell, 1986), which described OR practice with significant amounts of structuring messy problems, and "little explicit use of those mathematical techniques which are most commonly associated with OR (for example, mathematical programming and queuing theory). These and the insights they offer, along with many other technical devices, help constitute a tool-kit from which the practitioner may draw as need dictates. . . . Better tools may give better results, allow more jobs to be done and save on tedious work, but they seem to affect underlying methodology only slightly. Methods are renewed and extended but the essential methodology persists. The main methodological drive, as inferred by the Commission, is pragmatism. . . . [The means used] usually entail working closely with the client or his client, and almost continuous negotiation, stage by stage, of how the work should be moving."

Here I must, as author, declare my bias, and the bias in this book. I was trained as a mathematician and then as a traditional Operational Researcher in the 1970s in one of the first Operational Research Master's courses in the UK. And I firmly believe that mathematics, separate from the analysis of "real" social systems, has an important role in certain isolated areas. But for the main role of Management Science, that of taking real-world practical situations and using our analytical and modelling skills to bring greater understanding and better decision-making, mathematics divorced from reality is not helpful. The best exposition of the path that I have been on I think is summed up in one of my favourite books, *The Glass Bead Game* by Hermann Hesse, which was first published in 1943 (see Hesse, 2000). This book described an almost magical game: "All the insights, noble thoughts, and works of art that the human race has produced in its creative eras, all that subsequent periods of scholarly study have reduced to concepts and converted into intellectual property – on all this immense body of intellectual values the Glass Bead Game player plays like the organist on an organ." This wonderful game was attractive and satisfying, just as the mathematics of Operational Research can be to the experienced exponent. Indeed, in the Glass Bead Game, "Mathematicians in particular played it with a virtuosity and formal strictness at once athletic and ascetic. It afforded them a pleasure which somewhat compensated for their renunciation of worldly pleasures and ambitions." The game is almost weirdly like the attempt by Operational Researchers/Management Scientists to capture phenomena in analytical form, as Hesse describes: "Men like Abelard, Leibniz, and Hegel unquestionably were familiar with the dream of capturing the university of the intellect in concentric systems, and pairing the living beauty of thought and art with the magical expressiveness of the exact sciences." The people who played this game mostly "lived in a state of political innocence and naïveté such as had been quite common among the professors of earlier ages". They did not let the issues of "real-life" get in the way of their game, much like some modern-day Operational Research professors. But the hero of *The Glass Bead Game*, who rises to become the *Magister Ludi* – the most expert and most important player of the game – by the latter stages of the book comes to see that the whole point of such learning is to apply it in the real world and to bring useful benefit to the world. In *The Glass Bead Game*, this meant leaving the mountain where the game-players lived and moving into the world to become a humble teacher. For Management Scientists, the same understanding means that we must sacrifice beautiful, neat mathematical treatises for work that is practical and makes a difference to the world. (A colleague who read through the draft of this book pointed out that the hero of *The Glass Bead Game* dies after his first intervention in the real world – being useful in the world might not be the most comfortable path!)

When a group from a major business school in Europe, INSEAD, looked at the practice and literature of OR in 1993 (Corbett & van Wassenhove 1993), they concluded that the OR community and the management community didn't take much notice of each other's literature; OR tools were being used, but there was an expanding gap between OR publications, which were mainly theoretically orientated, and management publications addressing real practical needs (something I as an editor of a leading OR journal have been trying to change!). To take just one instance, the field of project management is one where there is a whole literature of complex mathematical works purporting to model "real" situations, but whose analysis is virtually never used or applied in actual real cases (Williams, 2003). So, Operational Research/Management Science is truly "the beautiful game" but it needs to bring benefit and use to the world, not just indulge in self-gratification (to take Ackoff's distinctive metaphor). And it is to avoid being tarred with this latter brush that this book takes the stance of the Management Scientist rather than that of the Operational Researchers – albeit these actual terms are fairly interchangeable nowadays.

This book is about "real world" Management Science: modelling situations we find in practice and trying to bring rationality and analysis rather than simply "nice" intellectually satisfying models.

1.2 The nature of problems

So, what are the problems that the Management Scientist investigates? The word "problem" here is surprisingly difficult to define. Mitchell (1983) has a go at this by saying that "The word 'problem' is used to describe many situations in which an individual finds himself. These situations have three common threads.

(i)   The individual is dissatisfied, or surprised, by what is happening. He might believe that his circumstances must be capable of improvement, or his understanding is at fault, or rules or beliefs which he has held inviolate are changing.
(ii) The individual believes he can and/or should respond, by action or by revising some or all of his beliefs.
(iii) The individual does not find it obvious what action he should take, or even if any is available, or how he should revise his beliefs.

These features of problems are subjective. They suppose that an individual perceives some normal state for himself which satisfies him and offers no surprises. . . ."

This certainly does define a problem situation, to which we can relate in our everyday life: we wish to change our job, or we need to work out the best airline routes to book, or the best ways to manage our finances. But (as Mitchell does go on to explain) the organizational problems with which Management Scientists deal are not as simple as that. And, indeed, the very word "problem" (with its associated assumptions that we can "solve" a problem and then we've finished) does not fully describe what it is that Management Scientists face in their work. The classic description of the various types of concepts in the area of problems was given, for example, in Pidd's (2003) illustration shown in Figure 1.1, which leans heavily on Ackoff's (1974, 1979a, 1979b) pioneering work. In this, the top axis is taken to be three points on a spectrum.

At the left-hand end of the spectrum are "puzzles". In these, there is no ambiguity about the formulation of what needs to be solved; the issues and options are clear, and the answer is unarguably the correct one. These require logical thought, and sometimes aren't easy to solve, but are not the domain in which we want to model. We come across such "puzzles" frequently: the popular

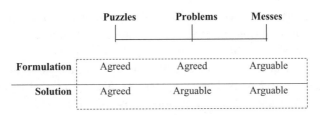

Figure 1.1 Puzzles, problems and messes. From Pidd. Copyright 2004 John Wiley & Sons Limited. Reproduced with permission.

"Sudoku" game would be an example, but so would many examination questions given to undergraduate students.

The nature of the real world is such that puzzles can only be hypothetical – in reality, issues and options are never perfectly clear. But as clarity decreases while we move along to the right-hand end of Pidd's spectrum, there is a range of real-life situations. In the mid-point of the spectrum comes what Pidd simply calls "problems", epitomized by the well-defined OR problems that were tackled in the 1960s. Here the formulation of the problem is usually pretty well agreed, but there are a variety of approaches to solving it. Pidd takes the seemingly straightforward question "how many depots do we need in order to provide daily replenishment of stock in all our supermarkets?", and then goes on to show how even this seemingly innocuous and unambiguous question can itself be questioned, and various aspects explored. Experience shows that two analysts will rarely have the same approach, although many approaches *may* tend towards similar answers. But, essentially, "problems" were what the Operational Research world started tackling, and where some mathematicians have got stuck. And many of these are important: "How do we schedule our railways?"; "how do we optimize loading of ship-containers so that we use the minimum number of containers?"; "how much stock should we order?" But such well-defined questions are fairly rare; and frequently, when they do arise, they arise only as the mid-point after the analyst has undertaken considerable problem structuring.

As OR proved adept at tackling a range of problems, it was faced with the requirement to tackle the many situations in which there is a lot of ambiguity, no agreement about the issues, or about concept relationships, or about what is going on, or whether a solution exists at all. These situations are termed "messes" by Ackoff. These are the sort of situations into which Management Scientists are often called, where the definition of the problem itself is not clear or agreed upon, let alone how to approach it. In such situations, an analyst cannot move straight in with his/her toolbox of mathematical tools and start modelling – the situation must be defined, structured, agreed and made amenable to analysis (Pidd talks about "taming" the messes). This is the "mess" – and the competencies needed to tackle such messes are quite different from the divergent problem-solving competencies needed to tackle well-defined traditional Operational Research problems. But these are the situations Management Scientists generally face: "it's all a mess – why?", or, "it's all going wrong – what should we do?", or "what are our options, and how do we choose?", or "I think I know what the problem is but the CEO thinks it's something entirely different".

This last phrase captures a further reason why our "messes" are so "messy" – the sort of situations into which Management Scientists are called usually involve groups of participants, indeed sometimes groups of decision-makers. If a problem for an individual, as defined by Mitchell above, is centred on an individual's beliefs, or rules or perceptions, then in a group – which is likely to have different objectives, beliefs, rules, or maybe even perceptions – then clearly the issues are going to be compounded. This was at the heart of Operational Research's identity problems in the late 1970s/early 1980s we discussed earlier: as Eden and Sims (1979) put it: "There is a major difference in emphasis between discussion within the profession and the behaviour of the OR consultant working within a social organization. In the first instance we see, within textbooks, journals, project reports, proceedings of conferences, an attention to the problem – its characteristics, structure, content – that is to say our attention is directed to an objective reality, a system of interacting variables that as a consequence of manipulation could be made to behave differently. The description of the problem is implicitly contained by the form of the model which is used for its solution; a solution is discovered (usually through mathematical/numerical manipulation) which will enable the system to operate in a preferred manner. . . . However, when we study what is going on in the process of behaving as a consultant we see a part of OR practice which we apparently feel unable to discuss, reflect upon, or theorize about. We see a complicated drama unfold which involves power, influence, negotiation, game playing, organization politics, complex social relationships with real people not merely office holders. In this environment problems are not self-evident at all; under the guise of the same problem title each actor sees a reality which is unique to him, that which comes to be known as the *real* problem for the consultant depends then upon his *own* reality and that belonging to those actors to whom he chooses to listen."

Because of this effect of the organization on our approach, some have taken up the simple classification given by Roth and Senge (1996). They take firstly the underlying complexity of the problem situation itself, which they call "dynamic complexity". More specifically, they say that dynamic complexity characterizes the extent to which the relationship between cause and the resulting effects are distant in time and space. This mirrors Simon (1982), who says that a complex system is essentially "one made up of a large number of parts that interact in a non-simple way. In such systems the whole is more than the sum of the parts, not in an ultimate, metaphysical sense but in the important pragmatic sense that, given the properties of the parts and the laws of interaction, it is not a trivial matter to infer the properties of the whole." But as well as this, Roth and Senge (1996) also take the complexity of the group effect, which they call "behavioural complexity": "Behavioural complexity characterizes the extent to which there is diversity in the aspirations, mental models, and values of decision makers." In political situations with high behavioural complexity they suggest as an example Jews and Palestinians in Gaza; as an example of low behavioural complexity they suggest a group of financial analysts solving a technical problem. They then propose a simple matrix as shown in Figure 1.2.

As we have seen, "tame problems" can be treated by ordinary, traditional Operational Research methods. "Wicked problems" are those where "complex underlying social realities are inescapable, and different groups of key decision-makers hold different assumptions, values and beliefs which are in opposition to each other." Messes we have already defined. Roth and Senge (1996) go on to say: "The research traditions that deal with behavioural complexity . . . and dynamic complexity . . . have remained largely separate. What

		Dynamic complexity	
		Low	High
Behavioural complexity	Low	Tame problems	Messes
	High	Wicked problems	Wicked Messes

Figure 1.2 Types of problem. From Roth and Senge. *Journal of Organizational Change Management* 9, Issue 1, page 92-106, Copyright 1996 Emerald Group Publishing Limited all rights reserved. Reproduced with permission

befuddles organizational decision making is that the two coexist and interact in what we have termed 'wicked messes' – needing new research methods and new synthesizing of the old methods." This is the area in which Management Scientists often find themselves, and the area we shall consider as we go through this book.

As we have moved away from treating tamer problems to dealing with wicked messes, Operational Research / Management Science has had to change also. One of the key texts in describing this movement is Rosenhead and Mingers (2001). They describe "traditional Operational Research" as dealing with the following:

- A single problem, which can be formulated with a single objective.
- A single person who has to weight the situation and make a decision about the problem: the "decision-maker". That decision-maker has objectives that could be defined. Furthermore, we could regard concrete decisions coming from that decision-maker through a chain of command to the workforce, who would carry out these actions.
- The problem is clear and unarguable, and we could assume consensus about what the problem was.
- Decisions are to be made based on these abstract objectives and then actioned; people in the analysis can be regarded simply as passive objects.
- Finally, they say that the aim of the analysis was to minimize or even abolish uncertainty about the future and as far as possible pre-take future decisions, to map out the future path.

The modern "alternative paradigm", with which they say we need to approach problems, recognizes:

- that there is a search for alternative solutions acceptable to a number of participants on separate dimensions, rather than a single all-purpose optimization;
- that the analysis and models are simple and transparent in order to be comprehended and therefore bought-into by the various participants;
- that the analysis needs to (both pragmatically and ethically) conceptualize people as active subjects;
- that the analysis needs to facilitate planning from the bottom up as well as, or instead of, from the top down; and, finally
- that we need to accept uncertainty, the aim of the analysis being to keep options open.

Now this argument covers a whole gamut of issues, but we can see the issues of multiple views of the problem and reality, and the need to deal with groups of decision-makers, with models that are transparent so as to keep them "on side" or "bought in". More of these issues will arise during the course of this book.

> This book will cover "messy" situations, in which not only is it unclear how to solve "the problem" but also it is not clear what "the problem" is. Since these problems are situated in real human situations, they will often be "wicked messes", in which perceptions, values, assumptions, even the underlying understanding or "reality" vary between the stakeholders.

1.3 The Management Science approach

If 'What is Management Science?' is a question that has not been answered satisfactorily, even more so does the question "What is the Management Science approach?" not have a uniformly agreed answer. Different authors give different answers (again with Operational Research and Management Science put together).

- Some answers are technique-based: "Management Science uses mathematical and computer techniques" or "Management Science uses mathematical techniques such as linear programming". And it is true – some Management Science does use such techniques, and we'll have a look at many of these techniques in Chapter 5. But this does not define the heart of Management Science.
- Some answers define the Management Science approach in terms of other approaches: "Management Science uses the System Analysis approach" or even "Management Science uses the scientific approach" – the former being too restrictive, and neither being helpful to tell us what this approach is.
- Some define Management Science in terms of quantification: "Management Science measures things"; "Management Science looks to optimize systems". Again, this is often the case, and Chapter 7 will look at issues of measurement and quantification. But there is Management Science that structures and does not quantify; and there is Management Science

that explains but does not offer solutions, let alone "optimum" solutions.

Mitchell (1983) comes down to the most inclusive definition that he can: Operational Research/Management Science "may be broadly defined as an activity which seeks: (a) to help groups (or individuals) to solve their problems (b) by using methods that would enjoy consensus support among scientists."

Underlying all of our work is the idea that we aim to apply the "Scientific method". This is an ill-defined term, but it is generally based on seeking an objective process (to avoid bias) by which empirical measurement data are collected to support, refute or help develop hypotheses about how the world operates. So, in many ways, this is our starting-point. Mitchell (1983) points to methods used by scientists that are clearly applicable to Management Scientists: using the rules of logic or mathematics to draw conclusions; checking beliefs or results for mutual validity; and so on. So the metaphor he comes out with is of Management Science as the intersection of two cultures: the culture of the problem domain (i.e. Management) and the culture of Science from which the analyst draws his/her methods – and s/he needs to understand both cultures.

But, following this definition, there are elements that seem to be agreed to come within the Management Science process:

- the need to structure the problem (or situation, or area);
- building some analytical framework of the issues, which is generally termed a model (this idea seems to be key, so we'll discuss it next);
- the need to collect data and measure, bringing the model into line with the "real world";
- a dialogue throughout with the "client" or "problem owner" (which very occasionally might be the same person as the analyst, but these are generally expected to be distinct).

We'll look at what a "model" is first, then we'll move onto where it fits into the Management Science process.

Pidd (1995) identifies six pictures or metaphors of Operational Research – the differences being to some extent the assumptions about the world upon which they are based. Two, *decision mathematics* and *optimization in social systems*

– similar to our third bullet point above – regard the underlying nature of our situations as non-problematic; his next two, *problem solving* and *management science* (defined in a more narrow sense) look further at the organization but still largely see this as a well-defined machine, and so fit into the picture above. But the final two perspectives, *systems perspectives* and *intervention and change*, start to look at issues of alternative perspectives of reality, the roles of the participants, and the nature of Management Science interventions. Therefore, we'll go on to look at these issues as we move through the final section of this chapter and Chapter 2.

1.4 What is a "model"?

At an intuitive level, modellers know what a model is – but it is surprisingly difficult to come up with an all-encompassing definition that tells us what is the essence of "a model", suitable for all types of Management Science models. A good start is always the dictionary. The Collins English Dictionary (1986) tells us that a model is "a simplified representation or description of a system or complex entity, especially one designed to facilitate calculations and predictions". This definition tells us that:

- a model *represents* or *describes* something real;
- a model *simplifies* that real entity;
- the production of a model has a *purpose*, generally to make some sort of calculations or predict how the entity will behave.

The first two aspects are our starting point: our models take something in the "real world", simplify it and attempt to represent or describe it. Now the term "the real world" needs some further consideration (as even this idea is not unproblematic), as does the word "simplify". But let's look first at the idea of "representing" or "describing" the world. Can anything that represents or describes the "real" world be termed a model in the Management Science sense of the word? We are all familiar with one popular form of representing the real world – that is, a painting or photograph. Does this constitute a model? Intuitively, management scientists would think that it doesn't, but why not? The answer to this question actually lies in the third point – the purpose of the model. A painting represents a single, static, representation of reality, which, having been created, is not changeable. As a contrast, we want to *manipulate* a model to tell us something useful, such as to explore alternative realities or to explain why the differences between these realities occur. This is because a model not only defines parts or conceptual elements of the whole, but must also define the *relationships* between the concepts.

Since we wish to manipulate these definitions, they must be *formal, theoretically based* definitions of reality that can be manipulated. This means that the "language" of the model will need to be as consistent, unambiguous and precise as possible. This often means using some form of mathematics rather than the English language, which tends to be inconsistent, ambiguous and imprecise. But we are not limiting ourselves to mathematical models, and indeed many of our quantitative mathematical models will be developed from qualitative models expressed in "English" terms – but in formalized formats so that the concepts are made as consistent, unambiguous and precise as we can make them and the relationship structures (for example, causal relationships) between these concepts are expressed.

Figure 1.3 shows an example of the most straightforward type of modelling, where we take something in the "real" world and express it in mathematical terms, and manipulate that model to gain some extra understanding. This is one of the oldest "Operational Research" type of models, dating back to Harris in 1913, although its development is normally credited to Wilson (1934). The example begs a lot of questions and makes unspoken assumptions – it is definitely *not* planned to give an idea of what real-life Management Science is like – but it is provided here to give a flavour of what a "mathematical model" means to any reader who may not have come across the idea before. It aims to illustrate how to approach a structured situation, take the concepts we have defined and express them as mathematical terms.

But we must have a vision for the scope of modelling. Those who see simple equations as the only sort of "model" will have a very jaundiced view of what modelling can do for them. In contrast, Management Scientists would say that modelling can be used – indeed must be used – to represent the whole breadth of reality as we see it (subject to various caveats below and in Chapter 8), and although one technique may be more useful than another, modelling must be available to model any aspect of our project.

So, let us say that we have an explicit representation of "the real world" – what is this "real world"? Traditional Operational Research at its most

Economic Order Quantity

Shop X sells 2 400 boxes per year of a product. Customers come along continuously through the year and buy from the stock of the product kept in Shop X's warehouse. Every so often, therefore, Shop X has to replenish its stock from the supplier. It is expensive putting in an order: Shop X estimates that it costs a total of £320 a year in clerical costs for processing the order and shipping costs to obtain the stock. So it seems sensible to put in only a few, large orders a year. But it's also expensive keeping the product in stock: Shop X estimates that it costs around 24% of the cost of product to keep it in stock for a year – in interest charges on the capital tied up (the product costs the Shop £40 per box) and storage costs (as well as breakages, pilfering, insurance etc.) That suggests it is sensible to put in lots of small orders a year. So, how many times per year should the Shop put in an order?

Let's build a model. Let's first look at all of the aspects in this description that we might need in our model, and represent them by a mathematical variable. It doesn't matter what you call them, but we'll use the some of letters traditionally used in this problems. Let's denote:

the size of the batch we order each time by	Q	(boxes)
the cost to Shop X for ordering each year	B	(£/year)
the cost to Shop X for holding stock each year	H	(£/year)
the total cost to Shop X each year	T	(£/year)

So, how do we calculate these costs? Well, the cost to the shop for ordering each year we know is £320 for each order. The shop is going to order 2 400 boxes a year in batches of size Q, so there must be 2 400/Q orders each year. The cost of ordering each year will therefore be:

$$B = 320 \times (2\,400/Q)$$

If we wanted to calculate the total cost of holding stock, we must think about how much stock is held during the year – and here we must start to make some assumptions. We don't actually know how

Figure 1.3 A mathematical modelling assignment: the "economic order quantity"

variable the demand is (nor for that matter how variable delivery times are), so we don't know how much so-called "safety stock" the Shop will hold. If they're very risk averse, they might still be holding a lot of stock when a new batch comes in. For the purposes of this example, we'll put that question to one side and *assume* that demand is regular and continuous, and that new batches come in just as the stock empties out. Thus the stock will start at size Q and gradually decrease to zero, then be replenished up to Q, gradually decrease, and so on. The *average* stock held is therefore $Q/2$. The cost per box per year of holding stock is 24% of £24. And so the cost of holding stock:

H = (average amount of stock held) × (cost per box per year of holding stock)
  = $(Q/2) \times (0.24 \times 40)$

The total cost is then simply:

$T = B + H = 320 \times (2\,400/Q) + (Q/2) \times (0.24 \times 40) = 768\,000/Q + 4.8 \times Q$

We can now plot a graph of how the total cost varies as the batch size varies:

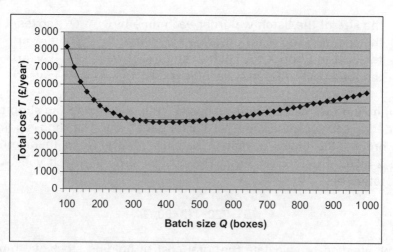

And this – or using calculus – will give the least cost when the batch size is $Q = 400$ boxes.

Figure 1.3 *Continued*

simplistic viewed the world as an absolute reality, which the modeller sought to represent. However, in practice the modeller gains much of his/her knowledge about the reality s/he is seeking to model through human actors who will each have their own world-views (or *Weltanschauung*). So first we may find ourselves modelling an individual subject's *perceptions* of the real world rather than the reality itself, and then we will be working with groups with perhaps inconsistent or even incompatible views of "reality" – and we shall need to discuss what we mean by "real" at all. We'll return to this area in a few pages, but it is worth noting that some would argue that models should not even try to be representations of reality, but simply inventions for debate.

The second bullet point on page 15 said that a model is a *simplified* representation of reality. This is a necessary fact of life – we cannot reproduce reality exactly in a finite period of time. This is not a disadvantage of modelling but indeed one of its most powerful advantages: that we seek to abstract the key elements of reality to provide us with the information we need. This enables us to analyse the model and come to some simplified conclusions about the real world which would be impossible to come to if we had to deal with all the richness, complexity and detail of the real world. Although perhaps not a model in our sense of the word (since it cannot really be manipulated), think of a metro map (an example taken from Pidd, 2003): this is a simplified view of reality – as in reality stations are not spread neatly around, nor are the lines straight, nor are the railway lines single lines in gaudy colours – but the map provides its readers with the information they need to travel on the railway. And, indeed, a precise map of the railway lines with all of the detail of crossing-points, branch-lines and differing depths, with all the lines coloured accurately (i.e. all a similar metallic colour!) would be totally useless for the purpose. So we're back again with our third bullet point: the degree of simplification that we impose on reality to produce our representation depends crucially on the purpose for which we are building the model. Again, this will recur later in the book, particularly in Chapter 8.

So, if the *purpose* of the modelling is so key, for what sort of "purposes" might we be modelling? This takes us back to the first few sections of the book – it might be to help a decision-maker to make a better decision, or help a manager control a system more effectively, or increase understanding in a system or a situation; any of the purposes we have discussed above.

Let's summarize all of the above in a definition that might not be perfect, but will be a start:

> A model represents or describes perceptions of a real situation, simplified, using a formal, theoretically based language of concepts and their relationships (that enables manipulation of these entities), in order to facilitate management, control, understanding or some other manipulation of that situation.

We've left some considerations of what "reality" is, which we'll come to in a few pages. And even on this simple view, there are many other important things that constitute a *good* model – this just looks at what a model is – but we'll leave those to Chapter 8, where we'll look at a much more structured definition of different types of model using various dimensions of model characteristics.

1.5   The Management Science process

So, modelling enables the analyst to build a representation of the real world that s/he can manipulate in place of manipulating the real situation. Indeed, some take this idea so far as to "allow modellers to create computer-based learning environments (or microworlds)" – in that case "for policymakers to 'play with' their knowledge of business and social systems and to debate policy and strategy change" (Sterman, 1988). A traditional view of Management Science looked to modelling a real situation and using that to come up with a "solution" or "answer" or "new understanding", which could then be fed back to the "real world" – that is, something like Figure 1.4.

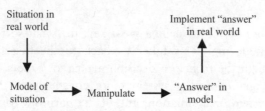

Figure 1.4 Traditional use of modelling

However, as we've been discussing, the types of situation in which Management Scientists have become involved have changed. Furthermore, the old social ideas that "problems" are best left in the hands of the "experts" who will come up with the "best solution" have declined, making the type of relationship where the analyst takes away a problem and comes back with a report now unsustainable. Problems are not objective entities we can point to, and give to the "experts" to solve: problems are subjective constructs, that are only problems as participants and observers perceive them. With our greater understanding of the client–consultant relationship, we shall be seeing in Chapter 2 that we have continuously to be discussing the situation with the client group, trying to model their understanding and negotiating what the "problem" actually is. Thus what we will be describing in this book is much more like Figure 1.5.

Thus we will describe continual iterations of the client-interaction process, in which we have to negotiate the definition of the problem with the client, and continue to analyse and build models in constant dialogue with the client. This modelling relationship in which we need to structure the problem, build models and collect data can be expanded in Figure 1.6.

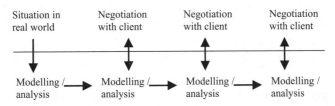

Figure 1.5 More current view of modelling

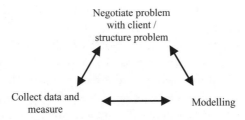

Figure 1.6 Modelling in the Management Science process

In Chapter 2 we will discuss in more detail what a Management Science "intervention" into a situation really means. But it is worth noting two points here first.

Firstly, the end of the process in Figure 1.5 is not nice and clean as it is in Figure 1.4. Indeed, as we'll see in Chapter 2, the whole idea that a "problem" is "solved" and then the Management Science work is complete is unhelpful to the analyst and confuses the process. Eden (1987), for example, says that the idea of "problem-finishing" is much more helpful than "problem-solving" – a problem can be finished in various ways, such as on reaching a "satisficing" solution (where the client "feels that it is obvious what must be done"), or the client might begin to feel equipped to manage the problem on their own, or the problem might be dissolved in that it has been redefined and no longer exists in its original form. This will be important in Chapter 2 as we consider what a "successful" Management Science intervention is.

Secondly, we will be considering an intervention into a complex decision situation to help decision-makers. We can differentiate this from a lot of Operational Research work, which can bring a lot of benefits by solving problems that are important in that they are repeated many times. For example, if you were to look at what are considered to be the best pieces of Operational Research work in the US, such as those that win the US IFORMS Edelmann prize (an annual prize, described for 2004 in Spencer and Graves (2005)), you will find that all of them (except one) describe an ongoing process, with regular incremental decisions, for which the task of the Operational Research group was to supply a "decision-support system" to enable these decisions to be taken, including a user-friendly computer program. Thus, typical of this work is scheduling containers in a terminal, or planning production, or scheduling rolling-stock. These are really "problems", in the sense we discussed above, and the skill of this work is in developing good, effective, fast algorithms. In virtually none of this work are the wider views of decision-makers described, as each individual decision is very small – the impact on the company comes as many thousands of such decisions are automated and optimized. This is not to deny the great worth of this work in solving problems – it is simply a different situation to the position in which Management Scientists generally find themselves, and which we will address in this book. (The one exception, incidentally, was described in Butler *et al.* (2005) and was, again, building a user-friendly decision-support system, but this time in support of looking at alternatives to reduce plutonium – effectively a one-off decision.

Here, the view of all stakeholders is considered and the paper looks at the rationality of their decision-making and at the surrounding decision issues and political factors – a paper following the sort of Management Science we will describe.)

1.6 What is "true"?

Before we explore in more detail how Management Scientists intervene into a situation, we do need to consider some underlying philosophy. Now, you might be surprised that we need to include philosophy in a book about "science", but experience shows that we do come across issues within modern Management Science practice (which, of course, deals with social and management structures and phenomena) that will lead us astray if we haven't thought through these questions beforehand.

There isn't scope within this book to give a full exposition of all the philosophical stances that have been taken towards research and consultancy within management. That would take a whole book – and, indeed, an excellent book has already been published (Johnson and Duberley, 2000) which does analyse the main management research philosophical standpoints; a quick introduction to some of the issues can be found in Chapter 3 of Easterby-Smith, Thorpe and Lowe (1991). Besides, the point of this section is not to lay out a completely philosophical foundation – it is to identify those areas where we as Management Science practitioners can come unstuck, and to give some of the background to what people have thought of these issues.

Essentially, the questions that arise come in two interrelated areas. The first area is ontology, or what is "real". Johnson and Duberley (2000) describe a spectrum of beliefs, from

- a "realist" or "objectivist" ontology, which assumes that a reality (including a physical, natural and social reality) exists independently of us, the observers – a reality exists whether or not human beings can actually cognitively perceive it, to
- a "subjectivist" ontology, which assumes that what we perceive (and thus assume is an external reality, again physical, natural and social) is merely a creation of our consciousness or our cognition.

The second area is epistemology: how we know what is "true". Again, Johnson and Duberley (2000) describe a spectrum of standpoints from the objectivist epistemology, which assumes that we can study the external world objectively, to a subjectivist epistemology, which assumes that this is impossible. (This doesn't mean there is a division between two opposed viewpoints; rather that there is a spectrum of emphases or views (Reed, 1985).)

Following on from these two fundamental questions is the issue of how we view interventions into organizations. However, we'll begin by looking at these first two issues – what views have been taken, and why does it matter to us as practitioners?

After describing all of the standpoints and how they developed, Johnson and Duberley (2000) give a diagram (which is reproduced in Figure 1.7) showing how the standpoints are positioned on these two fundamental dimensions.

Positivism underlies the scientific tradition, and can be traced through many major figures in the history of science: through Descartes (whose championed rationalism, and said that true knowledge could only be gained through an individual rationally looking at an external reality), Locke (who championed empiricism) and Hume (who championed empiricism and analysis of causality). But the key exponent of the idea of positivism is clearly Auguste Comte (1853), who saw true knowledge as only coming from that which is "positively

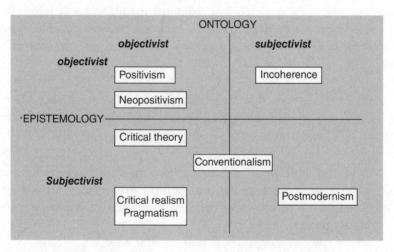

Figure 1.7 Main philosophical positions. From Johnson and Duberley. Copyright 2000 SAGE Publications. Reproduced with permission

given" – that is, which is directly available from the senses, making the assumption that the world outside the observer really exists in an objective sense, and that to find out about the world you should use objective observation and measurement methods.

A major move forward in positivist thinking came particularly from a group of intellectuals in Vienna in the 1930s, sometimes called the "Vienna Circle", who developed positivism into what we now would call "logical positivism". Taking Comte's view stated above, along with the claim that observation of the real world can be neutral and value-free, they would want to test empirically any theoretical statement or postulated theoretical mechanism – and any explanation for the world that cannot be empirically tested, cannot be sustained.

Positivist thinking took a further step forward with the well-known work of Popper (1959), who disagreed with inductive means of generating knowledge (i.e. collecting data, and inferring theories and laws from the data, particularly the causal relationships within that data) and laid the basis for deduction and falsification of theories (i.e. the idea that while the scientific method cannot prove a theory, by showing empirical data which disagrees with the theory, it can disprove it). Popper's work has been very influential in the social sciences, but we can now perhaps see two strains of positivist thinking: one inductive and one deductive.

What does this mean for our practice as Management Scientists? Positivism forms the basis for what most natural scientists see as "the scientific method"; in many senses it gives the foundations from whence Operational Research sprang. From positivist thought springs a number of implications about the way we carry out our analysis:

- observers who are independent from what they observe, and carry out their observation objectively and without influence from internal values or interests;
- the search for causality in the behaviour of the systems we study;
- the aim to operationalize the concepts we study so that they can be conceptualized and then measured quantitatively;
- the need to look at large samples, or repeat experiments many times, to be able to generalize about what we observe;
- we derive knowledge using the "hypothetico-deductive" methods – that is, by hypothesizing general laws and then deducing the types of empirical

experiment that will falsify (or demonstrate the truth of, if using the inductive method) these laws.

> Positivism gives the basis for Management Science work, and is a standard against which we will often be measured. Thus our starting-point should be as objective, independent observers, seeking operationalizable concepts and looking for causality to demonstrate "scientifically" and objectively results that can be relied upon.

So, why do we need go any further than positivism and the "scientific method". Well, as we look very briefly through some of the other philosophical traditions in Figure 1.7, we shall see that there are issues that arise where we have to modify our practice – life isn't always as simple as the positivist world would imply.

The first issue, which we can only look at briefly, focuses on the idealistic view of the independent, value-free observer, looking at a system with a completely scientific open-minded view (the first implication of the positivist viewpoint above). The ideas of conventionalism stem from the work of Immanuel Kant (2003), particularly the *Critique of Pure Reason* first published in 1781. His argument was that "pure reason" claimed access to knowledge of the real world beyond what it is possible for human observers to have: we cannot know the world as it is, only as we perceive it through our cognitive or mental structures; we come to view the world not with empty minds, but with minds that shape the way we perceive the world. Conventionalists will say that we cannot escape from the socialization to which we are all subject, and the pre-understandings that come from that socialization, so we cannot know the extent to which our mental structures have shaped the reality we observe (indeed, some would ask whether there is such a reality, or whether what we take to be an external social world is simply a creation of our consciousness – in other words, some conventionalists would take a subjectivist ontology, which we'll return to below).

But again, what does this mean for our practice as Management Scientists? Whatever your views about conventionalism as it comes to scientific research about the natural world, as we come to study the social world of management, it is clear that we come with pre-suppositions and assumptions that colour our observation.

More than this, as we come to collect data, which is key to our process in Figure 1.6, we need to consider what those data are: even when we believe we are collecting data on a "real" phenomenon (i.e. we have an objectivist ontology), often we are not collecting "real" data but someone's perception of that data, so our observation of the world is coloured not only by our mental processes but also those of the subject from whom we're collecting data. For example, if we were modelling the progress of a project (using the "Earned Value" method), one requirement would be to identify the progress on each sub-task of the project, which could involve measuring some physical progress (if it was, say, laying down a path, which could be measured), but might involve asking the participants how far through an activity they were (if, say, it was a systems engineering design task), which will elicit an entirely subjective response ("Oh, I think I'm around 75% of the way through").

And, of course, if this is true for apparently "real" data, there is a whole spectrum of data from the "real" to the clearly subjective. For example, suppose we are to investigate getting the best new production plan for a large factory ready. Some of our data will be physical: how big is the factory? how fast can our materials be moved? As we move to questions such as how many of each product will we sell, we can approach that using quantitative "hard" calculations of past performance, but that must be coloured by subjective beliefs about the future; if we ask what is the probability that new technology will overtake the products that we sell and make them obsolete, that is clearly a piece of "data" that is positioned firmly within the subjective and the social. If we move further to considering what is important to the future of our business – what does "best" mean in our assignment – then we are considering values that have no real physical realization but are socially constructed.

As we use such data, we need to be aware of the status of the data (i.e. how subjective it is) and the colouring that might have occurred both from any human data-provider as well as within us as data-collector. So, in our practice, the following are two clear modifications we must make to our positivist stance.

We are observing human systems, and so many of the data we collect are filtered through human perceptions. We need to be clear about the extent to which these data are objectively reliable and the effects those perceptions might have had.

> We ourselves are not value-free, independent observers: we must identify wherever possible our own *a priori* understandings and bear them in mind both as we analyse what we observe and as we make claims to the knowledge we generate.

Like Kant, Habermas (1972, as well as many other publications) rejected the idea of a neutral observer, which ignores the effect of the knower upon that which the knower is seeking to know, but he went further in placing the contamination of the "ideal" neutral observer within the social and cultural framework within which the observer sits. His work thus tries to take account of the power and dominating relationships that there are within all human relationships, and clearly within management situations. One particular focus is on communication: in his theory of communicative rationality (Habermas, 1984), he claims that it is the communicative structure which shows us where decision-making will be found, pointing out that where communication is dominated by sincere communicative speech acts (discourse unfettered by the coercive use of power) there will be good exchange of rationality (while, on the other hand, where power is being used to limit free communication, there might be failures in decision-making). From his work and other similar writers grew the ideas of "Critical Theory", which is particularly concerned with the effect of socially and historically constituted power relations on thought, and is closely related to considerations of privilege and oppression (more details are given in Mingers, 1992).

While this clearly opens up huge avenues of important epistemological and ethical debate (the latter returning in Chapter 12), we will limit ourselves here to a simple statement of an implication for our Management Science practice – although we will explore this more in the coming chapters. All study of management involves study of groups of humans, who will be placed within historical and current social structures.

> As we study management issues, we must be aware of the social and power relationships within the groups, and the effect that they will have on our perceptions and our ability to gather "true" data. This is true of all data, but most obviously for data that are a representation of social factors such as values and group views. This also affects the relationship between the analyst and those being analysed, and the effect of their power relationship must also be examined.

Critical Theory, or Habermas at least, still retains a realist or objectivist ontology. And surely, as Management Scientists, wouldn't we hold onto that ontology even if we have epistemological doubts? Well, if we turn to postmodernism, and the work of one particular author, Foucault, we do see some elements that are important to our analysis. Postmodernism is notoriously difficult to pin down, so we shall here restrict ourselves to a brief summary of some of Foucault (1980). The key idea within much of Foucault's work is the idea of a "discourse", which has become a widely used concept in the social sciences. Discourses are a "set of ideas and practices which condition our ways of relating to and acting upon particular phenomena: a discourse will be expressed in all that can be thought, written or said about a particular topic, which by constituting the phenomenon in a particular way influences behaviour" (Johnson and Duberley, 2000).

We can observe such effects in the management world in particular: by defining a particular way of looking at management issues, we therefore define how that issue is thought about and thus limit what is done or even thought. One example might be project management: as soon as an enterprise is entitled a "project", this defines how people within the project will be able to think about the enterprise; according to Hodgson (2002), although the proponents of project management claim its toolkit to be "universal and politically neutral", enforcement of project management terminology leads to an imposed ontology and specific way of thinking in a company, and he uses Foucauldian analysis to suggest that these claims "serve to establish significant power effects within organizations". In Hodgson (2004), he says: "The key effect of the application of project management models and techniques is enhanced control over the conduct of employees, based on close surveillance and the limited delegation of discretion to those subjects involved in project work. In particular, the quantification and detailed planning involved in project management serves to 'enhance the "calculability" of individuals through developing measures of routine predictability and control' (quoting Metcalfe)" (also incidentally showing a Habermas-ian interest in the power relationships involved). "Critical authors . . . [focus] on who is included in and who is excluded from the decision-making process, analysing what determines the position, agendas and *power* of different participants, and how these different agendas are combined and resolved in the process by which *decisions* are arrived at" (Cicmil and Hodgson, 2006). Fournier and Grey (2000) give three tenets of critical work, one of which is that it "aims to prevent oppression/exploitation" (typically exploitation of employees, women, ethnic minorities or the environment) (quoted in Cicmil and Hodgson, 2006). Some authors leaning towards a Marxist view have also argued against the false objectivity of Operational Research/Management Science and claimed that (traditional) Operational Research suppresses dialogue and works in favour of those in power, denying agreement by consensus (see e.g. Rosenhead and Thunhurst, 1982).

Again, what are the implications for our Management Science practice? Firstly, there is the point of power.

> As we study decision-making processes, we need to be aware of the underlying power structures and the effect on the situation under study.

We have also said that when we try to analyse a "real" situation, the ways we define our problems and approaches can themselves change that "reality" and, to that extent, our objective reality is only real insofar as we have defined it – hence, at least a nod towards a subjectivist ontology.

> As we study management, our formalizations themselves can change or even define the "reality" we are seeking to analyse, and such effects need to be recognized and action taken.

There is a further implication of these points for our modelling. We have already said that models represent or describe perceptions of a real situation – but some phenomonologists, such as Checkland, whose work will look at in Chapter 3, would argue that models are not actually representations of reality but simply inventions for discussion, and Figure 3.2 shows how "models" form part of the debate about how to proceed. Certainly, we shouldn't give our models a status of reality beyond that which they actually possess – as we will discuss in Chapter 12 when we look at the so-called Barabba's (1994) law ("Never say the model says"), this can be a real problem in how our work is used and viewed. The role of models in our practice – about which Checkland has been very influential – needs careful consideration, and this will come up throughout this book.

> Models are constructions that we use in our work – they are not the reality!

This has been an extremely brief gallop through centuries of philosophical thought, but has already made some points that will affect our practice. A pragmatic approach to praxis will need to be based on a certain degree of realism and objectivism in ontology and a certain degree of objectivism in epistemology; however, the expert Management Scientist will be wise enough to understand the limitations of an objectivist approach and take cognizance of the issues we have highlighted above, and their implications, which we will explore in the coming chapters.

Our views of these two fundamental questions – how we regard ontology and epistemology – will influence how we view interventions into organizations and how we regard the knowledge we can or should gather within our interventions. This will be covered in the following chapters, particularly Chapter 2.

If the reader is looking for the explicit methodology underlying this book, and has expected that to be expounded in this chapter, s/he will have been disappointed. The stance taken in this book is that there usually *cannot* be a single methodology – or, indeed, a single paradigm – to approach the work. Successful Management Science often needs to take a multi-methodological and multi-paradigmatic approach, viewing the world "through different lenses". Some might feel that we can't mix up apparently incompatible paradigms, but a pragmatic view is that this is often beneficial and sometimes even inescapable. This is a matter we will return to in Chapter 4.

1.7 Conclusion and going forward

In this chapter, we've sketched out the basis for exploring how to carry out Management Science. We've described the sort of problems with which today's Management Scientists get involved – messy, having regard to social and "soft" issues as well has "hard" physical issues. We've described the idea of intervening in management situations, with that intervention centred on an analytical approach using modelling as the distinctive feature of the Management Science approach. We've talked about some difficult philosophical issues, which are necessary as we take a critical view of management situations and need to have confidence in what we conclude.

But how do we carry out this work? The remaining chapter in Part I will discuss what a Management Science intervention is, and effective ways of interacting with the problem situation. Then, Part II will look at the toolbox of techniques we might use. Part III will describe some practical skills necessary as part of the Management Scientist practice. And finally, Part IV will continue this discussion with a wider look at what it means to practise Management Science.

2

Management Science
Interventions

We've seen what modern Management Science is about. And we have laid down some of the basic ideas with which we need to view the world. But how does Management Science go about its business? How do Management Science practitioners actually go into a problem situation and contribute usefully? To look at this, we'll need to consider first the environment within which Management Science practitioners work (based on the ideas in Chapter 1), then the way we perceive "problems", and this will show us some of the modes in which we can engage with a problem. The remaining sections of this chapter will look at issues that follow on from this argument: recognizing stakeholders in the problem; defining "success" in looking at problems; and so on.

Management Scientists engage with a situation either on their own or as a member of a team. And they can be external consultants, or function internally, giving advice within the organization ("in-house"). These, of course, are different ways of interacting with a client group, but this chapter will deal with the principles of Management Science interventions. Chapters 6, 11 and 12 will mention aspects that can differentiate these different ways of intervening – but the principles remain as we shall discuss them here.

2.1 The environment in which we work

In order to be able to advise organizations on their decisions and their decision-making processes, we need to understand the context in which decision-makers make their decisions.

Traditionally, Management Science has set out to support rational decision-makers make the "best" decision – and, indeed, this is true of traditional economics as well. However, this ideal of the supremely rational decision-maker does not exist. Our clients are human beings, which means that at the best their rationality is "bounded". The idea of "bounded rationality" appears in the writings of the Nobel prize-winner Simon (1972), who saw that people are limited in the extent to which they can make a fully rational decision for a number of reasons. The first and main reason is that they do not have complete information about the present and have uncertainty about the future, and so cannot make a fully informed, rational decision. Secondly, they will also have limits in the extent to which they can solve complex problems. Thus people have to make choices that are "good enough" (or that are "satisficing"). (Isenberg's (1991) well-known "How senior managers think" also illustrates the inherent boundedness of decision-makers' rationality and the intuitive aspects of decision-making.) Furthermore, managers' decision-making is affected by cognitive biases including hindsight (Barnes, 1984), overconfidence (or "expert bias"), ideology, perhaps even self-interest. Some of these we'll revisit in Chapter 7 (such as the work of Kahnemann and Tversky, for which the former received the Nobel Prize, Tversky no longer being alive at that time) – although we should recognize that more recent work, such as that by Gigerenzer *et al.* (2000), has shown how good humans are at developing "smart heuristics" to make good decisions in the circumstances of not being able to gather full knowledge. van der Heijden's well-known book about scenarios (van der Heijden *et al.*, 2002) discusses the psychological context, thinking flaws, and the impact that these have for managers as they consider the future (or decisions). It includes a chapter on "culture and cultural assumptions", which will be relevant in our consideration both within the formal organization and also as we consider the "social geography" (or informal social interactions) of an organization. And this is all before we consider any emotional element in people's decision-making!

The philosophical basis we have established in Chapter 1 gives us more to think about. We have pointed to ontological and epistemological stances that question the "reality" of the real world and the knowledge by which we understand that world. Writers such as Schutz and Luckmann (1974) and Cooper and Burrell (1989) start from the premise that knowledge is socially constructed, so that understandings of the organization and of the world will, firstly, differ from person to person and between parts of the organization, as individuals each construct the reality for themselves. But "socially constructed" says much more than this – it says that individuals within an organization participate together in the creation of their perceived reality, and to understand this we need to see how the social group together construct and institutionalize the elements of their social reality. Furthermore, that construction is often influenced by sometimes apparently extraneous considerations. This means that, rather than coming into a problem situation to investigate what is "real", we must to a considerable extent go in to investigate what is perceived or thought to be real by the participants, individually and as a social group – as this to some extent *is* the reality we have to investigate.

This leads on to the question about what an organization "knows". Polanyi (1962) established the idea of an individual's knowledge being internal and personal, or "tacit" and thus not necessarily easy to codify (as opposed to "explicit" knowledge, which can be expressed and shared in highly specified formats). Subsequent work on how people learn and what personal knowledge means is based on his seminal work. And what individuals "know" and what the organization "knows" are intrinsically bound up together: "All learning takes place inside individual human heads; an organization learns in only two ways: (a) by the learning of its members, or (b) by ingesting new members who have knowledge the organization didn't previously have. But . . . what an individual learns in an organization is very much dependent on what is already known to (or believed by) other members of the organization and what kinds of information are present in the organizational environment" (Simon, 1991). The idea of tacit and explicit knowledge led Nonaka and Takeuchi (1995) to develop their "SECI" model, which represented the creation of knowledge in an organization as a continuous process of transfers between tacit and explicit knowledge, as there is *socialization* (sharing tacit knowledge), *externalization* (making tacit knowledge explicit), *combination* (combining different people's explicit knowledge) and *internalization* (of explicit knowledge to tacit).

We also need to consider the influences within groups of decision-makers. Groups by their very existence condition decision-making and where strong structures exist and where strong power gradients exist between members of the organization, it might well be that decision-making becomes apparently less "rational". Perhaps the simplest example of this is what is known as "Groupthink", which is when the individuals within a group conform in their thinking with what they think is the group consensus – even to the extent of allowing the group to make decisions which each individual member might consider to be irrational. Janis' (1973) original use of the term was for conscious Groupthink, where a cohesive group strives for unanimity, although more modern uses of the term can also relate to the effect of powerful individuals in the group. And we've already discussed Habermas' ideas of "communicative rationality", which indicates the effect of the coercive use of power on the exchange of rationality; power can also be used to limit free communication and thus reduce the effectiveness of decision-making (see Noorderhaven, 1995, for example).

This all means that the ways that management thinking and decision-making proceeds within an organization is often not clear – some have even talked about it as "muddling through" (a term coined by Lindblom, 1959). "There is considerable agreement that conventional, universal statements of what management is about and what management does – planning, organizing, coordinating and controlling – do not tell us very much about organizational reality, which is often messy, ambiguous, fragmented and political in nature" (Alvesson & Deetz, 2000, quoted in Cicmil & Hodgson, 2006). But we do need to try to understand this decision-making process – otherwise, how can we influence it? And if our analysis work is at odds with the perception, rationality or decision-making process of our client organization, it will be in danger of being ignored.

One particular author, Nutt, has carried out a lot of research into how decision-making actually operates at the top of organizations. One study that is useful for us is given in Nutt (1998), which looks at how senior decision-makers (the so-called "C-suite" – CEOs and COOs and the like) evaluate alternatives. He defined four different approaches for assessing different types of data. Looking at the sort of advice in which Management Scientists get involved in providing, a tactic based on conclusions drawn from quantitatively manipulating data in records was used in a fifth of the sample, and a tactic based on conclusions found by quantitatively manipulating data extracted from field-tests was used in a tenth of the sample. These two tactics had very good results when the success rates of the decisions and the adoption of the decisions were tested, suggesting that our sort of advice can be well-received if the client group is approached in the right way. A seventh of the decisions had no justification at all! The best result seemed to be for a tactic based on conclusions drawn from qualitatively considering performance features found in data records and prioritizing alternatives, based on formal consensus-building or bargaining between stakeholders (so, clearly the inter-stakeholder effects we're considering are of vital importance in defining the problem); then, considerations of multiple alternatives or multiple criteria encouraged analytic-based evaluations. Hence there is scope for Management Science advice to help decision-makers, if we understand the way they make decisions and also the types of decision they are taking.

One area that we must consider, which is clearly a key influence on how decisions are made (and which Nutt included in his analysis above), is the politics of the organization – actions within an organization by individuals or groups of individuals (sanctioned or not) to influence others (Furnham, 1999). Our discussion of Habermas from Chapter 1 is useful here in helping us understand how and why these effects occur, and planning our interaction with a client needs to comprehend these influences. Often, though, patterns of political behaviour are routine, "even ritual in character" (Heiss, 1981), without reflection or even consciousness. People know implicitly what to expect from themselves and of one another in particular circumstances, in an implicit set of rules. So, as we look at the development of strategies of decision-making within an organization, and seek to influence that by our analysis providing "rationality" to the process, we will need to remember how decisions develop as the outcome of processes of bargaining and negotiation among interest groups, internal or external, some more powerful than others (Buchanan & Boddy, 1992).

The model of a rational consultant bringing objective analysis to bear in isolation from this decision-making process is clearly absurd. "Formal analysis and social interactive processes in organizations must be viewed as being closely intertwined rather than as mutually incompatible. . . . Formal analysis studies are carried out within specific social contexts involving different people linked together in hierarchical relationships," says Langley (1989). Indeed, she emphasizes that the very reasons for carrying out analysis are embedded within the social processes, and need to be identified as part of the analysis, be they for gaining information, communicating, direction, justification, understanding, and so on.

Before we can help an organization make decisions, we must understand how an organization makes decisions. This means understanding individuals and their bounded rationality; and also understanding the groups, with the group dynamics and political and social effects involved.

2.2 Defining "problems"

So, what are the implications of this environment on how we perceive the "problems" we are called to investigate? You will recall that we said in Chapter 1 that, although "problems", in Pidd's terminology, are nice and neat and can be treated by traditional Operational Research methods, in practice we are called on to look at various sorts of "messes". Chapter 1 identified that as one dimension of complexity in the problem – as we move from "tame problems" to "messes", in Roth and Senge's terminology, we get more complex and hard-to-define problem-situations.

However, our discussion in Chapter 1 about the nature of reality in human systems, as well as the discussion of the environment within which decision-makers sit, show that "messes" – or even "problems" – cannot simply be defined and then "solved". Even when we are assuming that there is just one "problem owner", we will have to negotiate with the client about what the problem is: how he or she sees reality; where s/he sees problems occurring; where the mismatch is between what the problem owner wants or thinks is a desirable future, and what s/he sees as the current reality or the likely future (and what is the effect of their mental models and what effect does their bounded rationality have). If we have been called in to look at a problem, we know that the client has perceived some issue – in the list provided by Mitchell in Chapter 1, the individual is dissatisfied with or surprised by what is happening; believes s/he can and/or should respond, by action or by revising some or all of his or her beliefs, and does not find it obvious what action s/he should take, or even if any is available, or how s/he should revise his or her beliefs. But to understand what we've been called in to look into, this implies that we must investigate and reflect upon both the position or situation of the client (which our discussion of ontology implies will be to some extent socially constructed) and also the ways in which the client's desired state differs from that position or situation, or the nature of the dissatisfaction or surprise (which by definition is subjective), even before we can start to apply analysis to consider how to alleviate the situation. And that is not a one-way investigation: we do not simply take a situation and then solve it, but our intervention "takes the form of a reflective conversation with the situation," in the words of Schön (1983) – the practitioner must then "impose an order of his own, jumping rather than falling into his transaction with the situation". This is quite a different way of approaching problems than the simple traditional approach, to which we'll return particularly in Chapter 13.

But usually there is not one single decision-maker; and even if there is, s/he is rarely in a human system consisting solely of him- or herself. This was the second dimension of complexity identified in Chapter 1 by Roth and Senge: "wicked problems" and even more so "wicked messes" are those real-world situations which show those characteristics we've just discussed in the section on the Management Science environment. The complexity in the underlying problem is overlaid – and sometimes dwarfed – by issues of different stakeholders having different perceptions of "reality", different understandings of "the problem", different assumptions, different values, different objectives, and so on.

This means that, as described in Eden and Sims' (1979) seminal paper, "when we study what is going on in the process of behaving as a consultant . . . we see a complicated drama unfold which involves power, influence, negotiation, game playing, organization politics, complex social relationships with real people, not merely office holders. In this environment problems are not self-evident at all: under the guise of the same problem title each actor sees a reality which is unique to him, that which comes to be known as the *real* problem for the consultant depends then upon his *own* reality and that belonging to those actors to whom he chooses to listen." Participants see different elements of the reality; they each form unique mental models to understand that reality; they interpret events and actions according to their own mental models; they perceive problems according to how they construct the world within their mental frameworks; they are influenced by various cognitive effects as well as the social power and political relationship structure within which they sit. Even more than that, as Eden and Sims go on to describe, the way a participant presents his or her perception of the problem "will be influenced by the way he wishes to present himself to [the] team" – for example, "if he wants them to think of him as competent, he is unlikely to present a problem in such a way that it could imply he has acted incompetently, even if this were his private belief about the genesis of the problem."

It is not enough therefore simply to talk about identifying and solving problems within organizations. The "problems" in which we are called to intervene are decision situations in which each stakeholder perceives both the reality of the situation, their interpretation of that reality, and their own objectives differently – and then proceed to express those perceptions in ways that will not accurately reflect their own perceptions. This means that the analyst needs to immerse him- or herself in the problem-situation and try to look at it through the minds of the participants. This means that in order to define "the problem" that the analyst is to solve, a negotiation process needs to be undertaken with a disparate group of participants to try to gain some agreement about reality, about the issues and the objectives. This implies that the path of this negotiation will reflect different participants' perceptions to a greater or lesser degree, reflecting (for example) the different levels of power, interest, credibility, difference between expressions and perceptions, the various aspects of social geography, and so on. (This isn't unique to Management Scientists, and in Chapter 13 we'll refer to an influential book entitled *The Reflective Practitioner* by Schön (1983), who describes practitioners such as architects and psychoanalysts in a similar way.) Dealing with the *process* of our intervention is not separate from dealing with the *content*: rather, "there is an intimate relationship between process management – understanding power, politics and personalities – and content management – capturing, structuring and analysing" (Eden & Ackermann, 1998).

In passing, it is worth noting that there has been increasing attention paid in recent years to these issues of complexity within the problems we are looking at, some of this coming under the heading of "complexity theory". It is clear that to model situations where the behaviour of client groups has a critical effect, simple models are insufficient – particularly simple linear models. Work firstly in physical systems showed how small events can have increasingly large effects (Lorenz's famous so-called "butterfly effect", often cited as a butterfly flapping its wings on one side of the world causing a hurricane on the other side of the world) and how patterns can develop from apparently chaotic systems. Similar work by Prigogine and others led to work in self-organizing systems, in which the underlying causality and feedback loops create complex emergent behaviour patterns. Early work in the consideration of human systems, particularly in the field of cybernetics and the work of Stafford Beer (1959, 1966), showed that such systems had three characteristics: complexity, probabilistic behaviour and self-regulation, and used modelling to show how such systems behave. As the work in the physical systems was used to inform study of human systems, we get initially to the ideas of "complex adaptive systems", which are self-organizing but can learn and adapt (e.g. McMillan, 2004). But, as we have been discussing, human systems involve systems of interrelationships, and so this work has been developed into a field of study led by Stacey (Stacey 2001, 2003, amongst others) under the title of "Complex Responsive Processes of Relating". This looks at the complex systems of human relationships as the humans communicate, negotiate power, status and politics, and work in joint action towards overlapping goals. These relationships form part of (and are influenced by) the wider organizational system. Organization emerges from these human complex responsive processes of relating, and also the individual's self-identity is influenced by them. While there is not the scope within this book to explore these ideas fully, this work describes very important effects that we need to take into our thinking as we look at organizational decision-making situations, particularly recognizing the complexity underlying the client organization, and the emergent properties that result from that complexity.

> To engage with a problem-situation, we must focus on the participants and the problem setting as much as the problem – which means concentrating on the process of engaging with the participants, and the joint client-group/ consultant issue-definition process as much as on the content of the problem.

In practice, this activity of negotiating "the problem" that the analyst is to solve with the client group does not come to a final resting place but is generally a continuing process. One key implication we will see from this is that, since the definition of the "problem" is under continual negotiation, the problem is rarely "solved", as tame problems (or indeed puzzles) can be. Our natural desire as analysts (or at least as Western analysts (Eden, 1987)) is to see a problem completed and set aside – or, at least, in Ackoff and Emery's (1972) words, a problem can be dissolved, resolved or solved. But this move to the new type of Management Science led to an emphasis particularly espoused by Eden (1987) on *problem-finishing*. This emphasis looks at managing meaning and sense in the negotiation process, turning the emphasis from being solely on the problem-situation to being on (or at least also on) the problem-participants. And this implies a much closer attention to the *process*: "to pay attention to problem-finishing is to pay equal attention to process management issues *as well as* content issues" (Eden, 1987). We'll look at some ways of doing this more formally in the next chapter (such as Checkland's work). And crucially, in Chapter 13, we'll look at how reflection on the process we follow and the development of our personal involvement will be an important part of our development as analysts.

> We do not necessarily "solve" a problem. We can finish a problem in various ways, such as when we have reached a "satisficing" point or the client's understanding of the situation has sufficiently increased so that s/he or they are ready to move forward.

So, how does this engagement with the participants take place? What strategies can we employ as we go about such "interventions"?

2.3   Modes of engagement

There are a variety of modes in which the Management Scientist can intervene in a problem-situation – some of which will depend on the type of decision we are trying to help, or problem-situation in which we are trying to intervene. Looking at Nutt (1993) again, he saw four types of formulation processes that organizations used in decision-making, which he called "idea" (ideas ultimately used that are available at the outset), "issue" (issues uncovered and used to identify solutions), "objective-directed" (objectives used to guide development) and "reframing" (a demonstration of needs or opportunities). Clearly we need to gear the style of advice we offer to the type of decision being made.

But our argument so far has led us to one key conclusion about how we interact with the client-group, encapsulated again in the description by Eden and Sims (1979). They describe three possible modes of engagement.

The first is a "coercive" mode, in which the client is coerced or feels coerced into using models or solutions devised by the Management Scientist. The status of the analyst in bringing "rational analysis" to bear, particularly if brought in by someone with a position of power within the organization, can sometimes endow the analysis with an aura of authority. This was certainly often the case with engagements in the 1950s and 1960s, when there were stronger social attitudes towards "scientific" analysis, rather than the move more towards an "anti-analytic, and indeed anti-intellectual, cast of management thought" (Rosenhead 1998). (This is a topic we'll look at in more detail in Chapter 11.) But even now, the politics of an engagement can mean that following the analyst's advice provides a participant with a rationale for his or her decision that can be invoked if the decision turns out to be less than satisfactory (sometimes impolitely referred to as a "cover your backside" strategy). But generally, in this mode, the danger is posed that the problem "solved" is the problem perceived by the analyst and considered to be the key problem by the analysis (possibly for his or her own reasons – such as because s/he can solve that problem!), and the solution offered will increasingly seem to be of limited relevance to the participant. This can lead to the situation in which, as Eden (1987) describes, "the client shows a loss of interest in the situation and [only] a polite interest in any work that has been undertaken by the consultant". If the client doesn't feel ownership in the problem that the analyst attacked (i.e. doesn't feel it's "his" or "her" problem), how can s/he feel ownership of the solution?

This mode is associated with the simple approaches to interventions where the problem is solved, or removed, and so can have attractions. And, indeed, it can be appropriate for straightforward "problems". But the "wicked" complexity of the problems we generally approach as professional Management Scientists, and the socially constructed nature of these problems, means that it is unlikely to be the best approach generally.

The second envisaged mode is an "empathetic" mode, where the analyst tries to empathize with the client's definition of the problem. This certainly deals with some of the basic ontological issues we discussed in Chapter 1, and is more likely to take a client along with the solution process. But rarely is a client a sole participant in a problem-situation, with no social interactions around him/her. As we have already discussed in this chapter, there is a need to understand the social setting of the problem-situation and the diverse perceptions of the various participants. (And we will often bring our own specialist knowledge to the problem-structuring situation also.) This empathetic mode can, therefore, only rarely be the best approach (although it can be the easiest sometimes!).

In general, when we move into "wicked" messy problem-situations, we need therefore to adopt the (third) mode of intervention that we have been leading up to: a negotiative approach, in which the consultant must negotiate between the various perceptions of reality, issues, values and objectives, in a problem area situated within an organization's social geography. Indeed, we have already found that in order to define problems, a negotiation process needs to be undertaken between analyst and client-group. Now, the analyst and client-group become co-producers of the whole structuring, identification and solution process. And, as we shall see, often that very process of negotiation provides the advance in understanding that the organization needs, thus in one sense "finishing" the problem. Many indeed take this idea of "negotiation" further and stress the dialectic between the analyst and the decision-makers in Hegelian conflict, where the activity of the dialectic helps the decision-maker to be actively involved in the knowledge-creation process – see for example Barabba (1994).

This will therefore have implications in this book for how we seek problem-definition and the multi-methodological approach we must take. It will have implications for the types of issue we must address within organizations. It will have implications for mundane issues such as how we make proposals and bid for work, and how we regard data and go about collecting them. It will have implications for the skills we need as Management Scientists – the ability to relate to participants with their bounded rationality, beset by political and social pressures, and with uncertainties about objectives and values. This is why authors such as Mulligan and Barber (2001), giving basic advice on intervention styles, cite the "Yin and Yang" of the consultant role, where "Yin" is soft-focus, inner-world-directed, exploring through experience, attuned to feelings/intuitions, attending to relationships, concerned with being, expressing and creating, and "Yang" is hard-focus, outer-world-directed, applying theories, attuned to thoughts and senses, attending to boundaries/rules, concerned with doing, diagnosing and tabulating.

> Problem-situations that are "wicked" or behaviourally complex require particular types of intervention. Normally the most effective mode of engagement will be a negotiative approach, in which the analyst negotiates with the client-group to gain a view of reality and problem definition – and the client-group will participate in, and feel ownership of, the definition of the problem and the approach taken.

2.4 Problem "stakeholders"

We have already identified that there are generally a number of different participants in a problem-situation, and talked about the need to negotiate the problem-definition with participants who have differing views of a wicked problem set in an organizational context and social geography. This is sometimes quite a step for an analyst used to thinking things through for him/herself – but an important step to take.

Clearly we're considering here a number of different types of involvements in the problem, and authors such as Eden and Ackerman (1998) (working in the area of strategy development) will recommend making an analysis of the various parties in what they call a "stakeholder analysis". This looks at stakeholders in the problem-situation in two dimensions:

- their *interest* in the path that the problem-situation takes, or the outcome of the ongoing process;
- their *power* to influence the problem-situation.

They then plot all of the stakeholders in these two dimensions in a power–influence diagram, as shown in Figure 2.1.

Actors have the power to influence the situation we are trying to understand, model or manipulate. We must take them into account in understanding what can be done, what are the perceptions of reality and so on. Some

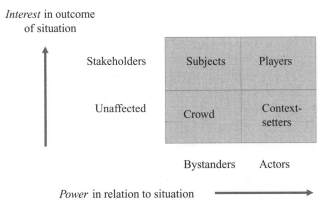

Figure 2.1 Stakeholder analysis. From Eden and Ackermann. Copyright 1998 SAGE Publications. Reproduced with permission.

of these actors are also interested in where the problem-situation goes, and are likely to wish to influence our Management Science intervention to support their interests – these are the main *players*. Our client or sponsor is likely to be a key player, but there will be others, and these are the first priority in understanding the geography of the problem-situation. Other actors, however, may have little interest in the outcome – these are the *context-setters*. Regulatory bodies might be one: we can't ignore them and have to work with them or around them, but they will have little interest in the resolution or progress of our problem. There might also be stakeholders who have little power over the problem, and it is easy to ignore them. However, some of these might have considerable interest in the outcome and could group together if they feel the problem-situation is being resolved in a direction against their interests, and possibly work to gain more power.

This latter point highlights two issues:

- Stakeholders are not in general individual stakeholders separate from the others: they form part of a system of interrelated relationships, forming a geography of relationships that we must recognize and understand.
- Some stakeholders who have an interest in the problem outcome may not have the same interest as the main client – indeed some, such as competitors, may have diametrically opposed interests.

Suppose we are analysing future production needs for an organization's management and planning a new factory, looking at what it should contain and what it should be like. Clearly there will be planning authorities and health and safety authorities; but those who are to work in the factory will also be interested in the outcome, as indeed would local residents who will have to live near the factory. So, the start of a power–influence diagram might be as in Figure 2.2. Of course, this grossly oversimplifies the social geography of the organization, and it would be much more complex than this, but the figure illustrates the idea.

In mapping out these stakeholders, we need to consider what the basis of their power is over the decision situation, and where it is derived from, and we need to keep in mind the Habermas considerations about the effect power-relationships have on the rationality of decision-making. We also need to consider the basis of the outlook that makes the participant interested in the outcome, which might have a different perception of the "real" situation

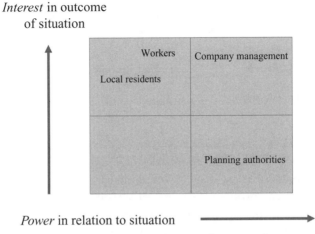

Figure 2.2 Highly simplified example of a power–influence grid

than other participants, and we will have to negotiate through these differing perceptions.

Eden and Ackermann's (1998) approach then moves on to managing these stakeholders, considering "how power-bases can be changed and how interest can be shifted", and this might need to be considered in our intervention into the problem-situation. The grids above are not necessarily static, but are a tool for us to understand the situation of which we are trying to make sense. Of course, other authors have used different dimensions to classify stakeholders (such as urgency, or legitimacy), but I have found these two dimensions a useful first tool.

> To be successful, our interventions need to comprehend the whole range of stakeholders, their interest and power, and the systemic structure of power–interest relationships.

2.5 "Success" in interventions

If these are the sorts of situations in which we are intervening, what then constitutes "success" in an intervention – particularly one in which we have

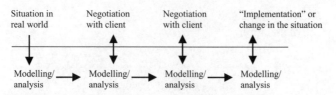

Figure 2.3 Implementation

tackled a "messy" problem? In puzzles, we can imagine that we would have been successful if we have "solved the problem". In simple "tame" problems we might propose a course of action and we might think ourselves successful if the client implements what we have proposed. But as we have said, in many of our interventions we are continuously negotiating what the problem is, and we might simply achieve success by finding a "satisficing" solution, or the client is simply helped to manage the problem on his or her own. "Implementation" in this world is *not* a separate issue for the Management Scientist; rather, it is an expression of the ongoing consultant/client relationship, so we could modify Figure 1.5 to look like Figure 2.3.

This is one reason sometimes why a very quick go at a solution can be effective (a so-called "quick and dirty" analysis): it can show the client what can be achieved and start to build the client/analyst relationship – and it can, by providing something on which to base the beginnings of a negotiation with the client as to the problem and its solution, start the process shown in Figure 2.3.

Knowledge and understanding is thus generated by the analyst and client-group together. Swart (2006) describes how knowledge for decision-making is co-created by two main processes: the socialization between parties, which helps to build common valuations, trust and "social capital", and "organizational structural capital", which establishes the basis on which the interactions and thus the co-creation of knowledge takes place. So the result of an intervention is a change in the real-world situation, aided and assisted by the interaction of the analyst with the client organization. "OR is generally considered to offer help to decision makers through the use of quantitative and analytical methods, i.e. a technical and specialist role. However an alternative definition could be 'intervening in a social process to facilitate feasible and desirable change', which places great importance on understanding and interacting sensitively with the employing organization's culture" (Fildes and Ranyard, 1997).

This word "culture" is important here. "Effective OR links closely with the culture of the employing group. Implementation of OR . . . is the activity which links the OR worker to the culture at all stages of the OR engagement. . . . Importantly, it includes the management of the process by which the OR worker makes himself aware of the content of the problem, of its whole context – why it is an issue, something of the relevant history and so on – and of the social processes in which he will be engaging and to an extent intervening" (Mitchell, 1983). Management Science (MS) is not a profession carried out from afar. Of course, we can never be fully immersed in an organization which we might be visiting for a short while, but as far as we can, we need to be embedded in the organization, to understand how issues have arisen, to have some idea of the corporate history and the corporate culture.

How we can best influence the client-group and its situation is something we will discuss in Chapter 11 when we look at what makes OR groups "successful". (We should note, though, that we have already looked at one aspect of this when we discussed the "coercive" mode of intervention, with its inherent danger that the problem solved is purely that perceived by the analyst and (to quote Eden, 1987, again) "the client shows a loss of interest in the situation and [only] a polite interest in any work that has been undertaken by the consultant".) It is the interaction with the client that lies at the heart of the OR/MS process shown in Figure 2.3. This is a truth that was slow to be espoused in the literature on OR/MS but has always been at the very centre of successful OR/MS. Rolfe Tomlinson in looking back on his OR Society Presidential Address in 1974, said that: "Thinking back, I believe I was particularly concerned to counter an attitude which implied that it was the function of OR to discover the truth, to present that truth to the decision-taker, and to leave it to him or her to accept the truth and take appropriate action. This view maintained that the OR analyst had to remain scientific, objective and separate. From his writings, it is clear that Blackett [one of OR's founding fathers, who we'll meet again in Chapters 9 and, particularly, 11] did not operate in isolation like that, nor did other successful practitioners. All my experience within the Coal Board led to a belief that although good OR workers were always respected by management, they were at their most effective when seen as part of the team. In essence, OR should not be done *to*, nor *for*, decision makers, but *with* them" (Tomlinson 1998).

> Implementation is not the last stage in an OR project – it is the outcome of the whole intervention process, in which the analyst and client-group interact technically and socially.

2.6 Beyond the individual intervention

This mode of interacting with the client in a collaborative venture to define and structure issues and move towards a solution, is perhaps more reflective of OR/MS in the UK in comparison with, say, the US or Southeast Asia, where Operational Research concentrates more on the solution phase of an intervention. It is in this type of working that perhaps UK OR/MS has distinguished itself (EPSRC, 2004) and is perhaps a reason for the UK's particular success in tackling messy "wicked" problems. And it is not only applicable in the UK – on the contrary, it is a direction in which other countries should be, and are, moving.

That is not to say that appropriate intervention in all countries is the same. As we have just said, organizational "culture" is important in carrying out OR/MS interventions, and this differs not only from organization to organization but also from country to country. The famous work in indicating the business culture in different countries is by Hofstede (2001). He differentiated countries by their scores on five different attributes: power-distance, individualism, masculinity, uncertainty-avoidance, and long-term orientation. Thus, if you were intervening in a culture with high power-distance (that is, the extent to which the less powerful members of the organizations accept and indeed assume that power is distributed unequally), such as many Southeast Asian and some formerly communist East European countries, it is easy to move into the "coercive" mode, in which the analyst feels as if s/he is bringing a word of authority to the workforce. Here, sometimes, an extra effort has to be made to promote the negotiation, and the client-group may indeed feel initially uncomfortable with an analyst trying to create an interaction in this way. Similarly, a culture with the high uncertainty-avoidance attribute (such as some Mediterranean countries, as opposed to, say, Scandinavian countries) will be less comfortable with uncertain or unstructured situations, and will want to impose structure quickly and avoid considering the ambiguities in a situation. Countries with a low level of individualism (such as South American countries) may be more familiar with working in cohesive groups and working for the good of that group. This is a large subject, and an analyst planning to work in a different national culture to his or her own – or indeed across national cultures – would be well advised to study Hofstede's work.

> To interact effectively with a client-group and understand its social geography, we must understand the culture of the organization. That culture will point to the way in which we can intervene most effectively.

There are two additional aspects going beyond an individual intervention. Good OR work clearly addresses the problem-situation, but a good OR analyst will be able to reflect on the intervention and gain more: reflection on the process we carried out helps to give us the ability to carry out such interventions in more effective ways. We'll discuss in Chapter 13 how reflection upon our experience enables us to conceptualize what we have learned, and this can enable us to change the way we intervene, which will lead to further experience – the so-called "Kolb learning cycle". We will also be able to use experience to mentor and apprentice younger analysts. And knowledge can be shared and built upon as the experience is discussed within the community of fellow analysts. All of these topics we will discuss in Chapter 13.

Further reflection on our work will often give generic insights into such situations that we can bring to other situations – indeed, academic Management Scientists will often carry out such work with the explicit aim of gaining generic understandings that they can add to our common understanding: this frequently comes under the heading of "action research". According to Eden and Huxham (2006): "For the research-oriented practitioner, there can be significant benefits that go beyond the moment of action towards some generality that is related to their expectation of implications for future situations. This circumstance provides the opportunity for collaborative or participatory research. For researchers, the generality will go even beyond this by having something to say about other contexts than that within which this specific practitioner operates. This may be through a recognition that the analysis of multiple cases can lead to a more general, less local, theory (Huxham, 2003; Marsick *et al.*, 2003), but it may also be through consideration of how the results *could* apply to other situations." Eden and Huxham go on to describe the attributes of good action research, and how theories can be developed and triangulated within this paradigm. We'll look at this area in more depth in Chapter 13.

The intervention is not necessarily the end. Reflecting on an intervention or a series of interventions can lead to learning that will help the analyst and colleagues to intervene more effectively in the future. And further reflection on work can produce generic results, which can be useful to a wider audience.

Part II
Modelling Techniques

3
Problem Structuring Methods

There are numerous techniques in the Management Scientist's toolkit that s/he can bring to bear on a problem-situation. In Chapter 5 we shall discuss the toolkit in detail, and run briefly through many of the tools that are available. But before we can analyse the sort of ill-structured "wicked messes" that we have been talking about in Chapters 1 and 2, we shall have to bring some structure to the problem-situation. So, this chapter will look into the sort of methods and frameworks that have been developed to structure these "messes" to make them more amenable to analysis. We have already said in Chapter 1 that Management Science has moved over the decades from tackling "tame" problems to tackling "wicked messes". A feature that has therefore characterized the change in the subject over these decades is the development of methods to structure these "wicked messes". This is usually so that they can be analysed – either by traditional methods that are also used on "tame" problems or by newer methods. Sometimes, though, the structuring itself can lead the client-group to such an understanding of the situation that they can move forwards themselves, and the analyst's role is over. A second feature that has also characterized the change in Management Science has been the need to approach problems by multiple means (particularly to get various analyses that can be "triangulated") – thus the development of "multi-methodology", and we will look at this in Chapter 4.

There is a wide variety of methods that can be used to structure problems. This chapter will look briefly at the two that are most popular in the UK, and then much more briefly outline one other that, while popular, has not so far captured the imagination of the UK analysts' world to the same degree. Other methods will be touched upon in Chapter 5. It is perhaps these areas of problem structuring and multi-methodology that distinguish OR/MS in the UK (EPSRC, 2004) and, as we said in Chapter 2, they are a feature of the UK's success in tackling "wicked messy" problems.

3.1 Why problem structuring methods?

The need for methods to structure the problems has arisen from three areas: we are tackling different types of problem-situations, we have a different understanding of those problems and, resulting from this, we have different aspirations in our interventions. Let's look at the first two of these – what characterizes these different views? The "wicked messes" we have been looking at in Chapters 1 and 2 are different from simple "tame problems" in that they have:

(i)   multiple actors rather than a single decision-maker;
(ii)   a "reality" that can often not be objectively determined, but for each different actor there is a different construction of reality;
(iii) actors who have different aims, different objectives and often different values – sometimes these can be conflicting; sometimes real underlying aims and indeed values can differ from those that actors espouse publicly;
(iv)   dynamic complexity that can be ill-understood – indeed, this element alone can be sufficient to persuade "traditional" Management Scientists that they need more organized or structured methods to approach problems, in order to understand them sufficiently to apply traditional OR techniques;
(v)   behavioural complexity – many actors interacting in complex behavioural ways, with underlying power-structures, organizational politics and social geographies that might not be apparent at all.

The way we develop methods to structure our analyses therefore needs to start from this point. But we also said in Chapter 2 that we have different aspirations in our interventions, where bringing structure and understanding may be as important as finding an "optimum solution" to the problem, if not more so – the very idea of an "optimum" can be rather naïve when the very definition of the problem is unclear, let alone the aspirations of the partici-pants, and, indeed, if we do look for a solution, it is likely to be a "satisficing" solution rather than an "optimum". This means that:

(vi) our structuring needs to be done transparently and in negotiation with the client-body, to ensure agreement and buy-in – a difficult requirement in view of (i)–(v) but an essential element that determines some of the aspects of the most common methods.

This means that we could also add a further requirement:

(vii) our structuring needs be inclusive, tending to retain solutions rather than reducing the set of possible solutions down to the "best" and perhaps ignoring or down-playing the complexity of the problem.

We can take a different approach to each of the points above, and these will lead to different types of method. In this chapter, we will look at the most common formal approaches, and see:

- what their underlying assumptions are, and how these relate to (i)–(v);
- the framework that is developed, and how this is derived from the assump-tions and the need for (vi) and (vii);
- the specific techniques employed and how a typical problem-structuring project progresses;
- a brief note of its foundation for further analysis;
- a brief summary of a particular classic example (for the first two techniques).

Now, three points need to be made before the methods are described. Firstly, these are just three particular approaches that three (sets of) prac-titioners have taken. The first two methods, it is true, have achieved wide popularity and are very well-known and thus could be argued to be well-proven as pragmatically useful; however, as in all Management Science, no particular technique is suitable for, or applicable in, all situations. This leads onto the second point: we will look at how the methods proceed, emphasizing their fundamental assumptions, but this should in no way be taken as a normative statement of how things "should" be done. If these methods are used like instructions in a recipe-book and just followed blindly, then this will miss the whole point of the techniques, which are offering structured ways of approaching and managing the complexity we've described above. These techniques are aids and prompts and supposed to complement the creativity that a Management Scientist must bring to analysis – not straitjackets that stifle creativity. Finally, the techniques are described very briefly in this chapter. A somewhat more full treatment of the methods is given in a famous book by Rosenhead, now in its second edition as Rosenhead and Mingers (2001). But as we look at each method, the key references to the original books by the authors of the methods will be given.

The first method we will look at ("Soft Systems Methodology") purports to be the more general method, and approaches the problem-situations with an open mind to gain as much understanding as possible. It was the first such problem-structuring method to be formally set out. Some analysts find it a useful way to structure situations – others find it overly prescriptive or simply unhelpful. The second, slightly later approach (SODA/cognitive mapping, part of the journey-making methodology) has a slightly narrower aim – so, in my personal experience, I have had more success in creating a way of thinking about problems using this method. The third method (SCA) is more of an all-inclusive framework for decision-making that some find useful, although others find very restrictive.

> The different types of problem that Management Scientists now tackle, and the different view they have of the world, mean that aids are needed to structure problems to make them amenable to analysis. But the methods described in this book are supposed to be aids to creative analysis, and *not* recipes to follow.

3.2 Soft Systems Methodology (SSM)

The ideas of Soft Systems Methodology, or "SSM", were developed over the 1980s and 1990s and are espoused in the key books Checkland (1981) and Checkland and Scholes (1990). The application of SSM to information systems is covered in Checkland and Holwell (1998). There are four key "thoughts" that determined the development of SSM, according to Checkland (1999):

- situations in which Management Scientists intervene are human situations in which humans are undertaking purposeful action;
- many interpretations of any declared "purpose" are possible;
- since there are many possible models of purposeful behaviour, it makes sense to create some and compare them with the perceptions of reality.

(There is not really scope in this treatment to cover the fourth point, which comes rather later in the methodology, which is that models of purposeful activity can provide a basis on which work on information systems can start, recognizing that these are "less than ideal in virtually every real-world situation".)

Now, the first two of these points are clear from the discussion we have had in Chapters 1 and 2. Indeed, the development of SSM mirrored the development that Management Science as a whole underwent during the 1980s and 1990s. And the influence was not one-way – the development of SSM was certainly an influential part of this development, although SSM's rather grand claims, such as Checkland's (1999, p. A9) effective claim to deriving the "soft–hard" distinction, are rather hard to reconcile with the general advances in philosophy in general and Management Science in particular during this period. But SSM certainly has reflected those general advances in Management Science thinking.

The third of these "thoughts", while fair enough, might strike some as already being slightly prescriptive in how to approach the structuring process. And this is a second issue that does arise with SSM. Its essence can be seen as normative, describing how a problem-situation ought to be approached. Indeed, the method developed into a seven-step method that we shall describe below, but Checkland's later developments move away from this sequence specifically because it "has a rather mechanistic flavour and can give the false impression that SSM is a prescriptive process which has to be followed systematically, hence its fall from favour". This is a clearly recognized error that can befall followers of SSM, but its frequency of occurrence does suggest a prescriptive flavour to SSM (as well as the seven steps, there are the three "E"s (later developed into five "E"s), "Analyses One, Two and Three" and so on – clearly giving a normative flavour to the methodology).

However, despite these issues, SSM is a well-used methodology that has helped many to make sense of an unknown problem-situation they have approached.

3.2.1 The underlying assumptions

The basic logic of SSM starts from the idea of a "system", a fairly well-known idea from the systems engineering tradition. Systems are complex, bounded, organized combinations of parts, which have (according to Atkinson & Checkland, 1988) two main characteristics:

- emergent properties (properties of the system beyond simply the sum of the parts, as expounded in the discussion of dynamic complexity by Simon and Roth & Senge in Chapter 1)
- a hierarchical or layered structure.

There are also two further attributes possessed by systems: processes of communication and control to enable it to survive in an environment.

However, SSM soon moves beyond the simple idea of systems in two ways. Firstly, we do not perceive systems in the world directly, we perceive them through a framework of preconceived ideas – and, of course, as discussed in Chapter 1, different actors will view the systems in different ways. But SSM goes further than this simple idea by pointing out that we as humans can think about our own thinking processes (although not those of others), which leads to the picture of the first ideas in SSM, Figure 3.1. (It is worth noting that Checkland always has hand-drawn figures, representing how this work is carried out in practice – the figures given in this chapter are therefore *not* as Checkland would draw them.)

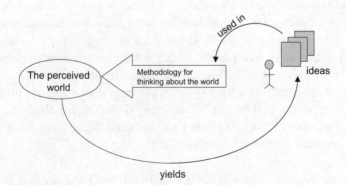

Figure 3.1 Using soft systems thinking to interpret the world. From Checkland and Scholes. Copyright 1990 John Wiley & Sons Limited. Reproduced with permission.

Thus we have certain pictures of systems, or ideas about systems (which we originally took from the real world and which form part of our thinking processes), and those are used in a methodology for looking into the real world. Thus we are *not* assuming that the world is itself made up of systems; rather, we are using hypothetical or imagined systems – or, to be more precise, what Checkland calls "holons" – and these are used in a methodology of thinking about the world.

This is all general so far. However, the problem-situations that Management Scientists study "all feature human beings in social roles trying to take purposeful action. . . . This was the thought which launched SSM" (Checkland & Scholes, 1990). Now, the thought might be clear anyway from Chapter 1, but this is fundamental to SSM. Checkland calls these systems "Human Activity Systems" (HASs) – remembering that these are "holons", or system models of reality; we are not claiming that the "real world" is made up of such systems. These are what are studied in SSM, although of course SSM emphasizes that there will be multiple views of any HAS and thus different representations. HASs by definition are purposeful; in SSM this purpose is always expressed as a transformation process in which some entity enters the system, is transformed, and then is output in a transformed state. Taking this model enables Checkland to give a "root definition" to each HAS to elaborate the transformation – and this idea developed into the well-known acronym used in SSM for defining root definitions, *CATWOE*:

- "C" "customers" the beneficiaries (or victims) of the transformation, which can be individuals or groups
- "A" "actors" those involved in the transformation, who form part of the internal workings of the HAS
- "T" "transformation process" the conversion of input to output, which is the core of the root definition
- "W" "*Weltanschauung*" the worldview (or ideas that we take for granted – see the discussion in a different context by Guinness (1973)), which puts this transformation into its perceived context, and looks at what is in the wider context having influence on the situation
- "O" "owner(s)" those who could stop the transformation
- "E" "environmental constraints" elements outside the system which it takes as given.

(Some users prefer the acronym VOCATE, where the "V" stands for "viewpoint" rather than the more technical "*Weltanschauung*" used above.)

The idea of "transformation" might strike some readers as rather a simplistic way to model real-world pluralistic systems, although the CATWOE definition does show how inclusive the definition can be. The CATWOE structure itself can feel rather prescriptive, but these ideas are key to the process that we will describe below (see Checkland and Scholes (1990, pp. 33–35) for more discussion).

Clearly so far the methodology has covered our points (ii), a "reality" that cannot be objectively determined, and (iv), dynamic complexity. It has recognized (i), the multiple actors. It has not yet explicitly dealt with (iii), the actors' differing aims and values, or (v), behavioural complexity. This comes from the following steps in the process described below. These steps look past the logic of the system and look first at the problem-situation as a "social system", and the second looks at the problem situation as a "political system". By this means, the methodology tries to capture the social geography and particularly the power relations within the situation (see the discussion of Habermas in Chapter 1).

3.2.2 Framework, and how a typical problem-structuring project progresses

SSM is therefore "a methodology that aims to bring about improvement in areas of social concern by activating in the people involved in the situation a learning cycle which is ideally never-ending. The learning takes place through the iterative process of using systems concepts to reflect upon and debate perceptions of the real world, taking action in the real world, and again reflecting on the happenings using systems concepts" (von Bulow, 1989). The principles outlined above can be put together in an overall framework describing this as shown in Figure 3.2 (taken from Checkland's retrospective of SSM in 1999). Analysts take their various "holons" representing real-world systems, and compare them with the perception of the "real world". By finding versions of the "real world" that the various conflicting interests can accept, accommodations are found which can be implemented to improve the real-world situation.

The process itself is described as a series of seven steps in Checkland (1975), and it is in this form that it is often seen. Checkland himself drew it up in a more descriptive format, rather than prescriptive, to avoid any "recipe-style" interpretation, as shown in Figure 3.3.

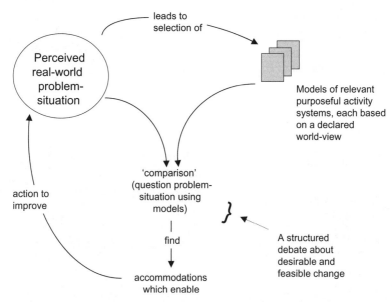

Figure 3.2 The inquiring/learning cycle of SSM. From Checkland. Copyright 1999 John Wiley & Sons Limited. Reproduced with permission.

Having made this point, it is simplest to consider the version of the methodology that breaks down the analysis into seven steps. These are the seven steps that are generally seen, and they can be seen as you move down the page in Figure 3.3.

- *Step 1: The problem-situation.* This step tries to set out what the participants see as the problem-situation. "Rich pictures" (see below) are the most common technique used in this phase. By using these with individuals and groups, this does try to recognize our requirement (vi) – that of transparent modelling, which maintains the participants' sense of ownership.
- *Step 2: The problem-situation expressed.* This is a key step, in which the problem-situation is analysed in terms of Human Activity Systems using three sub-steps referred to as "Analyses One, Two and Three".
  - Analysis One is a logical analysis, looking at the roles of the participants, and seeing who the problem owners are.
  - Analysis Two views social systems as an interaction between roles, norms (or expected behaviours) and values (or accepted standards), and analyses these aspects of the problem-situation.

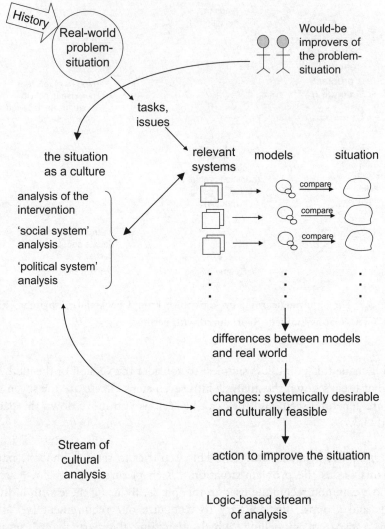

Figure 3.3 The SSM model as seen by Checkland & Scholes. From Checkland and Scholes. Copyright 1990 John Wiley & Sons Limited. Reproduced with permission.

- Analysis Three views the problem-situation as a political system, looking at the power relationships and the ways in which differing interests reach accommodation.
- *Step 3: Root definitions of relevant HASs.* Having identified the HASs, the CATWOE ideas above are used to specify their root definitions.

- *Step 4: Conceptual models of HASs.* This step takes the root definitions and builds a diagrammatic representation of those activities of the system and their logical connections, which must be in the system to satisfy the root definition. By Checkland's definition of a system, these activities must include communication and control. But rather than only building the models, Checkland also assesses the models by the "three Es":
  - *Efficacy* – does the means work?
  - *Efficiency* – what resources would be needed for a unit of output?
  - *Effectiveness* – is the transformation meeting the longer term aim?

(This has more recently been supplemented by two more "Es": *ethics* – is it sound morally? – and *elegance* – is it beautiful?)

- *Step 5: Comparison.* Step 5 takes the conceptual models built in Step 4 and compares them with the perceived "real world". Checkland uses the models to "walk through" either past situations or the current system, and comparisons of the model (either at a high level or at the detailed level) with the current situation. Following step 2, this is done both at the logical level and also at the social and political level.
- *Step 6: Identifying changes.* This analysis should enable changes to the current system to be identified that are both desirable (according to the logical analysis) and feasible (according to the social and political analyses). As we discussed in Chapters 1 and 2, it may be that the intervention is successful simply by increasing people's understanding of their situation – and, indeed, that more underlies the flavour of the SODA/cognitive mapping interventions that we are going to describe shortly; however, clearly the intervention is pointless unless some change is made in the real system or its actors.
- *Step 7: Action to improve the situation.* This step initiates implementation of the action in Step 6.

3.2.3   Specific techniques

The above describes a number of detailed procedures. Other than these, there are no particular techniques specific to SSM, other than the idea of Rich Pictures. This is a general term for a diagrammatic representation to describe particularly the relationships in the situation, consisting of icons, arrows, boundaries, phrases – in fact anything visual that can present the situation. This is often able to represent situations in their behavioural complexity in a way that pages of text could not. Rosenhead and Mingers' (2001) textbook contains many examples. Rich Pictures have been found to be particularly appropriate to represent the transformation process given by an SSM root definition. Construction of a root definition in succinct and precise text, together with developing a rich picture representing that root definition in an accessible visual form (sometimes by developing the Rich Picture first and looking for the root definition to emerge from the picture), has been found effective in maintaining both the rigour and the transparency (and client buy-in) in SSM.

The conceptual modelling on the other hand can provide the basis for further modelling – for example, Kotiadis and Mingers (2006) discuss a case in healthcare in which the SSM root definitions were used to construct a discrete-event simulation activity model, but the use of SSM here was much more than a simple "hard" modelling device; rather, it enabled the healthcare system under study, including the roles, viewpoints and aspirations of the participants, to be understood and thus shaped the whole study. Many therefore find the conceptual modelling Step 4 above to be the most useful part of the process.

3.2.4 Classic example

A well-known example of the use of SSM is that of Shell (given in Chapter 9 of Checkland & Scholes, 1990). This was work to help a division (called "MF") of the Shell Group define its "vision". The strategic planning work of van der Heijden and others in Shell was based on discussion and questioning of the "vision" of that part of the company. What was sought here was "an organized dialogue within which the MF 'vision' could be constructed and its necessary organization worked out". SSM was therefore used in the sense of the work we have discussed in Chapters 1 – there to help the client community construct understandings and interpretations of the world rather than any definitive analyses of what is "real". The role of the analyst, Checkland, as in Chapter 2, was negotiating the definition of the issue with the community (led by two managers who, in Checkland's term, 'orchestrated' the work). The issue was complex, partly due to the ill-defined nature of MF's role, but partly also due to the behavioural complexity both of the division itself and also as part of Shell (which Checkland says is effectively "a concept which arises in relation to a complex of ideas and events involving a large number of people who are prepared to behave *as if* some quasi-human 'Shell Petroleum Corporation' actually existed").

The work began with a collation of written material (which "revealed much recognition of the need for MF to reconcile irreconcilables"). This enabled a series of workshops to be carried out at which individuals and subgroups tried to define the core purpose of the division. This led naturally to the discipline of expressing those candidate core purposes as SSM root definitions; and these in turn were naturally formulated using CATWOE. Various root definitions were developed relevant to different core purposes (such as, relevant to relationship-managing, "An MF-owned and staffed system which manages fluid relationships between those involved in MF tasks in order to achieve a flexible non-fragmented organization which makes an impact on Shell business"; defining "C (parties involved), A (MF), T (relationships which become managed), W (the view that relationships can and should be consciously managed), O (MF) and E (the structure of MF and multiple client-groups within Shell)", and formally defining the concept of "a relationship". This led to further workshops on how the division should be organized to satisfy the role (with new root definitions), then later, naturally, to work on the information system that should underpin the organization set up.

> SSM gives an approach for taking a "wicked" human situation and expressing its core constituent systems in a standard way that is transparent and involves the whole client-group.

3.3 SODA/Journey-making

The use of cognitive mapping as a problem-structuring tool, SODA and Journey-making are steps along the way in the development of a methodology to help management develop strategy in a company. The main text for the methodology as largely developed is Eden and Ackermann (1998), although a step-by-step book of practical guidance on how to apply these techniques is Ackermann, Eden and Brown (2005). Of course, the aim of "Journey-making", that of strategy-making for organizations, is not the same as our purpose in looking for a problem-structuring tool. However, the basis of the methodology, cognitive mapping (Eden, 1988) and SODA (Strategic Options Development and Analysis: e.g. Eden & Ackermann, 1992), is essentially a way of making sense of a complex problem through the eyes of a client-group. It thus has a slightly more modest aim than that of SSM, but is significantly less prescriptive in its essence. I personally have found it a very useful problem-structuring technique, and it has found considerable favour in OR/MS and in the field of strategy formulation.

3.3.1 The underlying assumptions

Journey-making is firmly rooted in the existing body of knowledge of management theory, as described in detail in Chapter C2 of Eden and Ackermann (1998). We can only give a brief nod towards this foundation here. They lay out the various schools of management thought, then show how three of these schools particularly inform their work.

- Their emphasis on looking at the organization as a collection of individuals and the politics, power and social geography within that organization is particularly informed by what they call the "political" school of thought and the "cultural" school of thought.
- Their use of mapping and helping individuals to make sense of their construction of reality and their tacit knowledge is informed by the "cognitive" school of thought.

Forming inputs to these schools, they cite authors such as Berger and Luckmann (1966) and their work on the social construction of reality; Raimond and Eden (1990) on conflict and pluralism; Pettigrew (1977) in the "political" school; Silverman (1970) on actions arising out of meanings; and Weick (1985) and Johnson and Scholes (1993) in the "cultural" school. As the "journey" moves out into the forming of strategy and organizational learning, the work is further grounded on work in the "learning", "design" and "planning" schools of management thought, but this takes us beyond where we need to go for our purposes.

Their methodology therefore responds to our five issues (i)–(v) above as follows.

(i) *Multiple actors.* Proponents of SODA view the decision-making within an organization as a participatory activity, and emphasize the roles of individuals in the activity. This is different to those who think of the client organization as a single entity (or try to "reify" the organization).

(ii) *Individual constructions of reality.* The method looks at the individual within the client-group, and considers him or her to be involved in constructing his/her own reality psychologically rather than only perceiving an objective "real" world. Furthermore, the SODA methodology looks at teams that are deliberately brought together to bring different perspectives on the problem-situation – often being from a functionally different part of the organization, sometimes having a different level of seniority or simply a different background, and so having had different experiences. Thus, while members of an organization need common values and ways of thinking to some extent, the SODA/Journey-making methodology is specifically not looking for "groupthink" but rather for individuality in thinking to help promote creativity and new ways of interpretation.

(iii) *Different aims, objectives and values.* Point (ii) above might also imply that the groups have a mixture of aims, objectives and, sometimes, values, and Journey-making can explore this heterogeneity.

(iv) *Dynamic complexity.* The technique of cognitive mapping, which underlies the methods, allows for complexity to be encapsulated in maps, and the use of the accompanying software can assist in its management. But for our purposes, the crucial benefit of this approach is that it can capture and represent the complexity, and in Chapters 4 and 5 we will see techniques that can take that complexity and analyse it.

(v) *Behavioural complexity.* As we saw above, the methods are based on the ideas of the organization as a collection of individuals and the politics, power and social geography within that organization, and so specifically encompass the behavioural complexity of decision-making.

3.3.2 Framework

The behavioural complexity and the need for "facilitative devices intended to help manage political feasibility" (Eden & Ackermann, 2001) suggest a framework in which four perspectives come together (again see Eden & Ackermann, 2001).

- "The individual", who constructs his/her own view of the world in all its richness and complexity. The methodology is based on Kelly's (1955) personal construct theory, which looks at how individuals make sense of observations of the world and the events perceived in the world (and look for ways to manage and plan the future). This is heavily dependent on the use of language as the common currency of organizational life.

- "Technology and technique", which is the technique of cognitive mapping (to be introduced below) and software that displays cognitive maps, as a means of recording and to some extent analysing and managing the complexity – which explicitly supports our requirement (vii) above for inclusive modelling.
- "The nature of organizations" as negotiated enterprises, with the underlying theories of organization politics, decision-making and social geography that we discussed in Chapters 1 and 2 and which were covered in the "underlying assumptions" above.
- A "consulting style" that negotiates through the problem-structuring process (explicitly supporting our requirement (vi) for transparent and negotiative structuring to achieve buy-in). SODA is specifically geared towards taking a group of managers to the point at which they feel confident that they have sufficient understanding and can take appropriate action – following the idea of "problem finishing" to give a "satisficing" solution.

All of this passes in the framework through cognitive mapping and SODA as the facilitating device at the middle of the framework. (This, it should be noted, is the framework for SODA problem-structuring; this is developed into a full framework for a Journey-making strategy development in Figure P0.1 of Eden & Ackermann, 1998.)

3.3.3 Specific techniques and a typical problem-structuring project

Looking in turn at the techniques underlying the SODA methodology will show how a typical SODA problem-structuring project can progress.

3.3.3.1 Cognitive mapping

The SODA version of cognitive mapping picks up from the point in the first bullet point above, of "language as the common currency of organizational life". Cognitive mapping is a way of capturing the thoughts of an individual about the problem-situation, but in a diagrammatic form rather than textual, which is generally constrained to be linear. In this, it is not unlike the popular "mind mapping" technique (Buzan, 2003), but in comparison to mind mapping it is not as constrained or structured (depending on whether you think that to

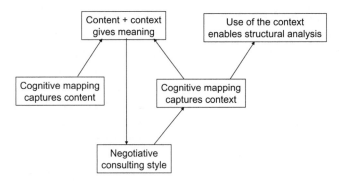

Figure 3.4 Example cognitive map

be good or bad!). The ideas are based on Kelly's (1955) personal construct theory and are explored in more depth by Eden (1988). The key point for our purposes is that, to understand the situation, we need to understand not only the particular points that the interviewee wishes to make (i.e. the content) but also the meaning and implications of the points (i.e. the context). By placing each point into a structure, we will then enable the bringing together of views and analysis. (Maps drawn up in structuring sessions can be quite large – tens, hundreds or even thousands of elements – but the use of software, as explained below, can enable the maps to be managed and analysed.)

Figure 3.4 shows an example of my thoughts as I sit here thinking about cognitive maps. Each element is simply a thought but there are lines that show implication or causality. Thus, it is the ability of cognitive mapping to capture context that enables the structural analysis. This linking of small discrete points (known in the method as "concepts") with (directed) lines of implication is what forms cognitive mapping.

Drawing up a cognitive map with an interviewee, while very simple in its essence, if done properly is a skilled task that requires attention to a number of matters and lots of practice. The reader who wants to become expert here is pointed to Chapter P1 of Eden and Ackermann (1998) or the step-by-step guide in Ackermann, Eden and Brown (2005). A key implication of the method is actually shown in Figure 3.4. Putting the thoughts into context is a large part of what gives those thoughts their meaning. This naturally leads to a discursive, negotiative style, which promotes the further and deeper exploration of context. The interviewee does not play a simple mute recording role; rather, the use of mapping enables a facilitative role in which the nature and meaning of the problem-situation is discussed and negotiated. This particularly comes from taking a particular concept and asking two questions: firstly "why?" (e.g. "what comes earlier in the causal process?" or "what is it that implies this concept?" or "why do you think this concept?") and, secondly, "so what?" (e.g. "what came later in the causal process?" or "what are the implications of this concept?"). This idea (sometimes called "laddering down" and "laddering up") enables exploration of the context and is very creative in helping the interviewee to think through the issues and come up with a good description of the problem-situation in its richness.

Because of this simple structuring, the use of cognitive mapping alone is perhaps the most powerful problem-structuring technique. It is an extremely useful method for the analyst in approaching a messy problem, with unclear attributes and measures, to come to an initial sense of what the problem is in a way that can be taken further into analysis (a point we will come to in Chapter 4).

3.3.3.2 Merging cognitive maps, and cause maps

A cognitive map will then give a view of how one member of the client group views the problem-situation. But we of course will need an idea of how the whole client-group views the situation, with all the differing views, aspects and objectives implied in that overall view. There are two key approaches to this, the first being the merging of cognitive maps to get an overall group map. This simply means the combining of the individual maps so that they are all put into one map. Of course, this might mean interpreting the content of individual concepts to see where these are the same, or can be combined or divided in such a way as to enable parts of different maps to come together. It might also highlight contradictions in fact, which might require going back to the original interviewees to obtain reconciliation if possible.

It is also good practice at this point to move on from "cognitive maps" – which are individuals' views of concepts, and in which the definition of a "concept" is fairly general – to "cause maps", in which the concepts are more properly ordinal (i.e. they can be "more" or "less" so, rather than simply statements of fact). Then the lines linking those concepts should suggest causality – that is, the first will make the second more so, or more likely. (Where this is done, it is also necessary to be able to draw negative links, where one concept increasing causes another concept to decrease.) A classic example is

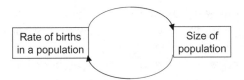

Figure 3.5 A cause map

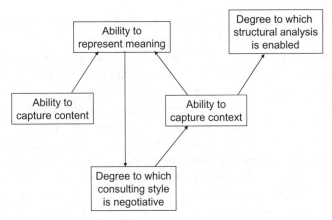

Figure 3.6 Cause map representation

Figure 3.5, in which the larger the rate of births in a population, the larger the population will get; but interestingly here, the larger the population, the larger the rate of births will be, which is an example of *"positive feedback"* (called "positive" because an increase in one element goes through the loop and causes the element to increase even more, and similarly a decrease in that element goes through the loop and causes that element to decrease even more). We will discuss these further below.

Figure 3.4 showed a cognitive map: if you compare this with Figure 3.6, you will see that this latter might be a cause map showing certain abilities of methods.

3.3.3.3 *Workshops and coming to a joint view*

The second of the two approaches to get an idea of how the whole client-group views the situation is to bring them together in a workshop. There are various orders in which these steps can be carried out. In some circumstances, it might be appropriate to start off with a workshop to get a joint view, then continue developing the maps individually. Alternatively, and more often (and more in line with Eden & Ackermann, 1998), individual cognitive maps will be produced, then merged, the merged maps analysed (see the following section) and then a group workshop can review the merged map and develop it.

Mapping with a group can be carried out manually or using computer software. Manual techniques will use individual pieces of papers, often shaped as ovals (Eden & Ackermann; 1998; Schnelle, 1979) in order to avoid producing rectilinear maps, although most common practice is to use "Post-its" as the easiest. Once the facilitator has initiated a workshop with a trigger-question or a trigger-concept, then the placing of concepts is done individually on a wall or flip-chart much as an initial cognitive-mapping session might be carried out. The facilitator will then interact with the group by clustering the concepts, then later by drawing links between the clusters with the group. These group sessions are very effective. Some prefer to use computer methods because of the increased efficiency in time they can bring, especially where the time of participants is particularly limited. These methods are similar to the manual methods, but use distributed lap-top computers, communicating to a central computer which displays on a screen. In this way, individuals can contribute concepts and even links between concepts. A typical piece of software to enable this is *Group Explorer* (Phrontis, 2008). Very detailed descriptions of how to carry out such workshops are given in Eden and Ackermann (1998) and Bryson *et al.* (2004).

Workshops are fundamental to the use of SODA/Journey-making. After all, as we looked above at the response of this methodology to our five issues, we said that this viewpoint sees the decision-making within an organization as a participatory activity, and emphasizes the roles of individuals in the activity. We said that this methodology uses teams deliberately brought together to bring different perspectives on the problem-situation and that we can also explore the mixture of aims, objectives and sometimes values. And we noted that the methodology comprehended the politics, power and social geography within that organization. The ability to facilitate such a workshop is therefore an important skill, to which we shall return in Chapter 10.

Whichever order is used, and whether manual or computer-based methods are used, the aim is to arrive at a map to which all of the client-group feel they have contributed, and can see how they have contributed (in other words, satisfying our requirement (vi) above for structuring that is transparent and done in negotiation with the client body), and which represents their varied views and concerns (thus capturing the behavioural complexity in requirements (i)–(iii) and (v)). The use of mapping and laddering up and down, rather than closing off avenues of structuring, also allows the modelling to be inclusive, in line with our requirement (vii) above.

3.3.3.4 Analysis

Possibly between the above steps, and almost certainly as a last step, the map is analysed. Here computer software is certainly useful, the most popular being *Decision Explorer* (Banxia, 2006), although some functionality can be gained from other packages (e.g. part of the *Vensim* package (Ventana Systems, 2006)).

There are a multitude of different analyses that can be carried out. Obvious examples are finding unlinked concepts ("orphans"), or starting or ending concepts (respectively "tails", concepts from which links only come out, and "heads", concepts to which links only go in; these should be, respectively, concepts that are root causes or triggering effects, and those which are the final consequences that you wish to consider – hopefully top-level strategic goals). Other analyses will look at the most "busy" or the most "central" concepts.

But a key analysis is the identification of feedback loops – particularly positive feedback loops. As we said above, a feedback loop is one where a line of causality starts at a concept, moves through other concepts and finally comes back to the starting concept (e.g. *A* causes or implies or exacerbates *B*, which causes (etc.) *C*, which causes *A*). Where these links are all positive (i.e. each concept increasing causes the next to increase), or an even number of the links are all positive, the effect of this is that where a concept increases it will cause itself to increase, and you have the classic "vicious circle" (or "virtuous circle") – the former name is used where the effect is undesirable, the latter where it is causes a desirable effect to increase. Figure 3.5 is the simplest possible form of positive feedback loop, but, of course, in a complex structure of related concepts, there might be many loops that are much more difficult to spot. Loops where an odd number of the links are positive – so that an increase in a concept is balanced by the effect through the causal loop which tends to make it decrease – are called "negative feedback loops" or "balancing loops". Negative feedback is the basis of control in such system, and for example will often control the runaway effects of positive feedback loops. It is the identification of these positive and negative feedback loops which forms one of the most powerful features of this type of mapping, as human brains find it difficult to identify, predict or understand such systems intuitively (Sterman, 1989). Indeed, in many circumstances it is precisely the uncovering of the feedback loops that unravels the dynamic complexity of a system, and this forms the basis of much of the logic of system dynamics (see Chapter 5). This aspect of cognitive mapping/SODA therefore is one of the aspects that gives the methodology the problem-structuring power for the Management Scientist.

3.3.4   A foundation for multi-methodology

As we will see particularly in Chapter 4, this methodology helps to structure problems in a way that opens them up to various forms of analysis. Even in a straightforward way, "it is usual for a SODA workshop to identify opportunities for further analysis, such as financial model building, simulation modelling, market research, and statistical analysis" (Eden & Ackermann, 2001). But the format of the structuring allows it to form part of a rigorous structure that will help to produce a simulation model, as described in Howick *et al.* (2008) and discussed further in Chapter 4.

3.3.5   Classic example

A well-known example of where the method was used, in a problem-structuring role, was the case of the *Shuttle* wagons described in Ackermann, Eden and Williams (1997). These wagons are the rolling stock that carry cars in the Channel Tunnel between the UK and France. A contract to build them had been let, but it had overspent significantly, and the contractor made a claim against the builder of the Tunnel. To help in the claim process, a team (Eden/Williams/Ackermann) were asked to uncover why the overspend happened, and model the project to show how the root causes led to the overspend both qualitatively and the actual quantum of the overspend. Cognitive mapping (aided by the forerunner of *Decision Explorer*) was used to interview managers and subsequently model the explanations given for the various circumstances of the project. This also showed differing views of managers in different parts of the project leading to the need to harmonize different accounts. As above, the resulting cause map was developed and validated working in a visual interactive mode with groups of senior members of the project team. The analysis and clustering methods within the software were then used to locate all the positive feedback loops (90 interrelated loops in this case). This in itself gave a qualitative understanding of the relationships between the elements and the feedback loops, and thus the basis of understanding the dynamic complexity that led to the overspend. But, furthermore, it provides almost immediately Influence Diagrams, which can provide the basis for the quantitative modelling, providing both the structure of a simulation model and subsets of the map also providing the bases for quantifying the difficult-to-measure "soft" effects (see Chapter 7). We'll explore some of these aspects of this example in Chapter 4.

Cognitive mapping/Strategic Options Development and Analysis (SODA) provide a useful set of techniques for taking a "wicked" problem, and using the mapping and workshops to bring some understanding to a behaviourally complex situation, in a way that is transparent and solution-inclusive. The mapping format provides a powerful tool for explicating dynamic complexity, which can form the basis of further (quantitative) analyses. It is particularly good at identifying positive feedback, which forms the basis of much dynamic complexity.

3.4 Strategic choice

3.4.1 The underlying assumptions

A third problem-structuring method is the "Strategic Choice Approach" (SCA) developed by Friend and Hickling (1997). We mention it here as it does have a small but loyal following – and it shows how a whole structure can be built up for decision-making rather than concentrating on understanding and structuring the problem-situation (but we will cover this in less detail). There is no obvious specific theoretical background to the method, but distinct emphases, which mirror those discussed in Chapters 1 and 2. As Friend states:

more emphasis on **STRUCTURING COMMUNICATION**	than on *REINFORCING EXPERTISE*
more emphasis on **FACILITATING DECISIONS**	than on *EXPLORING SYSTEMS*
more emphasis on **MANAGING UNCERTAINTY**	than on *ASSEMBLING INFORMATION*
more emphasis on **SUSTAINING PROGRESS**	than on *PRODUCING PLANS*
more emphasis on **FORMING CONNECTIONS**	than on *EXERCISING CONTROL*

(Taken from the SCA chapter of Rosenhead and Mingers, 2001)

While this gives a different slant to the aims of an intervention, it is clearly recognizing the issues discussed in Chapter 2, with a particular emphasis on the need to include consideration of uncertainty.

3.4.2 Framework, and how a typical problem-structuring project progresses

SCA identifies four complementary modes of decision-making, and the technique manages the movement between these four:

- "Shaping mode" – looking at the structure of the set of decision-problems faced.
- "Designing mode" – looking at what courses of action are feasible in relation to the current view of the shape of the problems.
- "Comparing mode" – looking at how to compare alternative courses of action.
- "Choosing mode" – choosing commitments to action over the time-future.

As can be seen, this is a whole analysis process, starting with an unstructured problem through to choosing action. A study essentially proceeds through these stages.

3.4.3 Specific techniques and a typical problem-structuring project

As the study proceeds, simple graphical techniques are used at each stage:

- A "decision graph" is used in the *shaping mode* in a similar way to a cognitive graph, where decision areas are plotted out and links shown between the areas. This aims at helping to select the areas to be concentrated upon in the study.
- Similarly, "option graphs" in the *designing mode* are used to show different options in each problem area and incompatible option combinations.
- Then in the *comparing mode*, various pair-wise and multiple comparison methods are used, as described succinctly in the SCA chapter of Rosenhead and Mingers (2001).

All of these operations are supported by a software package called STRAD2 (Stradspan, 2006) which again has a loyal following of those who have found it useful in choosing decisions.

3.4.4 Building on this framework

As we've said, this is a whole analysis process, starting with a problem that might not be fully structured – although giving much less help in approaching an entirely unstructured situation than, say, SSM – through to identifying options and evaluating them. It is therefore not solely a problem-structuring method but includes option-choosing and action-planning steps that can be tackled by more traditional methods (which we will look at in Chapter 5). This is therefore perhaps more often a stand-alone whole framework than one arm of a multi-methodological study. This means, though, that many analysts will find it much too restrictive to use as it stands. But it can give structure to a process that some might find useful.

3.5 Conclusion

These methods describe some ways in which a Management Scientist can approach the type of situation which s/he needs to tackle in modern Management Science practice: behaviourally and dynamically complex, and set in a political and social context, recognizing the issues we covered in Chapters 1 and 2. In some circumstances, this would be all the intervention requires. In many instances, though, this is the springboard to enable the Management Scientist to bring his/her toolbox of techniques to bear in the situation with the structure and increased understanding gained from this first stage. We'll look at some of these techniques in Chapter 5, but before that we'll look at how the "harder" techniques (which require more structure in the situation) and these problem-structuring methods and others can be combined in a discussion of multi-methodology in Chapter 4.

4

Multi-Methodology

4.1 Introduction

We described in Chapter 1 how Operational Research was founded on the solution of problems that could be described in clear and unambiguous terms based on a clear understanding of the problem structure. Over the past half-century, techniques have been developed which have enabled Operational Researchers to tackle such problems efficiently, particularly as computing power has steadily increased.

But we went on in Chapter 1 to describe how Management Scientists have had to move into addressing problems with multiple actors, with different views of "reality" and different objectives and values, in situations of both dynamic and behavioural complexity. So have we dismissed the old ways and moved on? We've said that we need to take a critical view of the situations in which we're intervening. And we've described a set of tools that could be described as "soft OR" in Chapter 3. For certain situations and some analysts, the answer is yes. Gaining some level of understanding and "satisficing" is enough for them. Other analysts will disdain these new methods and say that they do not give useful results – there is no "real" modelling. Some of these differences reflect differences in history, and some blind prejudice. Some analysts do indeed deal with well-defined unarguable problems and situations, and can justifiably claim that the traditional OR techniques are sufficient. Others analysts are called upon simply to guide clients in increasing their understanding, and they see no need to go beyond the "soft" methods.

For the majority of analysts, in the majority of situations, however, we do want to move more towards a solution to a problem, or a working model of a situation. Often we want some level of quantification to our answers. So we want to be able to draw upon those Operational Research methods that we mentioned in Chapter 1, but in situations of ambiguity and complexity. Therefore, before we look at the different techniques that the Management Scientist will have in his or her tool-box, we need to consider the context in which they can be used in practical situations. And this generally means that some mixing of methods will be called for. So, this chapter will consider why our tools need to be combined, and how they can be combined, to give practical ways of approaching real-life problems.

4.2   Complementarity and pluralism

Why do we need to use different types of method in our interventions? Look again at Figure 2.3 (which was a development of Figure 1.5). There you can see a straight line dividing two different lines of activity – one above the line in the "real" world, and one below the line representing the analytical activities of the Management Scientist. So the position of the Management Scientist is rather like the Janus figure of Roman mythology – the god of doors and gates and beginnings and endings, after whom January is named because he looked both to the old year and the new simultaneously – who is normally shown in pictures with two faces looking in opposite directions. In Figure 4.1 the Management Scientist is shown as a Janus figure looking simultaneously into two worlds: the "real" world, which the problem-situation and the client-group inhabit, and his/her "analytical" world, inhabited by his/her model and analytical processes. The first world is indeed messy and wicked in all the ways we've discussed. The analytical world – at least if traditional Operational Research tools are used – is well-defined and logical; certainly it should be constructed without the ambiguity and complexity of the real world. (An example of the latter is given in Figure 5.2, showing the use of "Linear Programming" – this formulates a pretend problem as a mathematical model. But in a real-world problem, the "messy" real-world would need to have been structured and approximated before it

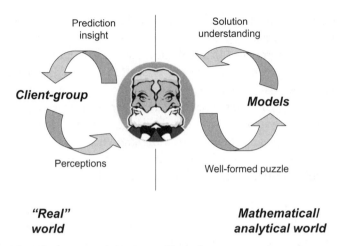

Figure 4.1 The Management Scientist as "Janus"

would be possible to carry out this (in this case simplistic) formulation.) As we've discussed before, the skill of the analyst is being able to translate from one to the other – "real" situations into models; models into insight in the real world.

It is clear, then, that the Management Scientist needs different tools for different purposes. For delving into the messy "real" world, s/he needs techniques that can uncover structure and help him or her to bring some sort of order to the dynamically and behaviourally complex situation – that is, s/he needs to look critically and will often be using the sort of "soft OR" techniques we discussed in Chapter 3. This is not to say that the "soft OR" models produced are any less within the "analytical world" than any other sorts of model – our models sit very definitely on the right-hand side of Figure 4.1. It is simply that the techniques used in their construction are particularly oriented to facilitate enquiry about structure, behaviour and complexity in the "real" world. Having done that, and gained some structure, the analyst can attack the problem using the analytical power of the "hard" methods in the "mathematical/analytical world". Where the model demands "data", the analyst goes out to the real world to gather perceptions and views – perhaps going via the softer models, as we'll see later. Where the client-group demands insight, the analyst interrogates the model to gain understanding in the light of his or her knowledge of the situation, and translates that into a message for the "real" world.

The Management Scientist needs to regard these two different worlds with techniques based on entirely different paradigms – that is, by different ways of thinking, with a different epistemological basis. Even in the most apparently straightforward intervention, his or her view of the real world has to be critical, has to consider issues of power and politics, of differing stakeholder views and values, has to recognize the perceptual influence that mediates data before being fed to the analyst, and so on. But the Management Scientist in constructing models and analysing them regards the analytical world on a somewhat different paradigmatic basis, since everything within those models has passed through the mind of the analyst and been used by that analyst in constructing the model.

This is not to say that analysts simply combine techniques. Jackson (1997), condescendingly, says that: "Almost all those who have shown an interest in 'pluralism' in operational research have decided to keep things easy for themselves. Methods, tools and techniques have been combined but under the hegemony of an implicit or explicit methodology embodying the philosophical assumptions of one paradigm. This, of course, was the typical case in classic operational research, when 'hard' OR methodology was employed to steer various models and techniques according to a functionalist logic." Of course, the work of 60 years of OR cannot be dismissed that simply, but there has been Management Science work that has tried to combine techniques inadequately. The true Management Scientist has to view the work in a multi-paradigmatic way.

So the message of Figure 4.1 is not that methods *can* be useful in combination. It is not the idea of complementarism (Jackson 1991) where different paradigms can be seen as consistent and different paradigms can be selected in different situations. It is the message that Mingers describes as "strong pluralism . . . which argues that most if not all intervention situations would be dealt with more effectively with a blend of methodologies from different paradigms" (Mingers 1997) – or, even more so, that the analyst by definition, in most situations at least, has to deal with competing paradigms.

Figure 4.1 is, of course, a simplification, and should not be regarded as representative of the process of an intervention. Some commentators think of an intervention as a "soft part" followed by a "hard part" – such as a SSM exercise followed by a hard analysis of the resulting model. But the Management Scientist needs to be aware of, and working with, two different worlds simultaneously all of the time. One pragmatic reason for this is the demands of transparency we made in Chapter 2 – the analyst does not go into a back room to interrogate his/her model away from the "real" world, but, as indicated in Figure 2.3, has to carry along the client-group with him/her and give them as much visibility of the working of the "analytical" world as possible. So our "soft" and "hard" models (in the analytical world) are developed in parallel with our interventions in the "real" world. But there are theoretical considerations also, and the argument about pluralism in Jackson (1997) has one of its main conclusions that "paradigm diversity requires that pluralism be observed at each and every stage of an intervention".

> Intervening as a Management Scientist in the sort of situations we have described in Chapters 1 to 3 requires the analyst to maintain views of both the analytical world and the "real" world simultaneously. This means using methods of intervening in the world, and maintenance and development of (often both) "soft" and "hard" models simultaneously, even though different paradigms underlie these activities.

4.3   Paradigm incommensurability

We have said that the Management Scientist regards these two different worlds with techniques based on entirely different paradigms. If these two views were to be entirely separate, there would be no theoretical problems. But we have said not that these are two separate operations, but like Janus we regard the two worlds simultaneously – and we will see soon how the two views inform each other constantly. So we have to be carrying different, indeed incommensurate – indeed sometimes opposing – paradigms in our thinking simultaneously. These paradigms bring with them fundamental assumptions about ontology, epistemology and the activity of research and analysis (or, "alternative competing 'truths' about the world" (Mingers & Brocklesby, 1997)). Can we do this without losing rigour in our thinking? Or are we bringing dissonances into our analysis due to irreconcilable differences between these paradigms? This is not a new debate – Kant's philosophy brought in the idea of the antinomy, where applying the logic of pure thought (the right-hand side of Figure 4.1) to the universe of sensible perception or experience (the left-hand side of Figure 4.1) gives rise to irreconcilable contradictions, but we shall see that it is key to how we approach Management Science.

There are numerous authors who have discussed the need to look at the underlying basis of OR/MS work and stressed the importance of theoretical coherence. Midgley (1997), for example, says that "critical systems thinkers are concerned to develop methodological pluralism in a theoretically informed manner" in perhaps slightly condescending contrast to "atheoretical pragmatism"; he goes on to look at a number of those authors who have "striven to demonstrate philosophical and theoretical coherence". On the other hand, there are some Management Scientists trying to use techniques practically to solve real problems, who are perhaps impatient with what can appear academic indulgence in these authors. So while we do not want to labour the theoretical niceties, we do need to be thoughtful and try to present an approach that makes sense theoretically and is coherent.

There is much literature on this subject, with Mingers and Gill (1997) giving some interesting discussion. Mingers and Brocklesby (1997) in particular concentrate on the topic of incompatible paradigms, and identify three levels of problems: (i) philosophical, i.e. paradigm incommensurability; and (ii) cultural and (iii) cognitive, i.e. the problems of, on the one hand, organizational (and academic) cultures and, on the other hand, individuals working with many paradigms or moving easily from one to another. The first of these (i) is clearly the key. They outline the basic problem of paradigm incommensurability, but bring in a range of literature and authors talking about "the ontological and epistemological uncertainties associated with any single paradigm" (Morgan & Hassard), paradigms "permeable at the edges" (Gioia & Pitre) and constructing bridges between paradigms. But perhaps more importantly they claim (quoting Weaver & Gioia) that the whole idea of paradigm incommensurability is fundamentally flawed, quoting for example structuration theory (which looks at reality as emerging out of the dialectic interplay of forces of structure and meaning). Their conclusion, after quoting much thought up to 1997, is that "although the paradigm incommensurability issue has to be taken seriously in debates about multi-methodology, the previous discussion gives us grounds for believing that multi-paradigm multi-methodology is philosophically sustainable" (Mingers & Brocklesby, 1997). Since then, there has been further philosophical thought (not least in the post-modern area, in which method and observation become intertwined) to strengthen that view. So, we can feel safer in keeping these paradigms simultaneously.

The second and third of the two problems that Mingers and Brocklesby (1997) raise are also interesting. Different personality types tend towards different types of view, and it is a rare type that can keep the views in balance. Most divisions of personality types would imply that a person would naturally lean more to one view than the other, be it the simply "left-brain, right-brain" distinction, or Jung's personality types, or whatever. And, moreover, the natural view of the world will to some extent also depend on the culture within which an analyst is working, as a person's basic assumptions about the world and his or her values arise to a great extent out of a considerable period of socialization. But we have established that the ability to work within both paradigms simultaneously is a key part of the skill of an analyst, so this apparently theoretical issue actually becomes a key distinguishing factor in the skill of a Management Scientist analyst, and it is an issue to which we will return in later chapters as we look at what makes an "expert" Management Scientist.

> The good Management Scientist has to maintain an analytical paradigm and a "real-world" paradigm in his/her head simultaneously. This apparent contradiction, or antinomy, is an essential element of good Management Science.

4.4   Combinations of techniques

So, in what sort of ways can these various methodologies and paradigms be combined? There have been a number of attempts to try to set up some sort of taxonomy of combination methods.

For example, Mingers (1997) tries to classify the different ways of combining methodologies into nine types using a five-dimensional classification:

(i)   Is there one or more than one methodology?
(ii)   Are these based on one or more than one paradigm?
(iii) Are they used in the same or different interventions?
(iv)   Is the whole methodology used (as opposed to only parts of methodologies)?
(v)   Is one methodology dominant or given overall control?

The first of these, of course, just determines whether there is a multi-methodology issue. The second determines whether we have a paradigm-clash problem. Unless both these questions are answered "yes" we don't have a problem! The third question is slightly more subtle, but if different methods are used in different interventions, then we have a clear division between the use of different paradigms, with a stop, a reflection and negotiation with the client, and any necessary communications between the interventions – certainly, we are not holding the paradigms simultaneously as in the "Janus" picture. So, the first three questions just ask: are we in a multi-paradigm situation? One possible answer to the situation might be to take an overarching methodology that claims to be all-encompassing (i.e. answering "yes" to question (iv)) – and we will look at this a little in Section 4.6 – but essentially, while such claims can often be appealing and can sometimes have strong followings, because of the wide variation of situations in which Management Scientists find themselves, their use is too specific for general use and they can be slightly discredited by disciples applying them to every situation. Another possible answer is "tweaking" a methodology to fit into an opposing paradigm (i.e. answering "yes" to question (v)), but this again is rarely satisfactory unless our view is mainly towards one paradigm. So, in the general case in which the Management Scientist finds him- or herself, we are in just one case – answering "yes" to (i)–(iii) and "no" to (iv) and (v) – and this classification doesn't give us much help!

Pidd (2004) presents a book of examples of different combinations, which we'll mention later in this chapter. He starts the book by suggesting three ways in which the different paradigms (simplified in this book to "soft" and "hard") can be combined – as distinct, incommensurable approaches, or as feeding off each other, or, since all Management Science must include some social construction, that soft approaches must include hard, as shown in Figure 4.2.

But these attempts logically to relate the paradigms do not seem to be helpful – and Pidd himself only presents the latter as a particular view of certain practitioners. In fact, we've already said that the skill of the Management Scientist is to keep these two world-views in mind simultaneously. They cannot be clearly reconciled – otherwise the Management Scientist's role would become simpler and could perhaps be codified into a "how to do Management Science". But within the mind of the Janus figure shown in Figure 4.1 has to reside two world-views simultaneously, looking to the "real", socially constructed world with a clear methodology based on a "soft" paradigm (to adopt the simple shorthand) but translating findings from there into the analytical world which the Janus mind regards with a "hard" paradigm. This is a clear

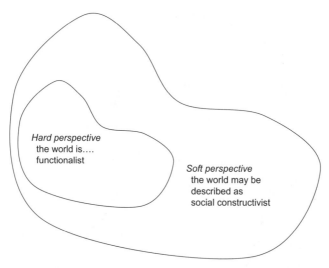

Figure 4.2 Soft encloses hard. From Pidd. Copyright 2004 John Wiley & Sons Limited. Reproduced with permission.

antinomy – but we do have to keep these two views simultaneously: let slip our view of the analytical world and we become sloppy pseudo-management consultants who cannot contribute to the "real" situation; let slip our view of the "real" world and we become "Glass Bead Game" players (as we discussed in Chapter 1) who carry out useless and inapplicable analysis. So the analyst's mind looks like Figure 4.3, with both paradigms maintained at the same time, talking to each other and informing each other – a topic we'll come back to in the next section.

This, of course, is not simply a view of how we model "reality", it is critically interlinked with how we intervene into a situation. First of all, we are not simply thinking about the content of the reality, we are thinking about the process of our analysis, and that rational thinking about process is affected by our interactions with the situation in a similar way to our rational thinking about content. But, more than that, we have dismissed the old idea of the disembodied analyst looking at a situation from on high; we are clearly part of a situation, recognizing the effects of our interrelationships, our emotions, our own cognitions and those of our clients, the structure of norms, language, values (see our discussion of Foucault previously) and so on. So, our thinking shown in Figure 4.3 has to include ourselves as analysts in the "real" world and to think about our intervention, our engagement with a problem-situation and with the participants and our process of issue-definition and process

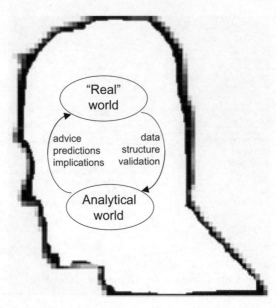

Figure 4.3 The antinomy within the Management Scientist

negotiation. This we can only do in a critical way, and this has to interface with our "hard" rational analysis.

4.5 How paradigms inform each other

The discussion so far has shown us that the Management Scientist simultaneously keeps both his or her view of the "real" world looking with a critical lens and his or her view of the analytical world looking with a harder, often mathematical, lens. But – despite the possible implications of Figure 4.3 – these aren't kept separate but form a part of a single analyst's view. The great advantage of this, of course, is that the two views can inform each other and support each other, producing a "virtuous circle" as one view improves and strengthens the other, which in turn improves and strengthens the first.

The initial move from the "real" world to the analytical world is fairly obvious. We have discussed how the analyst looks at the problem-situation and tries to find meaning and structure. A model in the analytical world will help the analyst see what data s/he needs to be looking for in the "real" world, and observations or perceptions in the real world can then flow back to the analytical world, and, as Figure 4.3 shows, advice or predictions or the implications of the model can flow from the analytical into the "real" world, hopefully to affect the problem-situation.

But that is at a fairly simple level, and so far the two views are forming quite different roles – it is not really the "strong pluralism" in which we have "a blend of methodologies from different paradigms" that the quote from Mingers (1997) referred to in Section 4.2 above. In fact, there are tighter circles of interrelationships.

- As we build a model of what we have found in the analytical world, we are forced to think clearly and define terms and variables unambiguously. The very action of doing this helps to highlight imprecise, ambiguous or even illogical data or statements from the "real" world, requiring the analyst to go back to the data sources and clarify the data or investigate reasons for inconsistencies.
- Once we have a structure to our model we will be able to test the structure to see whether there are any contradictions implied, or systemic properties that do not seem to accord with reality, and again maybe revisit the problem-situation for clarification.
- Once we have a model, we can see whether the model behaves in any significant way differently from what we believe is actuality, and compare implied behaviours of the model with data that our empirical work can collect.

But this is all flowing one way to "help" the model. In fact, benefits flow the other way also.

- The use of models to represent the multiple and possibly conflicting views that we know will arise from a behaviourally complex situation will highlight those conflicts, helping them to be explored with the client-group and helping the move, if not to a common view, at least to recognition and further understanding of the basis of the conflicts.
- Building a model can help to provide insights into the behaviour of a system that will help participants to understand the problem-situation and thus provide more informed and better-founded data.
- The use of multiple-methodology to build the models will, as we have said, help to foster ownership amongst the participants, especially in the not infrequent case where they have come from very different

backgrounds and the model can be seen to be a synthesis of all of those views.

While we have just talked about combining methodologies, we have already seen one procedure for doing this, in our discussion of how the Soft Systems Methodology *process* can help to generate conceptual models that can inform a "harder" paradigm, which can be used to develop mathematical models. We'll look at a similar idea with mapping methodology in an example to be described in Section 4.7, which will highlight many of the points above.

Even this picture is over-simplistic, because we have espoused a view where we look at the problem-situation with multiple methodologies or multiple views – not just two views. And we have discussed that a key reason for this is that there is no single "real" "truth" in "wicked", "messy" problem-situations; rather, there are multiple perceptions of different aspects of the situation, each with different interpretations – so that we are therefore particularly interested in what is known as "triangulation". This is the idea that we should check the validity of any results or data by approaching a question from as many different angles as possible (Denzin, 1989) – using different data to cross-check (the most common meaning of "triangulation" in this context) or using different methodologies or different analysts or participants, or any different way of attacking the same question. So we can use our "hard" analysis to model the expected behaviour of a system, and infer or observe behaviour in the "real" world, and use these to triangulate with each other. But more than that, as we move into the behaviourally complex world, we will collect different types of data, which we view with different lenses on the world, to triangulate each other. So we might collect "hard" numbers about personnel movements from the human resources department (which we'll regard with a fairly positivist view), but back these up or supplement them with anecdotes taken from the staff canteen (which we'll regard perhaps with an ethnographic view) and maybe perceptions and views from the Human Resources Director and so on.

We should sound one warning. Our different methodologies with different underlying paradigms give us different types of knowledge, and we must always be aware of the nature of the data we are collecting – otherwise we will misunderstand what we have and treat the data as if they were what they are not. We need to ensure "epistemological control at the methodological level . . . In order to learn we have to resist the lure of pragmatism. We cannot afford to allow the theoretically uncontrolled employment of diverse methods, tools and techniques that appears to occur in management consultancy," says Jackson (1997) (rather dismissively of the management consultancy industry!).

> Maintaining both the analytical view and the real-world view in the analyst's head simultaneously enables these two views to develop and support each other. Far from being incompatible, they are therefore actually synergistic. Furthermore, using both "soft" and "hard" models allows the former to be developed from the analyst's dual view, while the latter can be developed through the former to enable the mathematical models to become useful.

4.6   Structures of methods

As we mentioned in Section 4.4, rather than looking at situations with a variety of methods, some commentators have found it preferable to construct unified systems of methodologies that can be used for any situations. Now, in view of the multiplicity of different problem-situations faced by Management Scientists, and our discussion of the inherent wicked messiness of the management world, you might feel that this is a hopeless task (whether or not you think it a worthy aim). But such systems do have a very faithful, even if not large, following, so we need to mention them here.

The first attempts here were simple statements of different types of methodology showing the different strengths and weaknesses of the different types of method – in particular the "system of system methodologies" initiated by Jackson and Keys (1984) and later Jackson (1987), which classified methodologies by the type of relationships between the participants, and by whether the system is simple or complex (unlike Roth and Senge's later work quoted in Chapter 1, not differentiating between dynamic and behavioural complexity).

This really simply offers guidance to analysts. However, the development of this work into "Total Systems Intervention" (TSI) (Flood & Jackson, 1991) is described by the authors as a "meta-methodology". This is divided into three phases. The first is "creativity", which takes a series of "system metaphors" to help managers think about their organizations and choose a "dominant" metaphor that best highlights their concerns, which then gives the basis for what follows. The second phase is "choice" (choosing methodologies) and then "implementation". Critics would say this is simply one particular way of analysis; and you could make the further objection that by choosing a dominant metaphor, TSI is leading the analyst away from multi-methodology. TSI was later modified by Flood (1995), recognizing that a small set of metaphors is too limiting and also making the structure recursive, but the basic criticisms remain.

There have been other moves towards overarching grand schemes or universal methods, some of which are described in Midgley (1997), which also tries to set the methods within some of the important philosophical issues that we discussed in Chapter 1. However, it remains to be seen whether this search for a well-defined single "systems methodology" to analyse a complex "wicked" world will bear fruit.

4.7   In practice – and a classic example

In practice, I believe that many if not most good analysts pragmatically find they use a variety of methodologies in their interventions. However, there is little evidence about how much this is *formally* undertaken. Munro and Mingers (2002) attempted a survey of practitioners on the use of multi-methodology, but only got 67 answers, with the results suggesting (perhaps not surprisingly) that generally those with an interest in multi-methodology replied. But even for this survey, "most uses of multi-methodology are based in a single paradigm" although "there is a small but significant movement within OR/MS that is both multi-methodological and multi-paradigmatic." However, there are hints elsewhere of some formal multi-methodological work taking place (Mingers (2000) gives some further examples of mixing taking place in published papers). In the modelling of health services, for example, there are various examples. To pick some at random:

- Mixing Soft System Methodology and simulation in resource allocation (Lehaney & Hlupic, 1995; and, similarly, we mentioned Kotiadis and Mingers (2006) in the last chapter);
- Mixing system thinking with queuing and simulation in outpatient clinic operations (Bennett & Worthington, 1998);
- Mixing cognitive mapping with simulation in intensive-care patient flow (Sachdeva, Williams & Quigley, 2007);

- Mixing multivariate statistical analysis with analysis of interviews in high-dependency care (Kowalczyk, 2004).

The last example above comes from a book by Pidd (2004) specifically looking at how hard and soft methods are used in combination. This sets out a number of essays and examples by those applying mixed hard/soft methodologies in practice. However, while there are interesting illustrations (such as two examples of public bodies, one involved with tax and one with defence, which are faced with public scrutiny, so the "soft" part of the methodology has to be particularly rigorous and auditable), there are few actual conclusions.

One example mentioned in Pidd's book, which we have already discussed in Section 3.3.5, is the case of the *Shuttle* wagons (Ackermann, Eden & Williams, 1997, and there's a little more information, including quotations from the newspapers, in Williams, 2000). We'll explore this in more detail as it does illustrate some of the issues of this chapter quite well.

This was a litigation case that required an understanding of why a major contract to build railway rolling stock had overspent by so much. The problem-situation was just the sort of "wicked mess" that we have been describing – there were different perceptions of what had happened, and even if everyone had agreed on the facts, understanding how such dynamically complex projects behave is difficult. This being a litigation, there was a need to do three things:

- First, prove causality: that is, to show what the factors were that caused the overrun, and how these factors came together to cause overspending;
- Second, the lawyers would have to prove responsibility: that is, show which side should legally take responsibility for these factors and outcomes;
- Third, prove the quantum: that is, show that the factors caused a specific amount of overrun.

We have already explained how the analysts viewed the "real" world, using cognitive mapping to structure the problem-situation, and collect (sometimes differing) views. As is not untypical in such work, the resulting cause map is large (Ackermann, Eden & Williams (1997) describe 750 concepts and 900 links). However, we have also noted how the map was analysed to identify positive feedback loops, and both the events that caused them and their consequences. This in itself helped the various stakeholders (lawyers, analysts and engineers) to understand the behaviour of the project. The cause map was further developed and validated working in a visual interactive mode with groups from the client team. The description of the claim could rely on subsets of this map, giving detailed explanations of the trigger-events that must be made and describing both direct and indirect (i.e. systemic) consequences (Williams, Ackermann & Eden (2003): indeed, this reference also describes how the map can be used to produce "stories" of events that provide a useful "illustrative device" to explain the analysis to a judge or mediator).

However, in order to produce a claim, we must be able to take this qualitative model into the quantitative domain to calculate the "quantum", or value of the claim. The developed cause map is too big for direct quantification but, given the analysis we've just described, it can be reduced to its core components (and "Influence Diagram") and this can lead directly to something that can aid quantification. Once a model of the project "as bid" (i.e. as initially planned to happen) has been built, the disruptive effects on the project can be modelled by exactly replicating the Influence Diagram in a continuous simulation model ("System Dynamics", as we'll describe in Chapter 5): the same wording for the variable is used in each model so that their correspondence can easily be seen, giving a transparent model and an audit trail back to the original data-points.

Quantifying a few of the aspects of the System Dynamics model could be done by simply looking at the "real world" data. However, all of the variables needed unambiguous definition, and many of the variables required some degree of subjectivity in their quantification. So the qualitative model was used to define what was meant by specific variables in the quantitative model, and small subsets of the map used as a framework to collect data on the variables.

But the information flow was not simply one-way from the qualitative to the quantitative model. Analysis of the quantitative model showed ambiguities and contradictions in the qualitative model, requiring revision of that model and often the need to revert to the "real" world in order to investigate significant details. Furthermore, by modelling scenarios in the System Dynamics model in front of members of the client-group and letting them compare significant variables with their memories, enabled them to help validate the models (Howick *et al.* (2008) discuss these various steps in much greater detail).

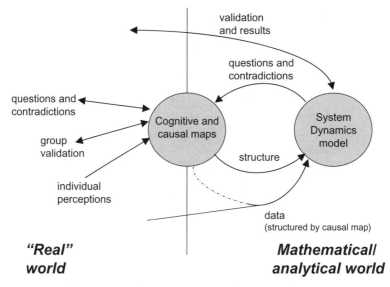

Figure 4.4 Simplified multi-methodology for case study

We thus have the structure in Figure 4.4. As you will see, the flows between the "real" world, the qualitative model and the quantitative model are rather more complex than the simple idea shown in Figure 4.2. And, indeed, what we have described above is more complicated even than Figure 4.4, as the simple element "cognitive and causal maps" in Figure 4.4 covers both the cognitive maps (collected from project participants and relating with the "real world") and also the summarized "Influence Diagram" (which provides structure to, and relates with, the System Dynamics model – and also provides structural subsets to facilitate data-gathering). (Actually, the description of this case in Bennett *et al.* (1997) is slightly more complicated again because it also brings in a wider view of the problem-situation using Conflict Analysis (see Chapter 5), making the multi-methodological view somewhat more complex.)

Analysts need to hold these seemingly different world-views simultaneously. But in so doing, we need a formal process in order to make our process both rigorous and transparent. Different interventions might require different processes, but the process does need to be thought through and the relations between the elements clearly laid down.

5

Management Science Methods

5.1 "Taxonomy" of methods

We have been discussing the use of various Operational Research/Management Science techniques, without actually describing any. And indeed, this is not the book to go into details of any technique. There are plenty of books that will give a rough overview of the techniques, but the important thing is to know how to approach your problems, and then what tools are available. If you decide that you need any particular tool, you can search for available resources to take you further into the topic.

The aim of this chapter, then, is to survey the landscape of some available techniques, to give an idea of which technique is used for what purpose – so you know what the Management Scientists' "tool box" looks like. Sample references will be given for techniques or groups of techniques – but references soon get out of date. This chapter will definitely *not* enable you to use any particular technique if you haven't come across it before: but it should enable you to understand which tools you should be considering, and what is available, and then you should seek out further information from those knowledgeable in that field. Examples are given of a couple of methods, for illustrative purposes only.

There are of course many methods not listed in this chapter. An encyclopedia of OR/MS techniques (Gass and Harris 1996) lists over 200 methods. This chapter only gives some typical methods – perhaps the more common – in each category.

This is a very pragmatic taxonomy of methods. There are attempts at more philosophical classifications, most notably by Mingers (2003), who suggests (but does not complete) classifying methods by their:

- ontology (i.e. what is assumed to exist)
- epistemology (i.e. the forms of knowledge the method uses)
- axiology (i.e. what the purposes or uses of the model are, and who develops and uses the model).

None of these, however, is unproblematic, particularly the last, but many of these issues will arise as we go through the methods. But since we are looking for tools to use in our analysis, our classification method will be to look at the purpose of the methods – which tools are used to do what? Even here, the classification is arguable, but I hope that you will find it helpful even if you can argue about some of the placements. And, of course, there are many more methods than are listed in this chapter, but I have chosen those that I think have proved most popular.

Fundamentally, following our analysis in Chapters 1–4, there are two types of individual Operational Research or Management Science methods:

- So-called "soft" methods, which allow us to attack problems that are either ill-structured or whose parameters are difficult to quantify, with the aim of bringing structure;
- So-called "hard" methods, which assume a well-structured, positivist, measurable universe and take advantage of that to gain further understanding of the situation.

These are by no means universally agreed terms, but, in general, the first of these categories helps us to look into the "real" world of Figure 4.1; the latter helps us to manipulate that well-structured, measurable understanding in the "mathematical/analytical" world of Figure 4.1.

Of course, our taxonomy below will only look at single methods. As we discussed in Chapter 4, many – if not most – good Management

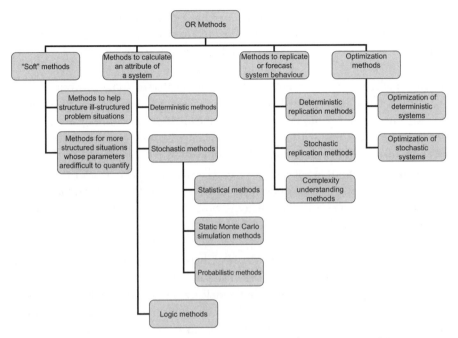

Figure 5.1 Structure of Chapter 5: Operational Research/Management Science methods

Science interventions will use a structured collection of methods, many consisting of one of the former type (to structure the problem) and one or more of the latter type (to come to conclusions). This chapter will provide the basis for such collections by reviewing the individual building blocks.

The methods are arranged by the division given in Figure 5.1. This does not show individual techniques, otherwise the picture would get too complicated, but it shows the overall structure.

The first division, then, will be into these two types.

- Section 5.2 will look at "soft" methods.
- The remainder of Chapter 5 will look at methods for working with well-structured, measurable systems, with the underlying assumption that the problem-structuring stage of an intervention has been done, and the "Janus" of Figure 4.1 is only looking inwards.

However, there are many reasons for analysing systems, and the latter section needs to be divided further into the various reasons why Management Scientists carry out such analyses. One simple division is as follows:

- We might want to carry out calculations to derive some attribute of the system as we have modelled it – Section 5.3 will look at such methods;
- We might want a model to try to replicate the behaviour of a system in order to understand it better, or to forecast its behaviour under different or future conditions – Section 5.4 will look at such methods;
- Finally, we might want to optimize a system in order to find the "best" way of carrying out an operation, with various different meanings of the word "best", of course, but always limited by the restrictions of the modelling method used – Section 5.5 will look at such methods.

There is no clear evidence about which of these techniques is gaining or losing credibility. Fildes and Ranyard (1997) summarize a range of literature giving surveys of usages of techniques, but much of this relates back to preceding decades; at that point, statistical techniques, forecasting and simulation, followed by mathematical programming seemed to be the most common techniques. This is not dissimilar to a study by Bennett (1994), which ranked statistics as the most-used technique, followed by simulation then forecasting. Abdel-Malek *et al.* (1999) surveyed US OR practitioners and asked for the methods to be ranked by pay-off. The highest rankings turned out to be as shown below, together with the business functions in the organization that often applied these techniques.

Highest average rank	Non-quantitative methods	Operations, marketing, distribution logistics, administrative
	Applied probability and statistics	Operations, marketing, finance, distribution logistics
	Simulation	Operations, management of information systems
	Heuristics	Operations, marketing, finance, distribution logistics
	Network analysis	Operations, distribution logistics

This already shows the market starting to change. It certainly seems in the twenty-first century as if complex mathematical reasoning appears to be less popular amongst clients, whereas the rapid increase in computing power has made simulation much easier to carry out. The rapid increase in computing power has also, though, made optimization techniques much more applicable – so, for example, some problems that were approached with mathematical programming, now that computers can evaluate hundreds of thousands of solutions, are now attacked with non-linear local search optimization heuristics of the type discussed in Section 5.5.1.8 (with more powerful methods ever being developed).

In parallel with these developments, as discussed in Chapter 1, our field of application has become much more complex, so we are requiring methods that can deal with both:

- *the dynamic complexity* – requiring computing power, developments in analytical, particularly heuristic, methods, and also sometimes needing to resort to the static or dynamic Monte Carlo simulation, and
- *the behavioural complexity* – requiring methods of modelling human-based systems and their complexity.

5.2 "Soft" methods

Soft methods are utilized when the more mathematical techniques are not applicable, which can largely be for one of two reasons: to allow us to attack problems which are ill-structured or whose parameters are difficult to quantify. This section will thus be divided into two parts:

- Section 5.2.1: methods to help us structure ill-structured problem-situations;
- Section 5.2.2: methods to help us work with more structured situations whose parameters are difficult to quantify.

5.2.1 Methods to help structure ill-structured problem situations

In fact, we have dealt with some of these already in Chapter 3. The nine most popular methods in the UK are probably those listed below. They are all very different and difficult to taxonomize; one convenient way is to consider the areas on which they focus – this is a very loose and somewhat personal characterization, but useful for giving some indications of which technique might be most appropriate in any given situation.

5.2.1.1 Soft Systems Methodology		possibly takes the most general view
5.2.1.2 SODA/Cognitive Mapping/Cause Mapping	focuses on	interconnectedness and causality
5.2.1.3 Scenario Analysis	focuses on	the future
5.2.1.4 Drama Theory/Metagame Analysis	focus on	conflict and co-operation
5.2.1.5 Hypergames		
5.2.1.6 Strategic Choice	focus on	uncertainty
5.2.1.7 Robustness Analysis		
5.2.1.8 Critical Systems Heuristics	focuses on	boundaries
5.2.1.9 Viable System methods	focuses on	organizational structures

5.2.1.1 Soft Systems Methodology

Soft Systems Methodology, or SSM (Checkland & Scholes, 1990), is an approach to understanding and modelling human activity systems (HASs), or systems that involve humans engaged in purposeful activity. In SSM, the purpose of a HAS is expressed as a transformation process; thus a "root definition" is given to each HAS to elaborate the transformation. The analyst defines the customers of, and actors in, the transformation, the transformation process itself, the world-view, owners and environmental constraints. The SSM process then looks to appreciate the problem-situation, understand the world-views of the key stakeholders, create the root definitions and conceptual models of HASs, compare these models with reality, identify desirable and feasible changes, and act to improve the problem-situation. This method is described in more detail in Section 3.2.

5.2.1.2 SODA/cognitive mapping/cause mapping

The basis of the methodology, cognitive mapping (Eden, 1988) and SODA (Strategic Options Development and Analysis) (e.g. Eden & Ackermann,

1992), is essentially a way of making sense of a complex problem through the eyes of a client group. It forms a key part of the more recent "Journey-making" process (key text: Eden & Ackermann, 1998). SODA assumes that power and organizational politics lie at the heart of problem solving and organizational decision-making; thus any action plan needs to be developed with shared understanding between participants to foster commitment to the plan within the team. SODA further assumes that each stakeholder has his or her own subjective view of the problem. Thus cognitive mapping is used, to make sense of individuals' construction of reality and their tacit knowledge. In this technique, the thoughts of an individual about the problem-situation are captured in a diagrammatic form, where concepts are placed around the map and joined by lines representing implication or connection (or, for more formal causal mapping, they represent causality). SODA then takes teams deliberately brought together to bring different perspectives on the problem-situation. A SODA workshop will bring together the individuals' cognitive maps to produce a group map, and it is this process that particularly helps to develop the emotional commitment to the final output. These methods are described in more detail in Section 3.3.

5.2.1.3 Scenario analysis

Scenario analysis, or scenario planning, is best known through the works of van der Heijden (e.g. van der Heijden, 2005; van der Heijden et al., 2002), and is most widely used in strategic management. It focuses on trying to learn about the future. It is a group process that uses techniques in workshops and transfer of knowledge to try to understand the nature and impact of those driving forces that will affect the organization – which are most uncertain and which have the most impact. The "strategic conversations" look at key points where events diverge, and develop "scenarios" – or stories of how the future might unfold – around these. The process of developing this conversation is as important as the end result in developing the view of the future.

5.2.1.4/5.2.1.5 Drama theory/Hypergames

There has been a stream of development starting from the well-structured ideas of Game Theory (see 5.2.2.2 below), which seeks to model formally activities between two or more competing or co-operating entities. Howard's (1971) metagame analysis was a development recognizing some of the contradictions within the thinking among the participants and trying to formulate the ideas in a more intuitive way to apply it to real situations. Hypergame analysis, mostly due to Bennett (1980), extended this by looking at the social construction of "real" situations and then incorporating the multiple perspectives that participants have into the analysis. Drama theory (see particularly Bryant, 2003) takes this further by recognizing the frequent irrationality of human actions, and using drama as a "framework of inquiry" (Bryant, 1988), incorporating aspects of role play, and so on. Rather than a well-structured analysis of rational actions, "it is more productive to view inter- and intra-organizational life as centring upon sense-making, and drama theoretic analysis as being about understanding and supporting how people negotiate meaning" (Bryant, 2007).

5.2.1.6/5.2.1.7 Strategic choice/Robustness analysis

The "Strategic Choice Approach" (SCA) was developed by Friend and Hickling (1997). It aims at helping decision-makers manage uncertainty at the strategic level of decision-making. It is not solely a problem-structuring method but includes option-choosing and action-planning steps. Robustness analysis similarly is a way of helping decision-makers when they have to make a sequence of decisions in the face of radical uncertainty about the future. It is summarized in Rosenhead (2001), and its most obvious feature is the use of decision-trees similar to those described in Section 5.2.2.4 below, looking for any decision at the number of acceptable configurations that are reachable from the end-point of that decision. SCA is described in more detail in Section 3.4.

5.2.1.8 Critical systems heuristics

"Critical Systems Heuristics" (Ulrich, 1983) states that it is a "framework for reflective practice". The main idea is that all problem definitions, suggested actions, and evaluations of outcomes depend on prior judgements about what the relevant system is. Thus we require what CSH calls "boundary judgements", determining which items – both observations and value judgements – count as relevant and which others are left out or are considered less important. Critical systems heuristics provides a framework of boundary categories that give "a checklist of twelve critical boundary questions", divided into sources of motivation, power (client, resources and the decision environment), knowledge and legitimation (Ulrich, 1983, 1987, 2000).

5.2.1.9   Viable system methods

The Viable System Model (VSM), rather than being a methodology, is a model for how organizations are structured in order to be viable (i.e. capable of survival), based on the cybernetics work of Beer (mentioned in Section 2.2). The cybernetics argument leads to the description of five different functions that need to occur: Operations, Co-ordination, Control, Intelligence and Policy; each is given a basic model. Development of this into a methodology (Beer, 1985) means it can be used for studying an organization and comparing it with the basic models, looking for weaknesses, or for designing a better organization from the start. Espejo *et al.* (1996) give more details of the use of the Viable System Model in practice.

5.2.2   Methods for more structured situations whose parameters are difficult to quantify

Where some structure can be brought to bear on a problem-situation – either because it is naturally more structured, or because some of the methods in 5.2.1 have been used – there are a number of methods available to help quantify and then analyse that situation. Below are six methods, roughly in order of how structured the situation needs to be for the method to be applicable (with the first being for the least structured). Again, one convenient way is to consider the areas on which they focus – again a very loose and somewhat personal characterization, but useful for giving some indications of which technique might be most appropriate in any given situation.

5.2.2.1	Influence Diagrams (Meaning 1) and Causal Loop Diagrams	focus on	causality
5.2.2.2	Game Theory	focuses on	actions
5.2.2.3	Conflict Analysis	focuses on	actions
5.2.2.4	Decision Trees	focus on	actions and probability
5.2.2.5	Analytical Hierarchy Process	focuses on	options
5.2.2.6	Multi-criteria/Multi-objective Decision Analysis	focus on	options

5.2.2.1 Influence diagrams (meaning 1) and causal loop diagrams

The influence diagram is a more formal type of cause mapping (see 5.2.1.2 above). Entities in the influence diagram are quantitative variables, and arrows between them show that the variable at the start of the arrow causally influences that at the end, either positively or negatively (shown with a "–" sign). If the set of influences shows that a feedback loop exists (either a negative "balancing" loop or a positive "reinforcing" loop) then this can be shown, forming a "causal loop diagram". This then provides a foundation on which a System Dynamics model (see 5.4.1.1 below) can be built. Lane (2000) gives a good summary of these methods. (Note that the term "influence diagram" has a second, quite different, meaning, as described in 5.3.2.3.2 below.)

5.2.2.2 Game Theory

The precursor of drama theory (5.2.1.4 above) and hypergames (5.2.1.5 above), game theory considers situations where "players" make decisions as strategic reactions or in consideration of other players' actions. A player is faced with a set of moves s/he can play and will form a strategy, a best response to his or her environment. von Neumann and Morgenstern (1944) introduced the idea of games, and also of "mixed" strategies where there is an element of randomness in a player's strategy. This led to a lot of work in developing "utility theory" (i.e. more representative measures of relative desirability between options than simply their monetary value) and different optimum utility criteria. Nash (1950) introduced the concept of a "Nash Equilibrium" (a point at which each player has chosen a strategy and no player can benefit by changing strategy while the others keep theirs unchanged) and later further work within collaborative games, which revolutionized game theory and led to a significant rise in the use of the theory within economics. This is now a huge field in itself, and it is beyond the scope of this book to cover all the various tools and techniques within the field.

5.2.2.3 Conflict analysis

Conflict analysis allows more general analysis of decision situations involving multiple players, each of whom may have multiple objectives, and multiple options from which to choose. Fraser and Hipel (1984) produced early work in conflict analysis (building on Howard's metagame analysis, see 5.2.1.5 above). A graphical model for analysing conflict and thus underlying a decision support system are given respectively in Fang, Hipel and Kilgour (1993) and Hipel *et al.* (1997).

5.2.2.4 Decision trees

A decision tree is a simple diagram of decisions and their possible consequences. It consists of two types of node. One, called a "decision node", represents where a decision has to be made. Branches from this node represent each possible decision. The other is called a "chance node" or "probabilistic node", and represents where a stochastic uncertainty occurs. Branches from this node represent each possible outcome from the event. The nodes and branches thus constitute a "tree" of possible sequential paths to all possible outcomes. Analysis of the tree is simply done by working from the end of the graph forwards, at each probabilistic node calculating the expected outcome, and at each decision node choosing the optimum decision (which can now be done as each branch will have a calculated value). It should be noted that the optimum is assumed to be based on *expected* values, which is a significant simplification. Decision trees are often used with "utilities" as values rather than simply financial values (see 5.2.2.2 above). Most basic OR/MS textbooks will cover this technique.

5.2.2.5 Analytical hierarchy process

The Analytical Hierarchy Process, or AHP, is a technique for choosing between a set of various options with multiple goals. It was developed by Saaty (originally Saaty (1980), with much updating in Saaty (1994)). The aim is to structure the criteria set hierarchically, with the overall goal of the decision at the top of the model, most strategic objectives in the next level and so on down a criteria hierarchy. Then the criteria are looked at by carrying out comparisons between pairs of criteria, and checking those comparisons for internal consistency. Pair-wise comparisons between pairs of options, given the decision-weight, allow options to be scored. The final result uses matrix algebra to give an overall score for each option and sensitivity analysis. (Software such as *Expert Choice* is based on AHP ideas.) Although very popular, particularly in the US, there has been extensive writing about the method with some criticisms identified, particularly concerning circumstances under which the mathematics gives results which are logically inconsistent.

5.2.2.6 *Multi-criteria/Multi-objective decision analysis*

Multi-criteria decision analysis, or MCDA, is a general term for methods to approach the problem addressed by the AHP: choosing the best option from a set of options, given a set (or hierarchy) of multiple criteria. Most techniques within this extensive field use methods for evaluating weights on the critieria (using its hierarchical nature where relevant), then applying those weights to the criteria scores for each individual option. Again, "utilities" are used rather than simply financial values (see 5.2.2.2 above). The SMART method (Edwards, 1977) is a simple way to use multi-criteria utility theory by using weighted linear averages, supposedly giving close to utility functions; this was improved in the SMARTS and SMARTER methods (Edwards and Barton, 1994). Two particular methods, known as "Electre" or "Promethée", rank results. Various software packages have been produced to help decision-makers score attributes and options, particularly using graphical methods of display. Belton and Stewart (2001) provide a comprehensive view of this field. Guitouni and Martel (1998) give a review of methods and some "tentative guidelines" to help choose an appropriate method.

5.3 Methods to calculate an attribute of a system

The remaining sections of this chapter assume a situation has been structured and seek to take advantage of that to gain further understanding of the situation.

The first set of such methods includes those that look at a model of a system and try to calculate some attribute of that system. Many of these methods are essentially mathematical manipulation methods, and will be covered very briefly below. We will divide the methods into deterministic methods and stochastic methods, with a brief note of one additional method at the end.

5.3.1 Deterministic methods

There are many models of typical systems that have standard solutions. The following three are examples.

5.3.1.1 Cost–benefit analysis

Cost–benefit analysis, or CBA, is simply the activity of calculating the total expected costs (which might need to be discounted to bring them to a common year) and calculating the total expected benefits (which again will need to be put into a common metric and may need to be weighted in some way) and then comparing the two. This enables a decision-maker to identify the "best" option, or to make a judgement on one particular option as to whether the benefits outweigh the costs.

5.3.1.2 Project network analysis or critical path method

Critical Path Method (CPM) is used to calculate the duration of a project (as well as some other features about a project's time-aspect), where a "project" for the purposes of this method is simply a set of activities that must be carried out along with certain precedence relationships between the activities. The simplest form is where the precedence relationships simply show that, after the start, each activity cannot start until one or more other activities have completed. A simple algorithm allows calculation of the project duration and the most constrained or "critical" activities. Developments include limitations on resources across activities (so activities might not be possible in parallel) and other types of precedence relationships, as well as stochastic elements (see 5.3.2.3.7 below). Maylor (2003) is a good textbook in this area.

5.3.1.3 Data envelopment analysis

Data Envelopment Analysis (DEA) is a method for comparing a number of similar *decision-making units* (DMUs), in particular to evaluate their *relative efficiency*. For each DMU, its inputs and outputs are measured. The basic idea is then that other producers should also be able to produce the same or more output with this input if they are operating as efficiently. Since there generally isn't a suitable comparison DMU, existing DMUs can be combined to give a hypothetical combined unit with combined inputs and outputs. We can then find the optimum hypothetical DMU for each real DMU using "linear programming" (see 5.5.1.1 below). If this optimum is better than the real one (either more output with the same input or the same output with less input) then the real DMU is *inefficient*. Graphical displays of DEA show the optimum DMUs as a "frontier" around all the inefficient DMUs.

Typical examples would be where there are a number of similar units operating – such as analysis of each shop in a chain of hardware stores, or an analysis looking at all UK doctors' surgeries. These can be compared to see which are less efficient (in this strictly defined sense) than others. There is again a huge literature building on this area. (Cooper, Seiford & Tone (2006) is a recent book by one of the founders.) One problem is that the data used are point estimates so it is sometimes difficult to distinguish between real inefficiency and simply "noise" in the data.

DEA is a subset of the field of performance measurement, which goes beyond OR/MS models and into ideas such as the "Balanced Scorecard" (recently published as Kaplan & Norton, 2005) – but this is venturing into the world of general management consultancy and beyond the remit of this book.

5.3.2   Stochastic methods

If there are many deterministic models of typical systems that have standard solutions, there are even more stochastic models. We can divide them for this purpose into statistical methods, static Monte Carlo simulation methods, and probabilistic methods. Only the last of these groups will be explored in detail below.

5.3.2.1   Statistical methods

There is, of course, a huge range of statistical methods for analysing sets of data. The OR/MS analyst needs a basic understanding of these because s/he will be faced with many instances in which patterns need to be discerned within data. To go through all statistical techniques is clearly beyond the scope of this book, but the analyst needs to be familiar with techniques both based on assumptions of normality and non-parametric tests, covering areas such as:

- relationships between variables (Pearson and Spearman correlation, regression, etc.)

- independence between treatments (contingency tables) or groups (t-tests, Mann-Whitney, etc.)
- the difference between groups or treatments (ANOVA, etc.)
- putting items into similar groups (cluster analysis, etc.)
- looking for a small number of explanatory factors (factor analysis, etc.)

and so on.

The increasing power of computers, and even more the increasing size of large data-sets concerning customer behaviour, has led to a huge increase in what has become known as "data mining". This involves sorting through large data-sets for summary information. These can be either to try to find out about something about the data, such as patterns of behaviour (using, for example, clustering, association and sequence rules), or to try to establish forecasts (using, for example, regression and classification, or by producing rule-based systems or neural networks).

5.3.2.2 *Static Monte Carlo simulation methods*

For many deterministic methods, there are computer packages available running Monte Carlo simulations of the method, enabling the method to be explored where parameters can be expressed as probabilistic rather than simply being known and deterministic. (Monte Carlo simulation means simply repeated sampling from streams of random numbers (or, more properly, when carrying out the operation on a computer, pseudo-random numbers), simulating a system many times over and looking at the probability distribution of the results obtained.)

The most straightforward and perhaps most well-known are Monte Carlo simulations based on spreadsheets (a common package being *@Risk* for *Excel* – see Palisade, 2007a). This simply allows cells in a spreadsheet to contain random variables subject to a probability distribution (with cells related to each other as in an ordinary spreadsheet), then a Monte Carlo simulation will populate the distributions with random numbers and calculate results many times over to indicate the distributions.

Other methods subject to such treatment include the critical path method (see 5.3.1.2), which has similar packages available (including an *@Risk* version – see Palisade, 2007b)

5.3.2.3 Probabilistic methods

There are probabilistic methods available to tackle a wide range of typical situations. These developed at different times, perhaps the first to come to prominence being "queuing theory" (see 5.3.2.3.8 below). These are used less frequently now than they used to be because the increasing power of computers has made Monte Carlo methods more accessible to users, and these can operate with fewer restrictions on the modelling. However, the probabilistic methods can often give useful insights into problem-situations not available from the simple application of Monte Carlo simulation.

We will take 10 typical sets of methods to illustrate the sort of tools that are around (in alphabetical order).

5.3.2.3.1 Availability/Reliability/Maintainability (ARM) analysis Reliability analysis concerns the distribution of "lifetimes" of components of an engineering system, and thus the distribution of the "lifetime" of the system as a whole. This is usually based on the idea of component lifetimes having probability distributions, or a probability of failure at any instant in time, and using these to calculate overall system reliability. Rates of failure are often characterised by a "mean time between failure", and the Weibull distribution has often been found to be a good approximation for failure-time distributions. Calculations can then be done using probability calculus.

Availability analysis is a simple extension of this – given that components or a system fail, for what proportion of time is the system available?

Maintainability looks at optimizing management actions to optimize reliability/availability. Should components be replaced on failure? Or should regular inspections be made despite the down-time this implies? Extensions of the probability calculus above will enable the availability and the cost of different management routines to be calculated and thus the optimum policy found.

5.3.2.3.2 Bayesian methods and Bayesian belief networks The title "Bayesian" applies to a whole approach in statistics, deriving from a simple result in probability theory derived by a church minister called Bayes in the eighteenth century. This result ("Bayes theorem") gives a means to update probabilities in the light of new evidence. This means that calculations can be done using estimates of probabilities, with initial estimates based on various sources – historical, judgemental, and so on – then these estimates can be updated as more evidence becomes available. Since, as we'll describe later in Section 7.6, many of our probabilities are estimated judgementally, this gives a powerful tool to combine judgement and quantitative measurement.

One particular OR/MS tool in which a Bayesian approach is taken is called Bayesian Belief Networks (BBNs). These can be used where many events are interlinked and interdependent in complex ways – and, of course, we are increasingly looking at dynamic complexity in our problem-situations. A BBN defines the various events, the interdependencies between them, and their conditional probabilities; it can then be used to calculate the probability that a possible cause was the actual cause of an event. It is a general method, so the ideas can be extended beyond straightforward random variables to include, for example, decisions. BBN graphs often take the name "influence diagrams" – but this is a technical definition that must *not* be confused with the much more qualitative type of "influence diagrams" defined in 5.2.2.1. More information on this whole area can be found in Bedford and Cooke (2001).

5.3.2.3.3 Credit scoring Credit scoring is an increasingly common application of data mining (see 5.3.2.1). The aim of credit scoring is to distinguish good customers (to be given financial credit) from bad customers (i.e. those likely to default), by looking at the best way to "score" each customer, given large sets of data on previous activity.

5.3.2.3.4 Forecasting A frequent position that an OR/MS practitioner faces is having to predict the behaviour of a parameter in the future, given its behaviour in the past. There is a range of techniques available for such a position, and we can only touch upon them here. They can be summarized in the three following sets:

(i) *Judgemental methods.* There are various methods used for helping experts use their judgement to predict (usually longer term) trends in variables. For example: Delphi Analysis, Technological Forecasting, Historical Trends.

(ii) *Associative methods.* For more sustainable forecasts, often used in the medium term, some methods try to relate the parameter to another parameter that we can forecast better or that we can control (such as, in the former case, relating sales of a product such as ice-cream to the weather, or, in the latter case, relating sales of a product to levels of advertising), accepting that there is also random "noise" in the system. Regression is the most common way of doing this, as mentioned in 5.3.2.1.

(iii) *Projective methods.* Perhaps the most common meaning of the word "forecasting" in OR, though, simply takes a series of observations (usually regular, given the name "a time series") and projects it into the future. There are two main sets of methods:

- The first set consists of the most simple methods, which allow the modeller to make some simple assumptions about the series and thus select the most appropriate method. "Exponential smoothing" and "moving averages" are common where series don't appear to have any discernable pattern. Holt's Method and the Holt-Winters Method are extensions of exponential smoothing where there appears to be (respectively) a trend and seasonality in the time-series. There are also similar extensions of moving averages.

- The second set consists of much more complex methods. These do not require the user to make assumptions about the time-series, but rather analyse the series as it stands to try to detect underlying patterns. The most well-known technique is Box-Jenkins, which provides an analysis tool for taking a series, identifying seasonality, trends, and underlying patterns, which are classified as coming from two clear archetypes: an autoregressive series (where observations depend on previous elements plus random noise) and moving average series (where observations are a linear combination of random noise elements) – not to be confused with the simple moving average method). This analysis then allows a more informed projection into the future. This method has been widely used, successfully, although it does require a substantial set of data, and also a degree of expertise in the user.

These methods can be combined: for example, one could explain as much of the variability of a parameter as possible using an associative method, and then project the outstanding part of the time series using a projective method.

Makridakis, Wheelwright and Hyndman (1998) is a well-known book covering much of this huge area.

5.3.2.3.5 Fuzzy methods "Fuzzy" methods are those based on the ideas of "fuzzy set theory", developed by Zadeh. Rather than elements being within sets or having particular attributes, as in normal logic, this theory is based on the ideas of elements having "membership functions" whose values range from 0 to 1 – 0 indicating "not in the set" or "not having that attribute" and 1 indicating absolutely "within the set". Numbers in between allow for subjective ideas such as "somewhat" or "very". The method is sometimes thought to be appropriate to represent such subjective ideas. (Note, by the way, that a fuzzy membership function is quite different from a probability.) The ideas are very well developed, and are used in elements of control theory, but their use in OR/MS has (as far as this author has seen) been much more in theory than in practical applications. Zimmermann (2001) describes a number of possible applications.

5.3.2.3.6 Stochastic/Markov processes A large set of OR modelling techniques come under the general heading of "stochastic processes", which as the name suggests are processes where a system can change state in a probabilistic way, and where the methods try to predict its path. A major set of such techniques assumes that there is a finite (or at least, countable) set of possible states of the system, and looks at how it moves from one state to the next.

The most common subset of such methods relies on the assumption that the system is "Markov" – that is, when the probabilities of moving from one state to any given state are the same no matter what the path to the current state was; this property is sometimes called "memoryless"-ness. Where this assumption is reasonably robust, it greatly simplifies the mathematics involved, and allows results to be obtained about how the system is likely to behave.

Where the movements of the system from state to state happen at discrete times, this is called a "Markov chain" and, since these are the strongest assumptions, it is here that the most results can be obtained. (The classic picture of a Markov chain is that of a drunken man walking down the road, who might veer left or right with each pace: hence the term "drunken walk" is sometimes used.)

This is a very wide category of analytical models, which have been used extensively where the situation allows the requisite assumptions. A good textbook such as Ross (2006) will cover these techniques.

5.3.2.3.7 Probabilistic CPM There is a large academic literature in the area of Project Network Analysis, or Critical Path Method (CPM), as described in 5.3.1.2 above, where some of the parameters are assumed to be non-deterministic. Some of these techniques have informed computer packages carrying out Monte Carlo analysis and help to optimize the use of resources within project networks (and so should properly come under 5.5.2 below), so-called "resource-smoothing" or "resource scheduling". However, the bulk of this literature makes assumptions that are difficult to fill, so otherwise a lot of this work is rarely used in practice (see Williams, 2003).

5.3.2.3.8 Queueing theory Queueing theory is one of the oldest areas of OR application, pre-dating even the expression "Operational Research", as it dates back to Erlang in the very early twentieth century. As its name suggests, it is the analysis of queues. The original work dealt with queues for telephony resources, and telecommunications has been a considerable application area (such as call centres), but any service situation in which items queue for attention could be a possible area of application for queueing theory. A common nomenclature for queue is given as $A/B/n$, where A denotes the distribution of inter-arrival times, B the distribution of service times, and n the number of (assumed identical) servers. Sometimes this is appended by other letters for various technical mechanisms, such as limits on the size of the queue or customer behaviour.

Where "A" or "B" are given as "M", this denotes a negative exponential distribution, giving that distribution the Markov quality and enabling many results to be found analytically. As in all analytical methods, it is often the case that the real situation is too complex for analysis, and analysts resort to simulation. However, even in these cases, queueing theory can often give insights into the behaviour of the system, enabling more informed models to be built.

Kleinrock (1975, 1976) gives classic treatments of the area.

5.3.2.3.9 Risk analysis Risk analysis is a very general term, denoting any activity identifying and evaluating effects that can cause uncertainty in achieving a goal. Many of the methods here in 5.3.2.3 and indeed any stochastic analysis tool can therefore be seen as "risk analysis" methods. Two common usages of the term, though, are worth noting:

- First is the idea of "project risk analysis". Because projects in organizations (i.e. initiatives with a defined, limited life-cycle) have (or should have) well-defined goals, then various tools have been developed to look at the risks of achieving those goals.

- Second, the term is also used in the finance field. In particular, the idea of "value at risk" (VaR) is defined, which represents the risk in the value of a portfolio of assets. VaR is given as the maximum amount at risk to be lost from a portfolio given a continuation of current conditions, over a specified period, at a specified confidence level.

5.3.2.3.10 Stochastic inventory/production models This item is more a large area of application of OR models rather than specific tools. Some of the models used here have become standard terms in OR, particularly the "economic order quantity" (which we looked at as an example in Figure 1.3). This is the order size that minimizes the total variable costs required to order and hold inventory. (It is another term that pre-dates the term "Operational Research".) From this beginning, a large number of different models have built up of the holding of inventory, and then to the manufacturing production of this inventory. Allied to this is the associated logic involved in manufacturing from a hierarchy of sub-products, which formed the basis firstly of (deterministic) "Materials Requirements Planning" and subsequent developments. This has been a major area of application for OR, although it is perhaps particularly in academic work in this area that the comments in Section 1.1 are most applicable, concerning hypothetical "models" which are developed with no real-world motivation nor any practical application, rather being simply mathematical exercises. Waters (2003) is a simple introductory textbook in this area.

5.3.3 Logic methods

5.3.3.1 Logic programming

One technique, which it is difficult to place within this taxonomy, uses quite a different computational idea. Logic programming specifies a computation in terms of a set of logical relations between the various entities concerned. The computer package used (*Prolog* is a common example) will incorporate a theorem-prover. This type of construction has proved useful in certain artificial intelligence applications and in developing problem-solving and question-answering systems. It is a specialized field, one into which few OR/MS analysts have moved, and interested readers are best advised probably to refer to the Association for Logic Programming (2007). It is mentioned here because of its occasional use in collaboration with a more common OR technique to provide specialist functions (Marsh, Williams & Mathieson (1990) give one example).

5.4   Methods to replicate or forecast system behaviour

The next set of methods are those to model a system and try to show how it behaves, or how it might behave, so that the model can be experimented upon rather than the whole system. We divide the methods into three:

- 5.4.1 Deterministic replication methods;
- 5.4.2 Stochastic replication methods;
- 5.4.3 Complexity understanding methods.

5.4.1   Deterministic replication methods

5.4.1.1   System dynamics

The most well known deterministic method for understanding and replicating how a system works is "System Dynamics" (SD). This models a system as a series of "stocks" and "flows", with material flowing continuously between the stocks. The model is given an initial state, then differential equations model how material flows from one stock to another. The method is particularly useful for showing the effects of feedback loops, information flows and time delays.

In practice, SD is carried out using a pseudo-continuous approximation, with a computer package carrying out the calculations. Thus the flow-equations actually show how material flows from one stock to another during a specified time interval ΔT (commonly referred to as "DT"). Apart from carrying out the calculations, the use of such packages is powerful in three ways:

- It enables the structure of the system to be displayed graphically, with the relationships between all of the stocks, flows and associated equations shown on the screen. This means that this is a very transparent technique, with no relationships used other than those shown, and these can be manipulated in collaboration with a client-group.

- Indeed, the very construction of such models flows naturally from the types of causal mapping we looked at earlier in the book (as described in Section 4.7). Some SD computer packages actually contain both mapping facilities and the SD calculation function.
- The displays can show the behaviour of variables over the course of the simulation, so that the output of the packages are not simply point estimates of results, but are time profiles, useful both for validating the models and also understanding the behaviour predicted.

(Later packages also allow some parameters to be random variables, but these essentially only allow random choices for what-if? analyses within what is essentially a deterministic method.) Sterman (2000) provides a standard textbook in the area.

5.4.2 Stochastic replication methods

The main stochastic method for replicating how a system works is dynamic Monte Carlo simulation, which comes in two types (although it is worth noting in 5.4.2.3 and 5.4.2.4 technological advances that can apply to either type).

Dynamic Monte Carlo simulation (which in its static usage we defined in Section 5.3.2.2 – based on the use of random numbers, with many iterations carried out to give an idea of the probable distribution of results) is perhaps the most frequently used technique in OR, allowing a degree of generality that cannot be achieved in analytical methods. The technique grew in importance as the power of computers developed. There are a variety of ways of implementing the ideas in practice, but the following are the common elements:

(i) "Entities" are the main elements whose behaviour is of interest – these might be people, or parts in a factory, or ships, and so on. They are usually the tangible players in the system we are trying model.

(ii) "Stations" or "work centres" (or some such term) show where an entity is at any particular time, and what it is doing.

(iii) "Queues" show where an entity has to wait for other entities to enter a particular state.

(iv) Rules and logical relationships describe what each entity does under particular circumstances, and links the different types of entities together.

(v) Random number generators give numerical figures each time a probabilistic parameter is used, with a given probability distribution.

(vi) Some mechanism is needed to control the time advance in the simulation. This mechanism will enable the positions and attributes of each entity to be updated subject to the rules and relationships above, then will move on to the next relevant time. There are two main ways in which this can occur, and this provides the two main different types of dynamic simulation (5.4.2.1 and 5.4.2.2).

5.4.2.1 Discrete-event (Monte Carlo) simulation

Discrete-even simulation keeps track of upcoming events, and at each time moves to the time at which the next event will occur. This was the basis of many early programmes, and is still probably the most used OR technique of all.

5.4.2.2 Continuous (Monte Carlo) simulation

This should rather be called pseudo-continuous simulation, as this technique moves the clock forward by a constant small time-step, much as in system dynamics.

Two advances have made the method particularly powerful.

5.4.2.3 Visual interactive (Monte Carlo) simulation

As computers grew in power, so did their graphical capabilities, and most simulation packages allow a single iteration to be run with a graphical display of the behaviour on the screen, many with capability for the user to interact with the run and input decisions or changes in behaviour. Visual interactive simulations can be discrete-event or continuous.

5.4.2.4 Agent-based simulation

More powerful computing has led to methods such as "agent-based simulation". In this, the concentration is on the individual entities in the model, and their internal state and decision-making. As the simulation clock moves forward, the internal logic within each agent will make its decisions. Such methods are very powerful for modelling complex systems where it is not clear what behaviour is likely to emerge from the interaction of the entities.

Robinson (2003) gives a very simple introduction to the area of OR simulation. However, this is a huge separate field in itself and many more resources can be found, such as through the Society for Modelling and Simulation International (2007).

5.4.3   Complexity understanding methods

5.4.3.1   Complexity theory

Section 2.2 referred to some of the techniques that have emerged from a variety of disciplines to model complex systems of entities without simplifying pre-assumptions of structure. That chapter referred to the work on "complex adaptive systems" by McMillan (2004) and particularly to the work on "complex responsive processes of relating" by Stacey (2001, 2003). There are clearly useful insights in these ideas, and it is hoped that they will be used for modelling of human systems. As yet, though, they are relatively unproven in the OR/MS field.

5.5   Optimization methods

The next set of methods includes those which seek to find the "best" or optimum from a well-defined set of possibilities. They by necessity assume a very well-structured problem, and thus are often misused. However, in the right circumstances – in particular, where the solutions allowed by the model are realistic and include all sensible realistic decisions – they provide one of the most important contributions that OR has made over the past 60 years. As before, we will divide the methods into deterministic followed by stochastic methods.

Optimization models generally have two elements: the objective function, a combination of the decision variables of which the modeller wishes to find the "best" value, and a set of constraints, in which a combination of decision-variables is $<$, $>$, $\leq$, $\geq$, or $=$ to a value.

5.5.1   Optimization of deterministic systems

Winston (2004) provides a useful textbook covering all of these techniques.

5.5.1.1   Linear programming

Perhaps the technique which is most often associated with the term "Operational Research", Linear Programming came to the fore in 1947 when Dantzig developed an efficient method called the "Simplex Method" for solving linear programmes, and it has been extensively used ever since.

Linear programmes have the above two elements of optimization models, but are restricted to problems in which:

(i)   there is a single objective function;
(ii)   both the objective function and the constraints are linear combinations of decision variables;
(iii) the decision variables are allowed to take any (non-negative) value subject to the constraints.

With these conditions, if there are any solutions to the constraints, then they form a continuous polygon in the multi-dimensional space of possible solutions, which will have a well-defined optimum (or a set of optima). While these are solvable by hand, there are many powerful linear programming (LP) packages on the market (as well as *Solver* in *Excel*).

Linear programming is such a fundamental – and iconic – type of optimization that it is appropriate to give an example of the method. Figure 5.2 shows a very simple "problem" with its formulation as a linear programme. As it says, this is not intended to be realistic, merely a simplified example to illustrate what the technique looks like.

5.5.1.2   Integer and mixed programming

If we relax the third of the three restrictions (iii) above, we can specify optimization problems where some of the decision variables are constrained to be only integers (this would be a "mixed" programme – an "integer programme" (IP) being one in which all of the decision variables are integers). This gives the method the ability to model many more situations – not only because some variables are naturally only integers (you can fly 1 aeroplane or 2 aeroplanes, but not 1½), but also particularly because we can use variables to denote yes/no variables, and to include logical IF-THEN conditions in the model (see e. g. the Williams (1999) textbook for some of this scope). Variables that take only the values 0 or 1 (0/1 variables) are widely used in this context and are a powerful tool for use in real-life problems.

Linear Programming

A very simple classic problem is given in the following. It is not intended to be realistic, simply a hypothetical grossly simplified example to illustrate the appearance of the technique.

A farmer rents 128 acres of land, of which 100 acres is available to him for growing cereal crops. He specializes in growing wheat and potatoes and would like to know how many acres of each to plant for the next year. A government order means that he can plant no more than 65 acres of potatoes. He estimates that the expected profit to be made on an acre of potatoes is £600 and on an acre of wheat is £900. However, he has only 480 man-hours of labour available to him at harvest time and reckons that he needs 6 man-hours per acre of wheat and 3 man-hours per acre of potatoes.

Steps in the process would be something like this:

Step 1: Determine what objective is
We will assume that it is to maximize the profit given the constraints.

Step 2: Identify and define the decision variables
The variables under the control of the farmer are the number of acres of the two crops he plants. So let us define:

W = acres of wheat planted

P = acres of potatoes planted

Note that we have made sure that both of these variables have units.

Step 3: Formulate the "objective function"
We decided that the objective was to maximize profit, so we need to express "profit" in terms of the decision variables. Since the profit per acre of potatoes and wheat is £600 and £900 respectively, then we wish to

Figure 5.2 Simple linear programming example

Maximize $900 \times W + 600 \times P$

Step 4: Formulate the constraints

We cannot use any value of W and P, obviously. If we look through the statement of the problem above, we can see four different constraints:

- "A farmer rents 128 acres of land . . ." So there are only 128 acres available in total:

$$W + P \le 128$$

- ". . . of which 100 acres is available to him for growing cereal crops . . ." So he can have no more than 100 acres of wheat:

$$W \le 100$$

- ". . . A government order means that he can plant no more than 65 acres of potatoes . . ."

$$P \le 65$$

- ". . . However, he has only 480 man-hours of labour available to him at harvest time and reckons that he needs 6 man-hours per acre of wheat and 3 man-hours per acre of potatoes . . ." So he can use no more than 480 man-hours, with the total number of man-hours used being the left-hand side of the following equation:

$$6W + 3P \le 480$$

And, to avoid impossible answers, we should remember that both W and P must be non-negative (that is: $W, P \ge 0$).

The accumulation of all of the above gives a "Linear Programme"

Figure 5.2 *Continued*

Maximise $900W + 600P$

Subject to:

$$W + P \leq 128$$

$$W \leq 100$$

$$P \leq 65$$

$$6W + 3P \leq 480$$

$$W,P \geq 0$$

This is such a small, simple problem that the result can actually be found by showing all of the possible values on a graph, using the equations for the constraint above to draw lines dividing feasible points from those that disobey each of the constraints above in turn. You will find that the corner of the shape for which the objective function is greatest is at:

$$W = 47.5 \text{ and } P = 65$$

Figure 5.2 *Continued*

Optimum solutions to integer programmes can be quite different to the solutions when the integer constraint is not imposed (see Figure 5.3 for a very small example). So, we need methods to solve these problems. However, the increase in applicability brings with it an increase in difficulty in solution. A typical method used to demonstrate how a solution is found is the "branch and bound" method, where successive integer-constraints are applied until the optimum solution is found, with an LP optimization needed at each step, and search-branches cut off as they are found to be non-optimal. Practically, though, integer programmes are only solved using one of the many powerful computer packages on the market.

5.5.1.3 *Special integer programming problems*

A number of problems have been found to fit within the integer programming framework, which have a wide degree of applicability, and have been given

---

IP models differing from LP models

Consider the following very small problem:

$$\text{Maximize} \quad x + y$$
$$\text{Such that} \quad -2x + 2y \geq 1$$
$$-8x + 10y \leq 13 \text{ and } x, y \geq 0$$

The methods above allow the best solution for x and y to be found:

$$x = 4 \text{ and } y = 4.5.$$

However, if we *add* the constraint that these variables are required to be integers (e.g. if they denote buses or aeroplanes or assignments) then the optimum answer is:

$$x = 1 \text{ and } y = 2,$$

a very different answer!

Figure 5.3 Example of IP models differing from LP models. From Williams. Copyright 1990 John Wiley & Sons Limited. Reproduced with permission.

generic names to identify them when they occur in practice. Some of these are as follows. Not all are best solved as integer programmes, and the more difficult are appropriate for dynamic programming (described in 5.5.1.6 below).

5.5.1.3.1 Assignment problems Where the problem is to assign items to resources, such as in assigning jobs to machines, or certain transportation problems, then this can be modelled as an IP using only 0/1 variables. However, there is a subset of such problems that can be solved analytically using the "Hungarian method" (which is described in Winston, 2004).

5.5.1.3.2 The set-covering problem Set-covering represents the problem of covering all members of a main set by group of subsets of the main set such that all members of the main set are covered, but at minimum total cost. The classic example would be choosing aircrew rosters so that all routes of an airline are covered. Such a problem is soluble by IP but special algorithms also exist.

5.5.1.3.3 The knapsack problem The knapsack problem has a single constraint, and is so called after the fictitious example of choosing possible items that can fit into one bag (of maximum weight) to be taken on a trip. Again, special algorithms exist, and have applications to project selection and so on, but they are rarely seen in practice.

5.5.1.3.4 The set-packing problem, and general cutting and packing problems Extending the knapsack problem, set-packing represents the problem of packing in as many subsets of the main set to maximize total value, but without any overlap in the members of the main set. Again, such a problem is soluble by IP but special algorithms also exist.

This problem can be extended to more general real-life problems of packing as much in as possible, such as in physical packing of transportation, or cutting shapes from pieces on a production line (such as pieces of steel for manufacture, or pieces of cloth for garment assembly).

5.5.1.3.5 Network-flow methods There are a variety of optimization problems that can be expressed in a network-flow representation (to be differentiated from activity networks, discussed in 5.3.1.2). The most straightforward is the "shortest path" problem, and simple algorithms (particularly that due to Dijkstra) exist to find the shortest path from the first to any other node in a network. More general is the "minimum flow" problem, which looks at finding the minimum-cost way of flowing through a network, such as in transportation problems. Where there are capacity limitations on how much can flow between the nodes in a network, then a second set of problems looks at the maximum flow through the network, for which again a standard algorithm exists (due to Ford and Fulkerson). There is also the "minimum spanning" tree problem, which looks at finding the set of arcs in a network that connect all nodes in the network at minimum total cost (or minimum total length).

5.5.1.3.6 Travelling salesman problem The "travelling salesman" problem gets its name from the idea of a sales-person (the gender-specific name of the problem was coined in the 1940s!) who must visit each of a set of cities once and once only, before returning home. Given the distances between cities, what is the best order for him to visit them? This can be easily represented as an IP and then solved. However, given that it is what is known as "NP hard" (very loosely, the difficulty in solution expands exponentially with the size of the problem), dynamic programming (5.5.1.6 below) is more suitable.

5.5.1.3.7 Vehicle routing The problem of planning deliveries to a number of customers using a variety of vehicles can in simple circumstances be reduced to a travelling salesman problem. However, in practice, there are numerous complex constraints that mean specialist software is required, and a number of such packages are on the market.

5.5.1.3.8 Job-shop scheduling Such techniques can be extended to more complex network type problems, such as scheduling a job-shop. This is where a number of individual manufacturing jobs have to move through a number of processes, or through a number of machines, and these have to be scheduled to maximize throughput. Again, this is "NP hard" (see 5.5.1.3.6 above) and dynamic programming (5.5.1.6 below) or specialist programmes are more suitable.

As in all such OR techniques, but perhaps particularly with these, the key is identifying the generic structure of such problems in practice, for which (in the network models, say) the arcs might be less concrete than distances but instead be interrelationships or costs, and the nodes might be decision-points or states.

5.5.1.4 Non-linear programming

If we relax the second of the three restrictions (ii) in 5.5.1.1 above, we can specify optimization problems where either the objective function or the constraints are not linear. This does allow more flexibility, but the problems are very much harder to solve. In some cases, the variables can be separated out and an approximation known as separable programming can be used. Computer packages are developing which can solve non-linear programming (NLP) problems, but it is probably fair to say that NLP is much less used in practice than LP.

One subset of non-linear programming that is popular within certain groups is where the constraints are all equality constraints, in which case the idea of Lagrange multipliers can be used, which will not only solve the problem but also directly supply sensitivity information.

5.5.1.5 Goal programming

If we relax the first of the three restrictions (i) in 5.5.1.1 above, we look at problems where there is not a single objective function, but a number of competing objectives. If these can be weighted, then frequently the problem can be re-cast into a single-objective linear programme (if restrictions (ii) and (iii) are observed, obviously) by using as an objective a combination of the amounts by which the various goals are unsatisfied. The key issue here is finding a single objective that does indeed optimize what the decision-makers are trying to achieve. The multi-criteria/multi-objective decision analysis methods described in 5.2.2.6 might be appropriate as a precursor to the use of this method.

5.5.1.6 Dynamic programming

Dynamic programming is a general technique (largely due to Bellman) used when there is a series of decisions to be made, which has a wide range of applications. It can be used when:

- The problem can be divided into stages, with a decision to be made at each stage.
- Each stage has a number of states associated with it, with the decision consisting of which state to move to in the next stage.
- The optimum decision for the decisions in the remaining stages must depend only on the current state and is independent of how the current state has been reached (i.e. not dependent on previous decisions). This is a real limitation, and care must be taken that this requirement is met before the method is used.
- The objective function must satisfy a recursive requirement, satisfied by additive functions such as cost or distance.

The method is essentially very simple: the problem is solved for the last stage; then solved for the penultimate stage, given the optimum paths for the last stage; then solved for the previous stage, given the optimum paths for the penultimate stage; and so on back to the first stage. This then gives the optimum cost and optimum path.

The method is obviously applicable to geographic problems, including good solutions to the travelling salesman problem above (5.5.1.3.6), as well as some problems in vehicle routing (5.5.1.3.7), and network problems. However, it is also applicable where the decision stages are not geographical, such as inventory replenishment, equipment replacement and so on.

5.5.1.7 Production scheduling

Production scheduling covers the general allocation of limited resources and sequencing of tasks over time. The key application area is, as its name suggests, in allocating production resources and sequencing the production tasks. This clearly builds on the techniques covered in 5.5.1.1–5.5.1.6, but it is getting much closer to real-life problems. This again is a large sub-field of OR – indeed a large field which overlaps with OR but also with engineering, computing, and so on – with its own journals and there is not scope to cover the whole application area here. Brucker (2007) gives some of the technical work in this field.

5.5.1.8 Non-linear optimization heuristics: local search techniques

If we can find the value of our objective function over a range of values of the variables of interest, then in trying to find the optimum we are sometimes in the situation of having to find an optimum for a non-linear expression of the variables of interest. This is a non-trivial calculation as soon as the number of variables is anything other than small. A range of techniques has built up, therefore, which will search the space of possible solutions for the optimum value. This section will outline three of the more common techniques. A textbook of such techniques is by Burke and Kendall (2005).

5.5.1.8.1 **Tabu search** Tabu search is a search procedure that iteratively moves from one solution to a nearby solution until some stopping criterion has been satisfied. The key problem with such methods is to avoid finding "local optima", where nearby points are all worse than the solution found but there is a better solution outside the immediate neighbourhood. To avoid this problem, tabu search changes how the "neighbourhood" is realized at each search point. A key way in which this is done is by the use of a "tabu list", which excludes certain solutions from the neighbourhood. It is the specification of the rules within this tabu list that differentiates the different types of tabu search and gives the method its power. Rules can be simple rules based on previous iterations (e.g. solutions that have been tested within the last few iterations) or some attributes of the current solution and nearby solutions (e.g. specific types of move).

Development of such methods, including the need to avoid local optima, showed the usefulness of adding an element of randomness into the calculation. These methods are still seeking to optimize one individual deterministic function, so although they use an element of stochastic search, they still come within this section "5.5.1 Optimization of deterministic systems".

5.5.1.8.2   Simulated annealing   This method operates similarly to tabu search in that it iteratively moves from one solution to a nearby solution, again with some predetermined stopping-rule. But by analogy with annealing metal, each iteration looks at a partly randomized nearby solution; if the alternative is better, the technique moves to that solution, but, even if it is less good, it can still be chosen with a probability that is a function of how much worse the solution is. By gradually settling down as this function changes, the method should be less likely to settle on a local optimum.

5.5.1.8.3   Genetic algorithms   The technique of genetic algorithms takes its inspiration from biology; the idea here is that candidate solutions should "evolve" towards a better solution. Again, the technique operates similarly in that it iterates with some predetermined stopping-rule. The iterations here, though, are not individual solutions but are populations of solutions that can be thought of as evolutionary "generations". From a starting set of potential solutions in one generation, the technique will iterate from generation to generation. At each step, each solution in the generation is evaluated, and a number of solutions are selected based on their values and with an element of randomness. The solutions can be combined and possibly also randomly mutated to form the next generation

5.5.2   Optimization of stochastic systems

The optimization of stochastic systems is not such an integrated field. Furthermore, the techniques are more complex and tend to require specialist knowledge. For the purposes of illustration, just three areas of application will be mentioned in this chapter.

5.5.2.1 Yield management

Yield management, or revenue maximization, is the process of reacting to customer demand by dynamically manipulating prices in order to maximize revenue. It is used for services that are subject to limited resources or in cases where, for example, goods become unsellable after a certain time. The method was pioneered in the airline industry, where prices for seats on aircraft would change as seats were booked up. The Internet made the method more powerful and more applicable, and other sectors (e.g. hotels) are starting to use the method.

The actual algorithms used in practice are generally commercially confidential, although their general characteristics are known. They clearly need to utilize stochastic forecasting techniques to predict demand given a particular price, and thus find the optimum pricing strategy. This technique again has given rise to a whole field of study, with its own journal and its own section of the US Operational Research society INFORMS.

5.5.2.2 Stochastic programming

Stochastic programming is simply the extension of mathematical programming from the deterministic methods discussed in Section 5.5.1. However, finding an optimum when there is any significant element of uncertainty makes the problems very much harder.

A common structure that has been studied widely uses a two-stage approach. In the first stage, an action is assumed to take place in the first stage, after which random event(s) occur and have an effect. What is known then as a "recourse" decision is then made in the second stage in the knowledge of the outcome of the random event(s), so called because it can compensate for any bad effects that might have been experienced. An extension of linear programming can then be applied to this two-stage model to minimize the cost of the first-period decision plus the expected cost of the second-period recourse decision and thus find the optimum policy.

The technique has been applied to risk problems in practice, but it is undoubtedly true that it is used very considerably less commonly than deterministic mathematical programming. Experience also suggests that the fit of models to the "real" situation can be harder to make credible for such methods.

5.5.2.3 *Real options*

Real option theory is an extension of the simple decision models discussed above, such as in 5.2.2.4 ("decision trees"). It has become widely used in sectors which make large capital investments whose benefits are subject to high levels of uncertainty, such as oil and gas. The technique's power comes from recognizing the staged nature of such investments. In particular, much as in the more structured stochastic programming above, the technique allows for the flexibility in decision-making that can come from waiting to see how events turn out – for example, that certain investments might not be made if information accrues that shows they are likely to be unprofitable, or that a decision can be made to make an investment if it appears profitable.

The idea of real options comes from the financial world. A financial "call option" is a contract that gives the buyer the right, but not the obligation, to buy a security at a specified price in the future. A "real" option refers to a physical capital investment today that gives the investor the future ability, but not the obligation, to make a further investment. Options analysis is now widely used for many types of financial instruments and services (electric power, communications bandwidth); real options analysis applies the same ideas to physical investments where there is insufficient historical knowledge of the risks to make a static analysis. The mathematics underlying financial options-analysis is complex but can be usefully transferred across to the "real options" case.

Again, this is a very large field, and the reader should study a relevant textbook in the area (e.g. Brennan & Trigeorgis, 2000).

Part III
Practical Skills

6

The Proposal Stage

6.1 The issues

This chapter looks at one of the most fundamental topics that a consultant can face: "How do I make a formal proposal for work?" Obviously, if a Management Scientist cannot get any work to do, then this book will serve no purpose other than a purely academic one. The most common route into a project will be preparing a formal proposal and gaining agreement from a client. This, of course, is true in many occupations – a builder or landscape gardener or often a car-repair garage or dentist will need to make a proposal of what they plan to do and gain agreement from their client as to the scope of work and the price before they can proceed to carry out the job. What makes this so fundamental to the Management Scientist, and so much more difficult in this case, are the various issues we have discussed in the last five chapters. To begin with, the client may be unclear as to the issues; the issues themselves will be socially constructed (and perceived differently within the client-group) and ill-defined (indeed, they are often undefinable until some of the work is done). The client will also be unfamiliar with the various techniques and approaches a Management Scientist may use. In addition, the planning done at the start will often, by necessity, be contingent on what is found, and so on.

There are two types of occasion were the situation is not so difficult. One is where the Management Scientist is called in to carry out some work where the issues of Chapters 1 to 3 are not particularly key – where the work is well-defined, and the issues clear-cut. In general, the way forward for "problems" is relatively straightforward – the situation can be formulated as a problem, even if it is not immediately obvious how to solve it. In this case, the only things we need to discuss are the practical issues of contracts, pricing and so on.

However, where we get involved in the sort of problems we have discussed in Chapters 1 to 4, the ideas we examined in those chapters have a number of implications. Before we can "solve" a "messy" situation we need to bring some sort of structure into the situation and formulate it, as we discussed in Chapter 3 and will discuss further in Section 6.4. And for "wicked messes", we have to deal with the social geography of the client-group, their social constructions of the problem and power and politics within the group. And there will be a need to manage individual expectations within the client-group. One implication of these points is that "problem-finishing", as we discussed in Chapter 2, is related not only to the analysis but as much to the problem-owner. Thus the focus in Section 6.2 will be on the consultant–client relationship.

There are also implications about what the word "implementation" means. "Implementation" is an ill-defined outcome, and more to do with the extent to which the decision-maker's thinking about his or her predicament has changed. "Implementation" is not a separate stage but, rather, is a continually changing part of negotiating an agreement to act. The emphasis in our work is on action and process rather than design (Checkland) or solution/end-point (Ackoff etc.). We need to pay attention to process management as well as content issues, and this will be important throughout the chapter.

There are also significant implications about how we are invited to tackle OR/MS work. It is more difficult to define terms of reference for a project if it is a "mess". Terms of reference can have a profound effect on the likelihood of OR influencing decision-making – problems change as a consequence of our working on them. As problems change during the course of a project, often we find that working on the original problem is the wrong thing to do – our focus needs to shift. So, there is a role for OR in the "management of debate". And consultants must be highly contingent, and prepared to do "quick and dirty" analyses (i.e. quick, rough-and-ready but robust analyses) to show which ways forward are useful, which might have scope for fruitful research and which are likely to be "dead-ends". These issues will be important as we plan our work and set it out in a proposal.

Sometimes these points cause us less of a problem in writing a proposal, and this is the second type of occasion where the situation is not so difficult. There are happy occasions where the Management Scientist is seen as so key that s/he can simply work as s/he sees best, charging a client for the amount of time used and the client will trust him or her to use the time wisely – much like you might in some circumstances use a lawyer. This takes a very well-established client–contractor relationship, preferably in a secure and well-defined contractual structure, but it does happen (I had this relationship with one particular client).

But this latter case is unusual, and the common situation we need to discuss is where the work is difficult to define, and we need to bring our ideas together into a formal proposal that will form the basis for our intervention. How do we approach our client? How do we bring order to the situation to lay out a scheme of OR work? And what about charging mechanisms, fees, contract types, reporting, contract monitoring and so on? This is the focus of this chapter.

The chapter concentrates on this one crucial step: preparing the proposal. There are important steps before we come to preparing the proposal – we are assuming that we know about an opportunity, or a client has approached us. And there are important steps after we have prepared the proposal, in particular presenting our ideas in person to a client-group (these issues will be covered in Chapter 10). This chapter will cover these practicalities within the environment of an ill-formed, socially constructed "wicked mess". This means, of course, that there cannot be simple recipes to follow but, instead, general principles. We'll look first at the aims of the proposal stage so we can align our efforts to what we and the clients want out of the process. Then we'll turn to what needs to form part of our proposal, which will give us a structure we can follow through the remaining sections, finishing up with some general guidelines about costing a proposal.

We'll talk in this chapter as if you alone are preparing a proposal, either for yourself or on behalf of a group. Of course, you may be part of a team preparing a proposal, but these points apply equally well. We'll also talk in this chapter as if you are preparing a proposal as an outside contractor for a client. If you (and your team) are representing an in-house OR/MS team, then some of these points may not apply – although it is worth having them as a checklist rather than making assumptions. The position of in-house consultancy teams will be looked at more in Chapter 11.

6.2　What does the proposal stage aim to do?

So, what does the proposal stage of a Management Science intervention actually aim to do? We need to see what ought to come out of the proposal – from the point of view of both client and consultant – and only then can we understand how to approach the preparation of that proposal.

Before we can look at the stage from the view of the client, we first need to identify who the client is – or, more often, who lies within the client-group. This might sound an easy issue with which to start, but often this is an important stage to pass through before we can try to orient the proposal towards the need of the client. Four questions perhaps best help identify the client(s). Two are more obvious:

* Who has identified that there is an issue to be tackled, or a problem to be resolved? Who has decided that "something needs to be done" or, perhaps more directly, has decided to call in a consultant?
* Who is paying for the work, or sponsoring it, or taking responsibility for supplying resources to the investigation?

And two follow from Figure 2.1:

* To whom does it matter whether the issue is actually tackled or the problem actually resolved? Who has a direct interest in the results of the investigation? Who will be affected by the study or will need to live with the results of the study or will need to use the results? Who (in terms of Figure 2.1) are the "stakeholders"?
* Who has power in this situation to actually make changes? If the results of the investigation require some sort of action to be taken, who has the authority to take such action? Who (in terms of Figure 2.1) are the "actors"?

There might, of course, be many people or groups of people fitting different parts of the above, and your work will have to be shaped around your perception of the direct client for whom you are preparing the proposal. But, as we will discuss below, the proposal will need to convince many of the above elements of the client-group, and help the direct client convince them. (And these considerations might be coloured by previous relationships with different parts of the group.)

Once the elements of the client-group have been identified, we can consider why we are actually putting forward a proposal, both from the point of view of the analyst and trying to see the question from the point of view of the client. Some good points here are given by Hussey (1998) (discussing management consultancy in general rather than Management Science in particular, but the points are still apposite).

The first reason may sound obvious, but it still needs to be stated. Fundamentally, the aim of this stage of the intervention is to give benefits to both the client and the consultant. Part of your thinking has to be "why am I hoping to engage in this work?" and you need to orient your plans and your proposals towards satisfying your aims as a consultant. But equally, it must be clear both to the direct client and the client-group why *they* should take up this proposal. And you need to make it quite clear in your proposal what the client is likely to gain from employing you. (Quite often I have seen proposals that look as if the consultant would gain from the work – or even that s/he would have great fun carrying it out – but don't make it clear at all what there is in the proposal from which the clients would gain.) If a client has to ask "why should we pay you money to do this?" then the proposal has failed in one of its prime objectives – explaining why the work would be beneficial to the client.

The second reason goes back to the issues we discussed in Chapters 1 and 2. We are not generally presented with clear-cut problems but as part of this phase of the intervention we have to come to an understanding of what the problem or issue actually is – for three reasons:

- Firstly, of course, unless we have at least an initial understanding of the situation, we can't think how we would approach the problem, what activities we're going to undertake and, therefore, how much effort will be required. In fact, we can't plan at all!
- But, secondly, we need to state our understanding of the problem clearly, as the whole of our proposal will be predicated on the issue we are tackling. If our understanding of the problem is different from that of the client, or the client thinks we are tackling a different problem than the one we believe

we are tackling, our proposal will not make sense to him or her. If our understanding is stated clearly and unambiguously, it will often be open to the client to say "actually, that's not how I see the problem; I see it like this – now can you reformulate the proposal?"

- Thirdly, though, we would seek to develop an understanding of the problem that matches fairly closely the view of the client. That might involve a dialogue that modifies his or her views – and likely will include mapping out where the understandings either differ or where agreement is uncertain.

We discussed in Chapter 3 how to approach structuring problems. Of course, at this stage of the work we might not be able to undertake a complete exercise to define the problem, but these ideas can be useful in coming to an initial understanding, and we will look at this in Sections 6.3 and 6.4.

We should, therefore, have come to the point where we realize that both sides need to gain something from the project, and we understand what the essential problem is. But this brings us onto the third set of reasons for this stage in the intervention: establishing why the client should choose our team (or you as an individual) as the one who should be given the work.

- We have to assure the client that we are able to do the work – that we have the skills, competencies and experience that will fit this piece of work. We may believe that we have, but this needs to be set out to the client, and s/he needs to be convinced. (Of course, first, we have to be clear ourselves that we are able to do the work – as we'll discuss in Chapter 12, it is unethical to take on work which we are not competent to carry out.)
- Furthermore, if we are in a competitive situation, we will have to convince the client that we are the most suitable candidate for the work. This will be a combination of what we can offer and value for money, and we will need to judge the relative emphasis the client is putting on capability and cost.
- More than that, we have to convince the client that our approach and view of the problem is a good match with the way they see the world in general and the problem in particular. This is less clear-cut than the first point and is more about flavour and reflecting a good client–consultant relationship.
- But even if the client likes our proposal, s/he will often not be making the decision to award the work on his or her own. In a private company, there

might be a group or a committee and the board may have to confirm the decision. In a public body there might be multiple levels of approval, with the general requirement that the decision-making process be open and demonstrably fair. This means that not only do we need to convince the particular person or persons we think are the direct client, we have to supply them with a sufficiently strong case to influence other stakeholders in the organization and, ultimately, if the decision is taken to give us the work, to demonstrate that that was a good decision.

• Part of convincing the client and helping him or her convince others is making them feel secure in choosing our company. The decision "I think this is the right consultancy to use but I'm not sure" is dangerous – we might lose out to a probably less good, but more certain, option. We need to give as much information as we can about our expected approach and the likely out-turns, as well as previous experience and anything else which backs up our case. We need to minimize any uncertainty the client may feel about taking on the proposed project.

These issues will be tackled in Sections 6.5 and 6.6.

Finally, we need to remember the objective of this particular proposal – we want to come to a contractual agreement to actually carry out the work. So many of the "practicalities" in Section 6.6 below will concern establishing the basis of that contractual relationship.

> We have to convince the client (once identified) that we bring understanding of the problem, that s/he will benefit from this intervention, and that we are the most appropriate consultancy to undertake this work, and to lay the foundation for the work.

6.3 What needs to be in a proposal?

The actual contents of a proposal therefore follow from what we have discussed in Section 6.2. The aim of this chapter is not to give a template or recipe for writing a proposal, but it will work through the essential elements, which follow logically from the purpose of writing a proposal. The proposal needs to comprise three sets of elements, as shown in Figure 6.1.

1.　ANALYSIS
(i)　Your understanding of the problem
(ii)　Methods and techniques

2.　PLANNING
(iii)　Division of job in stages/phases, major activities
(iv)　Timescale, milestones, deliverables

3.　PRACTICALITIES
(v)　Requirements on the client/data
(vi)　People involved
(vii)　Effort required, costs
(viii) A contract

Figure 6.1 Elements of a proposal

As we said, this is not a set format, but these elements will need to form part of your proposal. Most importantly, there must be a logical flow – your understanding of the problem will help decide what tools and techniques should be used, which will help to plan the project, and which will determine the practicalities. Your proposal should be a logical flow through these items, with each part logically (or, better still, necessarily) resulting from the previous one. This is the perhaps the most important point of all: if the rationale for one element cannot be seen from the previous elements, then the proposal is immediately flawed.

A second point that must flow throughout the proposal is that it must pay attention to process management as well as content issues. It must be clear to the client how the work will progress, how the stakeholders are going to be managed and their role in the project, how the social geography of the organization will be taken into account, and so on.

We'll now look at each of these sections in turn.

6.4　Stages i–ii: Analysis

We looked at length in Chapter 3 on "Problem structuring" how to structure a problem to gain an initial understanding. We examined various techniques such as SODA/Journey-making, which looked at process and content of analysis together, and which looked at both the individual (since it is based in sub-jectivism and uses language as the organization's common currency) and organizations (small teams and negotiation) using facilitation through the mapping technique. We also looked at Soft System Methodology, aimed towards learning about complex human situations. Understanding and structuring the problem using these qualitative techniques helps you understand what the problem is, who the client is, and hopefully align your understanding with the client's.

Here we meet a potential problem. Chapter 3 was written as if we had a blank sheet of paper, as if we were brought in by a client to look at a situation and do what we can to help it – a *tabula rasa* on which we can write whatever we want. But, of course, our ability to intervene is hardly ever that simple. Often – in fact, perhaps usually – we will have "terms of reference" on what to study, sometimes even how to study it. In other words, our client will have done essentially a problem-structuring activity before we come along, and is presenting us with "the problem" to solve. Now, sometimes – possibly rarely though – the problem is unambiguous and this doesn't restrict us. But in the type of wicked mess that we introduced at the start of this book, clearly we cannot simply accept terms of reference as they are set out without questioning them. They will often need to be discussed sensitively with the client, to see what flexibility there is – after all, proposing to solve a problem that the client fundamentally feels is *not* the problem that organization faces will not be very well received!

It is particularly important not to let the terms of reference restrict our problem-structuring or colour our thinking. It is very easy if, for instance, the terms of reference say "we have a problem scheduling our fleet of vehicles" to go into the problem with that particular mind-set and start to plan the best scheduling methods we know about. Instead, it is essential to look at the problem and find out whether that *is* really the problem, how the client's view has been constructed, and so on. This part of the proposal should be written in the way that a client can relate to easily, in particular taking account of the business need that the client perceives that s/he has. It is often at this point that the attention of the client will be won or lost: if the client does not see the relationship between the proposal and his/her perceived problem, then the proposal will be lost. In addition, don't forget that the client might need to influence others within the organization to accept your proposal if s/he is not the only decision-maker, so the description of the problem has also to reflect their perceived needs (i.e. you need to help the client be able to champion your proposal).

Having encapsulated the wicked problem-situation in an initial concise, structured, statement, as best we can at this initial stage, we set this out in the proposal, as the rest of the proposal will be predicated on that understanding. The proposal is a proposal on how to approach the situation *as seen by the consultant*, and if the client does not know how the consultant sees the situation, then the ground is laid for all sorts of misunderstandings.

If the problem is structured in the types of ways discussed in Chapter 3, then the proposal should lead naturally and logically into the second step: we should then be able to identify appropriate analysis techniques, particularly any quantitative techniques. The techniques you decide to use *must* be a logical consequence of the problem definition. Don't fall into the trap of listing every technique you've ever learned in the hope that one will be useful. Nor should you simply state "for this problem I will use Technique X" with no explanation as to why (let alone be the "technique evangelist" for whom every problem should be approached using Technique X). You should be aiming to say: "My analysis of this problem-situation is this and that . . . therefore it is appropriate to use Technique X because it is designed to help with exactly this sort of problem."

As we have discussed in previous chapters, often there is no "best technique". Rather, the best way is to mix the most appropriate methods/ viewpoints together, with the sorts of multi-methodology approaches we discussed in Chapter 4. Management Science intervention is a process, and at different points in the process we might want to use different techniques. For instance, the example in Section 4.7 used cognitive mapping and then causal mapping to structure a problem, then system dynamics to convert that structure into a quantitative model, with various mathematical methods used to analyse particular elements of the problem (such as learning curves, or productivity, etc.). Not only that, the problem-situation in a wicked mess is multi-dimensional, so we may want to look at many aspects at the same time. Finally, as discussed in Section 4.5, we will want to triangulate our results: often just getting the "answer" might not convince a client – or indeed ourselves. Using different techniques to approach the same problem can give much more confidence if the different techniques indicate similar answers.

So, our "techniques" chapter should be a carefully constructed set of proposed planned techniques to answer the questions as we perceive them. Of course, this careful construction may prove not to be the most appropriate set when we start to delve into the problem in detail, and in the next section we will have to look at contingencies and possible alternative plans. Sometimes it is appropriate to propose techniques and simply note the possible problems that might arise. But sometimes, when approaching the "wicked mess", it is appropriate to follow through at this stage the logical consequences of the various findings we might make and the different techniques that would be needed – as always, making the logical appropriateness (or even necessity) very clear.

In summary, the analysis section of a proposal should cover these questions:

– What do I think the problem is and why? What analysis got me to that understanding?
– Therefore, what style of analysis and which techniques do I propose to use?
– And what does that depend on? What would enable me to carry out the analysis (or inhibit me)?

6.5   Stages iii–iv: Planning

Management Science is like any project, and needs to be planned carefully using the various techniques that are established in project management: Maylor (2003) gives a good and simple account of these, and they are worth looking at in detail. We shall cover some of the main points in this section. Again, the key here is the logical flow: the tasks we identify in our planning should be a natural and logical consequence of the methods we discussed in Stage ii; the timescale and milestones should be logically based on the activities.

However, there are a number of clear differences between the sort of project outlined in the project-management literature and the types of intervention we are discussing in this book. Firstly, these projects are much more contingent: we can only come to an initial understanding of the problem, and even then we will be able to foresee various routes the intervention could take. They are contingent too because they depend on interaction with the client-group: they could be uncooperative; or unavailable; or give answers we do not expect or that change our view of the problem; or data could be unavailable; and so on. But there is also a second issue, which derives from the image in Figure 4.3 of the antinomy within the Management Scientist: the "hard" elements of the analysis can be predicted and estimated, but when we start we usually don't know what they will need to be; the "soft" elements of the analysis we can't estimate in an ordinary project-management way because of their non-positivist nature (positivism underlying standard project-management planning (Williams, 2005)). One possible way to alleviate this, as we shall see below, is to carry out some of the softer elements (e.g. the problem-structuring) in a Phase I, then we can make a firmer estimate for the harder elements in a Phase II.

Such projects (like all research-type projects) therefore cannot be planned with the logic of accepted project management. But it should be remembered that a key reason behind the proposal stage, as we described in Section 6.2 above, is to reduce the uncertainty the client may feel about taking on this project – hence we need to be as certain as we can about what we are likely to do, and what the client is likely to get out of the project; otherwise we will have failed in an important element of convincing the client to give us the work.

Of course, we can't (usually) simply make up our own timescale for the project. We need to identify what the timescale constraints on the client are, and plan our project accordingly. If we feel the timescale is unreasonably short, we might want to have an interim deliverable within their timescale, with further refining work after the initial deadline. In the same way, we should try if possible to find out what budgetary constraints there are on the customer, and again shape our bid within that constraint, if possible.

As shown in Figure 6.1, there are two sets of elements in the planning. Firstly, the work must be divided up into a logical sequence of activities, and secondly these activities must be planned out in terms of timescale and milestones, and the deliverables that the client can expect. In amongst these, the various contingencies must be identified. This section will go through these elements in turn.

6.5.1 Tasks

Firstly, the whole project needs to be divided into the main tasks that have to be undertaken. The discussion of the choice of techniques in the last section will have already explained what technical activities need to be undertaken, and their order, so, as in every part of the proposal-writing process, this part should be a logical consequence of the preceding parts, the problem definition and the subsequent analysis plan. Typically, then, these activities might be:

- a "softer" problem-structuring technique which will define the structure of the model;
- construction of a "hard" model;
- data collection for the "hard" model;
- analysis of the model and initial conclusions;
- discussions with the client about the initial results;
- completion and report writing.

Don't forget about writing the *final* report – and for that matter, don't forget, particularly if there is more than one consultant involved in the study, that you will need to project-manage the whole project, and that is an activity in its own right.

Typically in large projects the dependencies between the tasks will then be established (i.e. logical rules that say some tasks have to take place before others), and the whole project evaluated and presented using the "critical path method" (Maylor, 2003). And, of course, the dependencies are also important for us, but a typical Management Science intervention will only consist of a handful of activities, and a useful presentation will often be a simple Gantt chart (Maylor, 2003), as in the example below.

Let's look at the classic example described in Section 4.7. This was actually a large study, with a lot of person-months of effort involved. However, for now, let's look at a simplified version of the study. You could imagine the project consisting of 11 activities as follows (the first time this team undertook this work, as described in Sections 3.3 and 4.7, the plan would not have been so well defined – but, as Section 9.4 describes, a number of similar projects followed, which could be planned out in this way much more clearly):

- Task 1: Collection of individual cognitive maps about project disruption.
- Task 2: Creation of cause map of project disruption and validation with managers.
- Task 3: Creation of system dynamics model of project "as bid", including data collection.

- Task 4: Incorporation of cause map of project disruption with system dynamics model.
- Task 5: Data collection (subjective) about disruption.
- Task 6: Data collection (objective) about disruption and for validation.
- Task 7: Analysis of the model and initial conclusions.
- Task 8: Presentation of initial results to client and validation.
- Task 9: Any required amendment to model and analysis.
- Task 10: Writing final report.
- Task 11: Ongoing management of study.

This division of the project enables us to move on to the next part of the preparation of the project.

6.5.2   Timescale and milestones

The next task will be to estimate durations for each of these activities. Unfortunately, doing this is largely based on experience – it's difficult to give general guidance and so expect to rely on your experience and those of your mentors. Remember how "big" and detailed the models are likely to be – issues we will look at in Chapter 8 – and don't be too conservative. Of course, this estimation will also depend on how many people you have working, access to data and to the client and so on – issues we'll come to in Section 6.6 – but you can at least give initial thoughts on the durations, even if you need to revisit the estimates later on.

We also need to note the dependencies: that is, we can't start Task 2 until Task 1 is complete; we can't start Task 4 until Tasks 2 and 3 are complete; and similarly Tasks 5 and 6 follow Task 4; Task 7 follows Tasks 5 and 6; and then Tasks 8, 9 and 10 all follow in series one after another. Of course, this is rather simplified – we will start writing the report before Task 9 is complete (indeed, we'd hope to have it three-quarters complete by then), but this gives a simple illustration to show how the planning might take place. A Gantt chart using Microsoft *Project*® software is shown in Figures 6.2 and 6.3. This shows the sequence of activities and the dependencies.

Of course, Figures 6.2 and 6.3 also give us a visual overview of the progress of the project. In line with our views of how to intervene in management situations, as we discussed in Chapter 2, we will want to give the client an idea of the basic time-line. This not only helps to show him or her the structure of

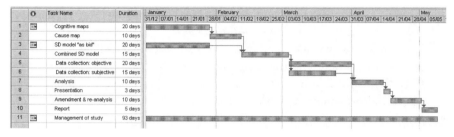

Figure 6.2 Gantt chart of simplified project

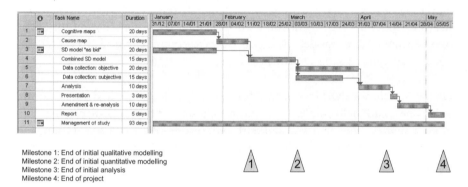

Milestone 1: End of initial qualitative modelling
Milestone 2: End of initial quantitative modelling
Milestone 3: End of initial analysis
Milestone 4: End of project

Figure 6.3 Gantt chart of simplified project, annotated

the analysis process, but also gives the client the idea s/he needs of what you are going to be doing at any stage – it gives the him or her a sense of involvement in the project if s/he knows at any point in time what you ought to be doing.

So, it is often sensible to set specific *milestones*, where we can draw breath and say "we have achieved something at this point", and show to the client some specific progress. It's all very well saying to the client "oh, we think we're three-quarters of the way through the first activity", but without clear evidence that something has been passed and we are moving on to the next activity, it is difficult for the client to be convinced that we're making progress. This means that, as well as the milestone itself, it is a good idea to assign to some of them specific *deliverables* – items that we are going to pass over to the client, either because they are of value in themselves, or as evidence of progress.

For our small example above, we might decide that appropriate milestones and deliverables could be:

- After Task 2 (Milestone: "end of initial qualitative modelling") – delivery of a "working note" on the *qualitative model.*
- After Task 4 (Milestone: "end of initial quantitative modelling") – delivery of a "working note" on the *quantitative model.*
- After Task 7 (Milestone: "end of initial analysis") – delivery of preliminary report and presentation (Task 8).
- At the end of project, delivery of a report containing the results.

Don't forget to specify the final deliverables! So, in our example, you would need to decide whether you were going to deliver only a report with the analysis, or a model that the client could also use. If you are unclear, and the client is expecting a usable model while you were expecting only to deliver a report, you could come to a disagreement.

Figure 6.3 shows the Gantt chart for our example, annotated to show the milestones and deliverables. The nomenclature or way of displaying this doesn't matter (this isn't the standard Microsoft *Project*® presentation, for example) – it is the information that is important.

6.5.3 Contingencies

As we've already said, approaching these situations of high behavioural and dynamic complexity and uncertainty, we can hardly have a firm, unchanging, detailed plan. So, what can we do? Firstly, the level of uncertainty will lead us to different types of contractual arrangements, and we'll talk about that in the next section. We'll also talk there about some methods of protecting ourselves against one of the biggest areas of uncertainty – a capricious client. But let's suppose that we're in a situation where we can put together some sort of plan of campaign: even then, it is still necessary to think about the key uncertainties, and build contingencies for such uncertainties into that plan. For our simple example above, we've said that we'll deliver a preliminary report and presentation to the client after we've done our analysis – and it is clear that this might give rise to some changes or problems with the modelling, no matter how carefully we have brought the clients along with us in our work. It was therefore sensible to include the activity "Any required amendment to model and analysis" in the plan above. More than this, you should be ready to prepare in advance what would be likely to be alternative analysis routes if your plan doesn't succeed or turns out to be infeasible for some reason.

In summary, the planning section of a proposal should cover the following questions:

– What tasks will actually be involved in carrying out the work described in the "analysis" section?
– What will the overall time-plan look like, and what will be the main milestones in the work?
– What will the client actually receive, not only at the end of the project but also at the interim milestones?

6.6 Stages v–viii: Practicalities

A proposal for a Management Science study needs to be an intensely practical document, and there are four areas in particular that must be contained in the proposal.

6.6.1 Requirements on the client/data

Management Science interventions, in the spirit of Chapter 2, can only proceed with a continuous relationship with the client organization. Your plan that you carefully produced in Section 6.5 will require you to collect data, and some of those data will have to come from people within the client-group or from the client him/herself. Data collection rarely runs entirely smoothly, and no doubt you will have built in some allowance for delving into data sources. But if the data are not available, or the people you want to interview or find out about are not available or not willing to discuss your study, or the data are inconsistent, your plans will be disrupted and the study might even fail. Indeed, it is not even sensible for the client to agree to your proposal unless s/he knows what is being required of the client organization: are you going to collect all the data yourself or are you expecting the client to hand you the data ready prepared, or what? And that is apart from all of the considerations we discussed in Chapter 1 about the complex social geography of client organizations, with multiple hidden agendas and members who will not want to help, and maybe even hinder, the study, or give biased views.

It is essential therefore to set out with as much clarity and precision as possible:

- What input have you assumed from the client and/or the client's organization when preparing your plans?
- How much effort would be required from the client in carrying out this work?
- To what extent will you require the client and people within the client organization to be available for meetings during the study?
- What data have you assumed will be available, and in what form do you expect those data to be in?
- And who is going to collect the data: you – and if so, how – or is the client going to supply the data?

Indeed, you should be making it clear that your planning depends on these assumptions, and the proposal is null and void if the client cannot satisfy these requirements. Of course, you do not suddenly make this statement without knowledge of what the client's expectations are, and you tailor your requirements to what s/he is prepared to offer during your discussion setting up the project. And even then you will have built in some contingency against some problems in this area in your planning. But you do need to protect yourself against clients who are not available, either in person or in providing data, or who are not willing to support the study, and since this is outside your control, your proposal needs to be very clear on this point.

6.6.2   People involved in the study

You need to tell the client which people are going to be involved in the work. Not only that, you need to explain why they are the most appropriate people for this study – which should, of course, like all elements of this chapter, follow from the definition of the work in previous sections. We will talk a little more about selling the members of the team in Section 6.7, but you will certainly need to include the curricula vitae of team members, highlighting their previous experience, skills, competencies and so on. Clearly, there is also a fine judgement in choosing a team if you have a pool of available consultants; in a competitive situation, you need to convince the client that you are the most suitable candidate for the work, and this will be a balance between having the most experienced and effective people versus the cost of those people. Part of your discussions with the client must be to judge the relative emphasis the client is putting on the quality of the work and its cost.

6.6.3   Effort required and costs

Eventually, we have to come to the point where we estimate the cost of the work. This will come in two parts: first, the cost of the time of the people involved and, second, the other non-labour costs. Let's look at the first of these.

Again, this section follows the work above. Firstly, you have listed out the tasks required in Section 6.5 above and decided who is going to work on these tasks. Then you need to estimate how many person-weeks would be involved in each task, which, again, is largely a matter of experience, looking back on similar projects, and consulting with experienced peers and mentors. Remember all of the tasks. Have you forgotten any additional work that would need to be done? Have you taken into account project-managing the work, and administrative or organizational tasks? Or report writing, which can take quite a long time? Or preparation of interim deliverables that we offered in Section 6.5? What is the nature of the final deliverable – just a report, or a program or piece of software as well? These all need to be included in the estimate.

Once you've allocated people to each of these tasks, you need to calculate their cost in £ (or $) per person-week (or per person-day or per person-hour). Your organization will normally have standard ways of costing labour. Often, if you've not carried out the calculations, the rates will seem higher than you expect – Figure 6.4 gives an illustrative calculation of a labour-rate which comes higher than many might initially expect. If you are quoting rates in £ per day or £ per week, remember to include a note in the proposal about what defines a "day" – is it 7 hours? Or 7½ hours? Or what?

Other non-labour costs might include travel and accommodation, and this can be estimated from the tasks which need to be done. You might also need computing facilities, stationery and secretarial support: you need to think of everything you will require to carry out the work. Some will be assumed to be an additional cost and can be put in the cost quoted in the proposal; some, such as stationery, might be included in a standard labour overhead rate (as described in the example in Figure 6.4). Your proposal needs to be clear not only about what is included in the day-rate for personnel, but also how extra items are charged to the client.

Costing your time

You are a keen young consultant. Let's say you want to earn £50,000 a year. There are 52 weeks in a year, 5 days a week, so that's 260 working days – so you want to earn £50,000/260 = £192 a day. How much should you charge per day for your services? Obviously, the calculations here are illustrative, but they do give you an idea of how these calculations are done.

Firstly, of course, you don't work 260 days a year. Let's say you work 46 weeks of the year and have the other days as holidays. Then, you are sick for, let us day, 5% of days. Then of course, not every single hour of the day is spent working on work that can be charged to a client – you have to go to conferences, work on privately funded developmental work, marketing, and so on. An 80% utilization rate would be a pretty good record (a more realistic level might be between 50% and 70%) but, even so, let's say that in fact you work 46 × 0.95 × 0.8 = 35 effective weeks per year.

Then you have to write proposals to get the work – a major part of your job that doesn't actually directly earn income. Let's suppose that proposals take on average 2 person-weeks to prepare, and the average contract you win is for 40 person-weeks, and finally that only 35% of your proposals are successful (again, quite a good average!); therefore you would be carrying out 2/0.35 = 5.7 person-weeks of unpaid work writing proposals for each 40 person-weeks of paid work. Therefore, only 40/45.7 = 87.5% of the effective weeks actually earn you money. That is, you gain fees from you consultancy for:

$$35 \times 87.5\% \text{ person-weeks} = 153 \text{ days per year}$$

Now, let's look at your salary again. You wanted to earn £50,000 per year. But the cost of employing you will be more than that – your employer will need to pay (in the UK system) "employer's National Insurance" (say, 10%) and will need to contribute to your pension (in the UK system called "superannuation" – for the sake of argu-

Figure 6.4 An example of how to cost your time

ment, assume this is also 10%). So your salary of £50,000 would actually cost the employer 120% × £50,000 = £60,000.

So, where are we? So far, we've found that rather than the £192 per day, in order to cover the cost of your salary you need to charge:

$$£60,000/153 = £392 \text{ per day}$$

– almost double the original estimate.

In fact, the cost of carrying out consultancy is much more than that. You will need an office, a computer, internet, personal indemnity insurance, maybe a secretary, invoicing services (unless you're going to do that yourself) and so on. These will usually be charged as an overhead on your time. A *very* low cost for this would be 50% (it could be 200% or even more). But at just 50% then you need to charge:

$$(£60,000 × 150\%)/153 = £588 \text{ per day}$$

– over three times the original estimate.

In the UK, finally, value-added tax at 17.5% is charged on such services, so you would actually have to charge:

$$£588 × 117.5\% = £691 \text{ per day}$$

So: your final day-rate – just to cover your costs, not to make profit for the company, don't forget: simply to cover what has to be paid out – is £691 per day. Don't take this as the "right" answer, but it does illustrate the type of considerations that need to be taken into account.

Figure 6.4 *Continued*

6.6.4 The contract

Finally, you need a contract – that's the point of the proposal! Often again, the organization for whom you work will have standardized forms of contract, although there are still likely to be some decisions that need to be made – especially if your client also has standardized forms of contract that differ from your organization's!

The aim of this part of the proposal is clear: for the contractor, you want to sign a legally binding contract that results in the fees being paid once you've done the work – you need the confidence that you can enforce payment, otherwise you won't want to do the work; for the client, s/he needs to sign a legally binding contract that will result in the benefits being delivered – s/he needs the confidence that the work can proceed and the benefits will actually be gained.

Having said that, there are some important issues you will need to consider in specifying the contract. The first is, should this be a "fixed-price" or "time-and-materials" (or "cost-plus") contract? In other words, are you simply going to declare a price and keep to that, or are you going to charge for all your labour by the hour (or by the day), however long the job takes? (Note that different countries may use slightly different terms – in some circumstances, "fixed price" means the price is fixed and cannot vary (the sense we shall use it in here); in some countries, though, "fixed price" simply means that no bargaining is possible. In many circumstance in the US and UK, "fixed prices" can change under certain circumstances, such as with inflation, or changes in costs of materials, whereas "firm fixed prices" cannot change – you do need to be aware the of possibly different legal terms in different countries and spell out what you mean.) In a fixed-price contract, both parties know what the price is, which brings clarity – and you can often justify a higher mark-up – but what happens if the study takes longer than you expect? In "wicked messes" it is very difficult to predict with clarity what activities are going to take place and what is going to happen. Or, even if you can predict the behaviour of the project, what happens if the client's interpretation of what you're supposed to be delivering is different from yours? This latter situation is a common problem: because of all the issues we discussed in Chapter 2, often it is not clear what will result from a study. If you state that you will deliver a "report" for £X, say, then the client will want to be satisfied that it's going to be a comprehensive, full report, not a three-page summary. On the other hand, if you state that you will deliver a "computer program" for £X, then you will want the confidence that when you deliver your working program the client is not going to insist on a massively bigger, more complex program than you envisaged.

Because of these problems, many contracts are let on a time-and-materials basis (i.e. the client pays for labour at a certain rate and expenses). However, this contract type also has the problem that the client is then uncertain how much s/he will need to pay before results are gained, and this type of contract does need an increased level of trust between contractor and client. In addition, if the client him/herself has to convince others in the organization to let the work go to you, that might be more difficult if the final price cannot be guaranteed.

Sometimes, one of these contractual approaches will be clearly the right one to take. Sometimes, there are ways to combine these approaches to try to bring a compromise. One way might be to carry out the work in multiple stages: a small cost-plus contract could be used to structure the problem and define the work more clearly, and prepare a detailed fixed-price contract; that way, there is much less uncertainty for the client, and you are protected by having the time and scope to plan the work much more thoroughly. Or, you might have a number of "if-then" clauses in the proposal ("if we find this, then the cost will be X, otherwise . . ."). Or, there are variations to these contract types, including incentivization and cost-sharing, maximum and minimum profits (see In't Veld and Peeters (1989) for some simple explanation).

As well as the contract form itself, you will need to include some level of contract monitoring, so that the client is confident that the contract is continuing acceptably. This will include some level of reporting by you to the client. Its exact form will depend on the circumstances of the project, and will be related to how payment is made – is it on deliverables? At the end of the project? By monthly invoices? An up-front payment? This needs to be carefully specified in the contract.

Whichever type of contract is used, deliverables need to be defined as closely as possible, to try to avoid misunderstanding. And don't promise more than you can give! There are a few other details that the contract will need to cover:

- The governing law of the contract (English or Scottish law, or the law of the country within which the client resides). This can be a particularly contentious issue if the client is within the US.)
- Under what circumstances can one side or the other cancel the contract?
- Who keeps what at the end of the contract? In particular, who has the rights to the "intellectual property"? The data are presumably the client's – but the results? And the methodology? And the copyright to the content of the final report?

This last point is a complex but especially important legal issue. A contract is a binding legal document, to which you can be held, and against which if necessary you can be sued. Unless you are experienced, it is essential to gain legal advice on how to set up such contracts before you start. And even when you propose some contract terms, it is likely that the client will want to negotiate these terms, and you must be very careful unless you are confident of your ground.

> In summary, this section of a proposal should cover every practicality that is required to enable the client to give you a contract – costs, rights and duties for each party, including what you are expecting of the client, who is going actually to undertake the work, and the contract terms you are proposing.

6.7 Selling yourself

The aim of the proposal is to sell yourself to the client. You need to describe your past assignments that are relevant to this piece of work. Describing these will not only show that you are experienced, but will often help to explain how you work, and how your methods have turned out in practice. It is important to be specific. Rather than simply saying that you are a very experienced consulting firm, a client will want to know that you have the experience to be working on his or her specific problem and that s/he can put trust in you. The curricula vitae (see Section 6.6 above) will show the experience of your consultants. Indeed, Hussey (1995) goes as far as to suggest that you should present your strengths relevant to the assignment in such a way that the client will want to probe your competitors' bids to see whether they possess such strengths. Whether or not this is done, you certainly need to try to persuade the client that your bid is the one to accept. We'll return to this in Chapters 10 and 11. And in Chapter 12 we'll turn to the need to act ethically (including, say, respecting the confidentiality of the client), which is also part of the trust relationship.

> To summarize this chapter – plan the study and sell your plan to the client!

7

Data

"Not everything that can be measured is worth measuring and not everything worth measuring can be measured" (*quote often attributed to Einstein*)

7.1 Introduction

We have used in previous chapters the picture of the Management Scientist looking at the "real" world and receiving data from it to inform the models being built. Figure 4.3 shows the Management Scientist keeping the "real" world and the analytical world in one head, both worlds talking to each other and informing each other, and in particular with "data" as part of the flow from the "real" world to the analytical world. Clearly, if we are constructing models, and particularly quantitative models, and those models are supposed to represent a version of reality, then we must gather facts, quantities, structures and other representations from the real world to inform those models. And often we are not so much interested in the attributes of entities themselves as the relationship between them – so that we have to be able to measure relationships between variables as well as the variables themselves.

Therefore, data collection forms a key part of the Management Science process. Indeed, it has always formed an important part of the process, and textbooks such as Mitchell (1983) have chapters describing how to collect data, looking at different types of data sources, and pointing out some potential pitfalls or common errors. A key distinction that is usually made is between "primary data", which is collected for the particular study under question, and "secondary data", which is data already available having been collected for a different purpose. This stresses the need to consider the purposes for which the data were collected and possible shortcomings in the quality of that data. And there are key traps to avoid, such as bias in samples taken, or having ill-defined and inconsistent definitions of variables. Some of these will be touched on below, but the important reason for having this chapter here is the change in the problems modern Management Scientists are investigating, as we discussed in Chapter 1: as we move to modelling "wicked messes", the issues about constructing those models, including structure then populating the models with data, become more subtle, and need to be considered from the basis that we set up in Chapters 1–4.

In such scenarios, we cannot necessarily consider even apparently "obvious", "hard" quantities as given, but we must accept that the reality we are modelling is to some extent socially constructed – and constructed not by one mind but by a whole group of people in a complex social geography with the ontological issues implied.

Furthermore, since we are modelling behaviourally complex situations, many of our variables will not be representing "hard" quantities but "soft", ill-defined, human-oriented aspects. These are obviously more difficult variables to handle, but often these are the critical aspects that explain how systems behave. In the UK, we came to appreciate this rather quicker than in some countries; in 1998 a leading US operational researcher wrote: "Our current models are concerned with tangibles . . . It seems to me that the field would make a vast creative step if it were to look seriously into models that handle intangibles and their measurement, because most of our problems deal with such factors" (Saaty, 1998). Difficulty in defining and measuring a variable does not of course imply that that variable should not be included in a model – Forrester, the founder of "system dynamics", almost 50 years ago said:

"There seems to be a general misunderstanding to the effect that a mathematical model cannot be undertaken until every constant and functional relationship is known to high accuracy. This often leads to the omission of admittedly highly significant factors (most of the 'intangible' influences on decisions) because these are unmeasured or unmeasurable.

To omit such variables is equivalent to saying they have zero effect . . . probably the only value that is known to be wrong. . . .

A mathematical model should be based on the best information that is readily available but the design of a model should not be postponed until all pertinent parameters have been accurately measured. That day will never come (Forrester, 1961).

Besides, while "soft", human-oriented aspects are difficult to model, there are two aspects that generally make this easier for us. Firstly, we'll in general be looking at the *effects* of the aspects; we won't need to define absolute measures of the aspects themselves (which in general would be very challenging) but model the relationships between aspects. And, particularly, we will often be in the situation when an intangible variable starts to affect tangibles, which can give us something to measure more directly. For example, suppose we consider that staff pay levels affect staff morale, and that this in turn affects productivity. Now, measuring "morale" would be quite a challenge, but we can look at the relationship between staff pay and productivity, and infer a relationship with an intermediate variable, which we're calling for this study "staff morale". A second aspect which also makes things a little easier is that we'll in general be looking at the effects of changes or perturbations in the aspects – so we can look for relative rather than absolute measures – "an intangible, by definition, has no scale with a unit" claims Saaty (1998). But clearly there are epistemological issues that will need to be handled carefully but pragmatically.

There is, however, one further level of complexity. We have already discussed in Chapter 2 that we are not generally in the situation of an outside analyst simply structuring the problem, populating a model and then analysing in three straightforward steps. Rather, we are intrinsically engaged in an intervention, which has an ongoing relationship with the client-group (as in Figure 2.3). As we gather data, our views of the problem-situation change and our problem-structuring models might change – or we might return to the client to revisit where the problem actually lies – or data might be difficult to retrieve and we will need to revisit the situation to develop a more pragmatic plan – and so on. So, our data-collection enterprise will look less like a simple linear process and more like Figure 7.1 before we even get to the stages of making recommendations and seeing them implemented.

So, as we look at collecting data, clearly the problems are not trivial. We'll look first at some ideas of what measuring data actually means – Management

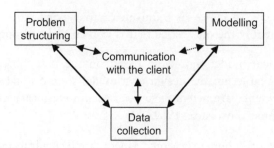

Figure 7.1 Data collection

Scientists sometimes have a very weak understanding of the basis of measurement, which can lead to erroneous analysis. Then we'll look at the easier issues of "hard" data, and then move on to the (ironically, harder) issues of "soft" data, on which we will concentrate most (as this is the area of most concern to the Management Scientist), before looking at the issues of triangulation we mentioned in Section 4.5.

> The ontological and epistemological issues we have discussed are intrinsic to the process of data collection in a behaviourally complex "wicked mess". We need to be aware of these issues, and the cyclic nature of problem structuring, modelling and data collection as part of our client-centred intervention, to ensure a sound analysis.

7.2 Measurement

So let us stand back briefly from Management Science and ask: what is measurement? What does it mean to take an entity or concept in the "real" world and measure it? What does scientific learning as a whole tell us that might help us in our particular enterprise?

It is fairly clear what the essence of measurement is – it is a way of assigning firstly an ordering, then numbers to levels of an attribute to help us understand the differing quantities of the attribute. But that hides different levels of measurement: we can actually distinguish four different levels, which will be increasingly useful to us in our modelling the further down the list we can go.

(i)   The simplest level – which is not measurement, simply the first step – is to be able to classify our subjects into exclusive categories (land use might be classified as "agricultural", "residential" and "industrial", but there is no sense of order between the categories). Such a variable is called *nominal*.

(ii)   The next level is where the order matters, but not the actual difference between numbers: "Likert" questionnaire scales are often like this (1 for "strongly disagree", 2 for "disagree" and so on). Such a variable is called *ordinal*.

(iii) The next level is a measurement where the difference between numbers is meaningful but not necessarily the actual numbers. The difference between 20°C and 10°C is twice as much as between 10°C and 5°C. However, the value zero is not meaningful in a measurement sense (although it does have a physical meaning) – so 20°C is not twice as hot as 10°C. Such a variable is called *interval*.

(iv)   The final level, measurement that can give us the most information, is an interval variable where the value zero has a meaning, so that we can talk about ratios between values – to continue the last example, temperature on the Kelvin scale is a ratio scale, and 300 K is twice as hot as 150 K; 100 kg is twice as heavy as 50 kg. Such a variable is called *ratio*.

This is all very well, but it does beg questions about our understanding of what it is we are observing, and the status of the attribute. The simplest, and most traditional, understanding of this would be the "realist" stance, in which the idea of a quantitative phenomenon means that the phenomenon is intrinsically or inherently quantitative in the "real" world, and that in measuring we are trying to get close to a "true" or "real" value of the phenomenon. This idea clearly underlies concepts such as "accuracy" or "error" which seek to express the difference between measured values and "real" values. This view is expressed for example in Michell (2005), who describes the history of the realist view of measurement, and concludes by effectively seeing no problems with the underlying ideas of measurement:

Measurement is always based upon the hypothesis that some attribute is quantitative. . . . The scientific methods of critical inquiry, according to which hypotheses are only accepted following serious attempts to put them to the test and given evidence in their favour, applies to this hypothesis as much as to any. When the hypothesis that an attribute is quantitative is accepted, then along with that hypothesis, as part of the same theoretical package, it is accepted that different magnitudes of the attribute stand in relation of ratio, these relations being instances of real numbers. . . . When scientists set about devising practical methods for measuring, it is precisely these real numbers that they are attempting to measure.

However, irrespective of the ontological issues in realism that we have discussed in previous chapters of this book, there are a number of intrinsic problems with this viewpoint.

Firstly, it ignores that many variables are defined not as "real" quantities but by scientific models and hypotheses postulating the existence of such a variable. This has always been true in the physical sciences: for example, if you want to measure the position and momentum of a particle. Traditionally, based on the current models of the physical universe, it was assumed that as measurement instruments got more accurate, these measurements could be made with more and more accuracy. We now know by what is known as Heisenberg's uncertainty principle, that there is a limit on the accuracy with which it is possible to measure (even define) such a pair of variables. But – particularly in Management Science – variables are generally defined by some underlying model of "reality", implying that the measurement of that variable cannot represent the underlying reality itself. This brings a fundamental circular argument (similar to that shown in Mari, 2005):

- We use models of the world to understand the relationship between entities;
- We base these models on measurements of the entities;
- Those measurements are based on our models;
- The models have been defined by measurement of the entities.

Mari (2005) also points out a number of other epistemological issues involved with the realist view, such as the definition of "quantities" and "non-quantities"; the length of digits of measurements; the continuous-ness (or otherwise) of physical phenomena; and so on.

An understanding of measurement that sees the words "a quantitative phenomenon" simply as an abbreviated expression for "a phenomenon represented by a quantitative expression" is the "representational" view of ontology, "stressing the importance of the relation by which the phenomenon is represented" (Mari, 2005). Finkelstein (2005a) says this: "The dominant paradigm for the process of measurement has been that of measurement in the physical sciences, and was philosophically rooted in the approaches of logical positivism and operationalism. The important representational theory of measurement is based on this standpoint." However, this does not avoid many of these problems. Certainly, even in the more quantitative disciplines, measurement has lost its foundational position since these problems have been realized: "Several scientists ... are now proposing a 'non fundamental' standpoint, according to which no absolute foundation is possible for science, because human knowledge is essentially based on a continuously iterative, try-and-revise, adaptive, autopoietic process ... in which progressively some element become more and more solid but nothing is definitive" (Mari, 2005). In this view, knowledge is seen as a "network of components" in which attributes are not defined absolutely but in reference to the whole network.

And as we have said above, in many Management Science analyses, as well as economics, sociology and psychology, the attributes we are trying to measure are in themselves "soft", ill-defined attributes. Here the non-foundational nature of measurement is clearer, and we need to beware of the circular argument quoted above, perhaps defining our models on the qualitative analyses we have discussed before trying to define how to measure these attributes. Even for apparently "hard" measurements, an ISO guide (International Organization for Standardization, 1995) states that any measurement must be specified as an estimation of both the value and its uncertainty, and that evaluating the latter requires consideration of personal experience, beliefs, and other "softer" issues. We will move on to the softer factors in Section 7.4.

> Our view of the measurement of variables depends on our ontological stance. A realist stance poses problems, such as the definition of quantities, and a circularity between the use of models to define measurements and the use of measurements to support those models. We need to bear this logic in mind when devising measurements and drawing conclusions: our measurements cannot be fundamental in the traditional sense, particularly when we consider the "soft" variables that come into Management Science analyses.

7.3 How "good" is data?

On first consideration, the most straightforward data to collect are those associated with clearly quantified or quantifiable attributes that are unambiguous in their measurement – normally termed "hard" data. In fact, as we shall see, this ideal view of data rarely pertains in practice, but it is an appropriate place to start.

Mitchell (1983) talks about three types of data in a management problem situation: "physical data", "data about the organization surrounding an issue and the organization's behaviours" and "data about policy and the limits and constraints relevant to an issue". The first of these – physical data: how a system works physically, the physical dimensions of an entity, distance and so on – seems to be the clearest "hard data". Put another way, Mitchell defines this category as, "data about which there is a relevant consensus that it is measurable". Of course, having a consensus that something is measurable is one thing, but having a consensus on what those measurements are is quite another. There can be different ways of measuring (internal/external dimensions, for example, or road distance vs direct distance). Mitchell includes "how much something costs" in this category, about which it is notoriously difficult to get agreement: ask even accountants within a company the "cost" of part of the operation, and there are a whole list of questions that must be answered to make it unambiguous (do you include "overheads"? which "overheads"; do you mean net-present-value? in procuring an item, do you include the cost of labour within the company? do you include set-up costs or just marginal costs? ...). We are rarely to find ourselves with simple measurements of unambiguous variables.

Where are the data likely to come from? Mitchell (1983) points to five sources of data:

- Recorded information: accounts, procedures, files, sets of data and so on. Here we will sometimes find clear data – but with different sources disagreeing. Sometimes, even after having worked through all the reasons for differences between two data sources, there are still contradictions or discrepancies that remain unexplained – this is often a mystery to practising Management Scientists!
- Personal knowledge. For "soft" data, this is sometimes the only source, but it is also a useful source of information for simple factual statements, remembering to take into account biases in the interviewee, which we will discuss below.
- Measurement and observation.
- Stimulated or elicited data – i.e. where the analyst sets up some forum for collecting data, such as a workshop or meeting (mentioned also in Section 7.5).

- "The sponsor". Having thought about the argument of Chapters 1–3, we know that the "sponsor" is rarely a unified body, and we need to work through the social geography, politics and power-relationships within the client organization, as well as the cultural setting of that organization as a whole. This can lead to multiple understandings of what a variable means, or how something should be measured, or how that measurement should be interpreted, let alone multiple biases. This means that, rather than measuring a variable directly, we are often looking at that variable through multiple lenses, with each layer of the organization through which we are viewing the variable putting a different slant on our observation.

What are we looking for in a measurement mechanism? Traditionally, it has been considered that there are a number of attributes, six in particular of which we'll discuss below (the last two really being simply practical issues). But as we'll see, this traditional view poses ontological problems with our new understanding of a Management Science intervention.

The first three attributes are straightforward to understand – if we take a realist view of the world. If we are simply trying to measure an aspect that has some independent existence, then the two key measures of the "goodness" of our measure are the following.

- The first is *precision*. This simply denotes the amount by which the measurement differs from the "real" or "true" value. (This is sometimes called "accuracy", but this is not unambiguously defined.) Of course, since we cannot measure the "real" value, we can only estimate precision. It might be estimated by summary statistics, such as the average of the absolute value of the difference between the measurement and what we believe is the "real" value, or mean square error (MSE, the average of the squared value of the difference between the measurement and the estimated "real" value).
- The second is *bias*. This denotes systematic error, where the same effect generally happens when we try to measure a variable. It is generally used for the case in which errors in the measurement tend to be all in the same direction – that is, tending to be all overestimated or all underestimated. There are many different types of bias, and the important examples are discussed when eliciting subjective probabilities in Section 7.6 below.

Figure 7.2 gives a pictorial illustration of these two simple concepts. But, of course, they do rely on the idea of an "error" in the measurement being the

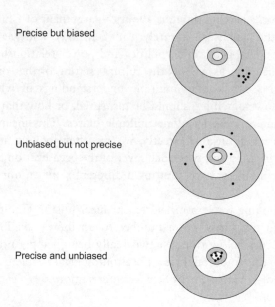

Figure 7.2 Bias and precision

deviance from a "true" value, which does not necessarily concur well with the philosophy of Chapter 1. But they are still useful concepts when we look at measures: if there really were a "real" value of this attribute, how precise/ biased would this measure be?

This all, of course, assumes we're actually measuring the right thing – which brings us to our third and fourth attributes. In practice, we're often not looking at an aspect that has an independent existence that we can touch or actually measure. Instead, many of the aspects we would like to use in our analyses we cannot measure directly; we have to use an approximate measure, or indeed a proxy measure (where we measure something that we feel is representative of the aspect in which we're interested).

The third attribute of a measure is its *reliability*, which essentially refers to how consistent it would be if it measured the same aspect more than once. Obviously, precision affects this (a wildly imprecise measure would not give the same results if used more than once), and the effect of lack of precision needs to be removed from our consideration of reliability – imprecision refers to the attempt to measure something directly when our measuring instrument is not able to capture precisely the correct number, while lack of reliability refers to the attempt to measure something with the best instrument that we can but we are not sure it always measures the right aspect. The use of a ruler, for example, would be pretty well fully reliable for measuring a short length, but not necessarily precise.

Lack of reliability can come from a variety of sources, and we need to consider each of these when considering the reliability of a measure. The intrinsic reliability of measures can be investigated by simple repeated measuring, assuming a measurement does not change the measure (for example, if you repeat an IQ test immediately, memory of the previous test might affect the second test) or the time between tests does not change the answers. Instruments such as questionnaires measuring a concept can have multiple questions pertaining to that concept, and the results to the different questions can be compared. Reliability relating to the measurer can be studied by more than one person administering the test to similar groups that could be expected to have similar scores (this can help to reduce the problem of measurers being more likely to see what they expect to see). And so on.

This does all assume we are actually measuring what we think we are measuring. The fourth attribute of a measure is *validity*. A measure is *valid* if it really does measure what we are trying to measure – in other words, if the measurements we are achieving do tell us something valid about the aspect we think we are measuring. Sophisticated studies are sometimes carried out which find interesting results about a measure, but where the measure doesn't actually represent the aspect in which the investigators were interested.

Let's think about practical examples:

- Take for example productivity. You might measure the resources used by a factory (money, manpower etc.) over the space of a month, and the output on that month, and you might feel that the ratio of one to the other gave a good indication of productivity. If there was a long production time, you might consider putting time lags (otherwise you would be comparing, say, August's output with August's input, but the output was actually the result of inputs stretching back the previous 6 months).
- If you wanted to measure "anxiety", there are two parallel measures invented by Spielberger (1983), and much research over the past 40 years has gone into checking the reliability of those measures. The fact that two different measures are given ("state" and "trait" anxiety, looking at short-term and longer time aspects) indicates that you need to be careful to

ensure that the aspect you are interested in is indeed measured by these statistics.

- If you were measuring "morale", you might issue a questionnaire amongst your workforce asking "How positive do you feel about the company's prospects" and so on. This is starting to get slightly more problematic, as you would need to be aware of bias if the questionnaire was not anonymous (so there should be some way the forms can be returned without identifying the respondent), or indeed bias in that perhaps only the disaffected will respond (so perhaps an attempt should be made to ensure as complete a return of the entire workforce as possible is made). Careful validity consideration would have to be made of whether the questionnaire was actually asking about morale in the sense that you want.

- You might feel at this point that the "softer" or more human-oriented the statistic, then the harder it is to establish a reliable, valid measure. But consider, say, the issue of crime statistics. If we want to know the rate of crime in England and Wales, there are two sets of statistics, police recorded crime figures and the British Crime Survey (Walker *et al.*, 2006), which often give differing results. The first is objective and appears to measure a real entity; however, for example, this is only reported crime and does not include any crime not reported, and so it is skewed away from particular types of crime that people are reluctant to report. The second is an objective survey but measuring more subjective aspects, in that it asks people about their experiences and their feelings. Some feel that this gives a more complete estimate of crime. More definition would be needed as to what you actually wanted to measure, and whether these two types of statistics were representative of this aspect, or which was the most valid measure.

This idea of validity being the instrument actually measuring what we wish to measure is a very positivist idea – it suggests a realist view of an entity that really exists, and an objectivist view of epistemology that we can actually know the value of this variable and try to get an instrument as close as we can to the real value. A more phenomenological approach would be to ask whether we know as much as we can about the views, meanings and knowledge of the subjects on whom we are using the instrument.

The other two attributes of our measures are pragmatic issues rather than intrinsic attributes: *availability* and *timeliness*. Clearly, data which are not available, or impractically difficult to get hold of, are not useful – and where data are difficult (but possible) to obtain, a careful judgement needs to be made as to whether they are sufficiently "good" (by the criteria above) to be worth the while. Timeliness of data relates to how out-of-date they are, both single instances of getting data (do they still adequately represent the variable you're trying to measure?) and particularly if you are setting up a system for repeated similar decisions, which will rely on a data source – for example, if you set up a production-planning system based on sales figures, and because of difficulties in collating the sales figures you find that they relate to sales a year previously, this is likely to call the production plans into question.

Three further issues must be mentioned before leaving this brief summary of issues.

The first is that often we are offered, or we find, data that seem to match our purposes but they have already been collected for another purpose (so-called "secondary" data). This can, of course, make life easier, but there are a number of issues that need consideration before you make use of secondary data. There are the issues we have listed above: how old are the data (timeliness)? are the data attempting to measure something that represents the variable of interest to us (reliability), or can a transformation of the data reliably give us reliable information? But we also need to consider issues such as: what were the original reasons for the data being collected? (looking into why a set of data was collected can often reveal underlying biases or partiality), was the data collected properly? And, how much sifting or organizing of the data would be needed before the information we need becomes available?

The second issue is that often we cannot take a complete measure of the population we're interested in, so we will need to take a sample. This is not the place for a complete summary of statistical sampling, which can be found in many good textbooks on business research (Collins & Hussey (2003) give some very simple pointers). However, there are some points to look out for, which can be summarized as follows:

- Carefully choose the type of sampling. Completely random sampling is usually the least efficient. To get more information from the data you collect, a good common technique is to divide the population into strata. If you think the variable of interest might be different due to particular attributes of the members of the population (e.g. gender, age, etc.), then independent samples can be taken from each stratum.

- Beware of any biases inherent in non-probabilistic sampling (e.g. picking people in the street, or waiting for returns from postal surveys).
- Similarly, make sure the set of people from whom you're sampling is representative of the whole population, not an unrepresentative subset of the population. This is a common error when there is a body "representing" a population, which will often consist of activists. (I am currently working in a Children's Hospital in the US where there is a patients' parents committee which advises the hospital. This is likely to give views representative of the general population of patients' parents, but with some biases because they are the type of people willing and able to serve on such a committee. Of course, if I were actually seeking, say, (recovered) patients' views rather than their parents', I might need to do different data gathering.)
- Make sure you have thought about the sample size – too big, and you're wasting effort; too small and your results won't be reliable.

The third issue is the so-called "Hawthorne effect". This term refers to a factory in Chicago where a number of observations of workers were made in the late 1920s and early 1930s (see Roethlisberger & Dickson, 1939). A series of studies manipulated various conditions (such as lighting, rest periods and pay) and worker productivity was measured before and after each change. The surprising result was that each change resulted in an improvement in productivity, even when the changes had worked full circle and eventually returned to the original condition. The traditional understanding then, and since, is that this result was because of the workers' knowledge of being measured or in general of being studied. This is what is generally referred to as the Hawthorne effect, and clearly this is an important effect that we as management scientists need to guard against. In fact, there has always been controversy over whether the effects observed were due (or were entirely due) to the knowledge of being observed, and many other explanations have been put forward – the effects of learning, the workers being prompted to reflect on their work and improve, the effect of feedback about their performance being given to the workers, the feeling of being valued and thus being happier, so being more productive, and so on (see Gillespie, 1991). There are also similar (or maybe overlapping) effects with other names, such as the expectancy effect (Rosenthal & Jacobson, 1968) whereby workers will often tend towards the expectations placed upon them (some of which may be due to the so-called Parkinson's Law (Parkinson, 1957), in which workers slacken off if they are over-performing their set target), and, less well-known, the John Henry effect (Zdep & Irvine, 1970) in which a group being used as a control group compares themselves with the experimental group and tries to match them.

> When measuring "hard" data, we need to consider the precision, bias, reliability, and validity of our measure. The last of these, particularly, needs careful consideration; sometimes it is not immediately obvious what the most valid measure is. We also need to consider the availability and timeliness of our data. There are pitfalls in Hawthorne-type effects, in using secondary data and in sampling, and we need to make sure we have addressed these issues.

7.4 "Soft" data: principles

Although "measurement" has traditionally been concerned with "hard" data, with which the last section largely dealt, we're often interested in "softer", more human-oriented, and often more subjective, data. How can we approach measuring these? We'll look at some principles in this section, then at a few issues about practical methods in Section 7.5.

The basic idea of Section 7.2 gives us our guide. "Modern theory of measurement, which embraces all measurement, in physical science and in other domains, is based on model theory" (Finkelstein, 2005b), and it is on this idea that ideas of measurement have been based (Krantz *et al.*, 1971–1990). And as measurement of "hard" concepts has moved to this model-based idea, it makes the measurement of "softer" concepts feasible. Of course, we still have the circularity we discussed in Section 7.2 – measurement is based on models, which are themselves developed based on measurements. And, indeed, we have more problems here about measurement, when we come to look at model validation in the next chapter, and because for example we can sometimes only measure the outward manifestations of complex systems and not internal variables. For this reason, we are often looking at what Finkelstein (2005b) calls "weakly defined measurement":

> Strongly defined measurement . . . follows the paradigm of the physical sciences. In particular, it has precisely defined empirical operations, representation by numbers and well-formed theories for broad domains of knowledge. Measurement that constitutes representation by symbols of properties of entities of the real world, based on an objective empirical

process, but which lacks some, or all, of the above distinctive characteristics of strong measurement, may be termed weakly defined. . . . The power of a measurement scale depends on the richness of the empirical relational system that it represents. Formulae in terms of representative symbols that do not correspond to empirically determinable relations are not meaningful.

So, we should not be frightened of "measuring" the softer aspects, even if in this weaker form of measurement.

The main quantitative difficulty in developing a measure of such aspects is not so much gaining a descriptive or nominal measure (i.e. one that categorizes different responses), or even being able to order the categories into an ordinal measure, but to gain a quantitative measure in which the ratios between the difference categories can be established – essentially, the problem of *calibrating* the measure.

The main reason for this is clear. We have addressed a number of problems relating to measuring any aspect. But if the *unit* in which that aspect is measured is a known unit with a ratio scale, then we can start to work with that measure, subject to the all the caveats above. For example, take the measurement of unemployment or of gross national product. For both of these, there are many problems of definition (what defines unemployed?), definition of units (what about inflation; or income in different currencies?) and particularly practical measurability (what about hidden unemployment? what about the black economy? what about the subjective "bundling" in price indexes?). But with the caveats concerning these difficulties, the final unit used is numbers of people (for unemployment) or pounds sterling (for GNP). These are ratio scales, and it is clear that (subject to the caveats on measurement) 1 million people unemployed is twice as many as 2 million people unemployed. When measuring "soft" aspects, this is not true. When we measure (say) intelligence, although a numeric score is developed, and that score is calibrated to aim towards *reliability*, it is not clear at all that this is a ratio scale – in other words, someone with an IQ of 200 is not (necessarily) "twice as intelligent" as someone with an IQ of 100, who him/herself is not "twice as intelligent" as someone with an IQ of 50.

This means that what we can do with such measurements, where they cannot be formed into a ratio measurement, is much more limited. "The task of developing valid, reliable interval measurement . . . is the central theoretical and methodological problem in scientifically oriented sociology," says Wilson

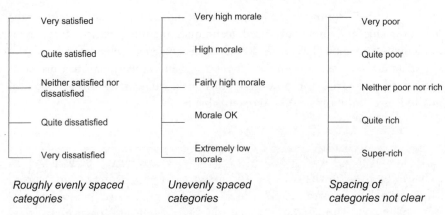

Very satisfied	Very high morale	Very poor
Quite satisfied	High morale	Quite poor
Neither satisfied nor dissatisfied	Fairly high morale	Neither poor nor rich
Quite dissatisfied	Morale OK	Quite rich
Very dissatisfied	Extremely low morale	Super-rich

Roughly evenly spaced categories *Unevenly spaced categories* *Spacing of categories not clear*

Figure 7.3 Spacing of categories

(1971) because "the ordinal level of measurement prohibits all but the weakest inferences concerning the fit between data and a theoretical model [that is] formulated in terms of interval variables." We can sometimes set out numerical scales; and, in the simplest of cases, it is sometimes clear whether categories are roughly in equal ratio or not – see for example Figure 7.3. But even here, the final example is not clear whether this is a linear scale, a log scale, or simply an ordinal scale without any sensible mapping into a ratio; and even in the others it is not clear that these are actually ratio scales. (One interesting approach is in Linacre (2002), who uses what is known as Rasch measurement theory using the idea of log-odds to formulate a ratio scaling from an ordinal construct, which is applicable in some circumstances.)

A particular issue with such factors in management research is that we can often not measure them directly, but have to measure aspects that are accessible that we hope will be a proxy for the variable of interest. Indeed, quite often the aspects we are interested in are complex and encompass a whole range of issues, each of which we could look at separately. Segars (1997) uses the example of "technological diffusion" within a company (the extent to which technology has been dispersed throughout the organization). In looking at this, he uses five different questions in a questionnaire, each looking at specific aspects, such as "our divisions/SBUs are dependent on centralized hardware" (strongly agree to strongly disagree), "most major data processing is centralized in one location" and so on.

Such multiple measures then need statistical manipulation and checking to make sure they are robustly measuring a unidimensional aspect. Cronbach's

alpha measure (Cronbach, 1951) provides an indication of the strength of the measurement, and more advanced techniques include comfirmatory factor modelling (Anderson, 1987). Segars (1997) sets up a carefully defined underlying structure for assessing the effectiveness of unidimensional measurement, with various metrics for how good this measurement is. These statistical methods are really outside the scope of this book.

> Measurement of "soft" aspects is even more dependent on the underlying conceptual models than the "hard" aspects. Often the obvious measures are ordinal or even nominal, which does not give much power to our modelling. Developing ratio scales can be a challenge, particularly for complex aspects that might represent a portfolio of aspects, but is necessary if these measures are going to be used in Management Science models.

7.5 "Soft" data collection

The most basic tool for measuring subjective concepts is the questionnaire, and establishment of questions to be asked, of course, depends on the measurement of the aspects being studied, which relies on the issues we have discussed above. There are some obvious pitfalls or simple lessons to be followed in developing questions, and there are many textbooks covering this area, but some of the simplest points are:

- Questions should be understandable: jargon, inappropriate technical words, slang, overly complex phrasing and ambiguity should all be avoided.
- Questions should be answerable: that is, if the respondent has the knowledge, can s/he answer the question? It should be well-defined, and if possible you should avoid questions that overly dependent on assumptions, memory or hypothetical reasoning.

Questions in a questionnaire are of two types, leading to two different types of analysis. Closed questions have only a limited set of answers, either a nominal set of options (including yes/no) or, very commonly, a Likert scale (Likert, 1932). The most common type of Likert scale makes a statement and then gives a series of options asking for the degree of agreement with the statement, such as:

1. Strongly disagree
2. Disagree
3. Neither agree nor disagree
4. Agree
5. Strongly agree

Open questions, on the other hand, allow textual entry in any form for an answer.

Clearly, the data from closed questions are available for traditional statistical analysis – more usually non-parametric analysis (Spearman's correlation; Mann-Whitney or Wilcoxon tests etc.) as answers generally consist of nominal or ordinal data as described above. This is taking a fairly positivist view of the problem. Open questions often require the analyst to take a more phenomenological approach. By definition, they offer fewer opportunities for statistical analysis, although there are methods for analysing qualitative data, even though it is unstructured and text-based (*NVivo*, for example, is software to help "manage, shape and make sense of unstructured information" by helping you "analyze your data and discover patterns, identify themes . . ." etc. (QSR International Pty Ltd, 2007)). But often we are searching for deeper meanings within individual responses rather than statistical generalizations across the whole sample. (Methods such as protocol analysis (Ericsson & Simon, 1993) allow more in-depth search for meaning within textual data.)

The questions for a questionnaire are clearly prompted by the research question we are trying to answer. If we have an idea of some of the independent variables that might affect the issues in which we are interested (e.g. demographic data) then these have to be asked. Then the outcomes in which we are interested (the dependent variables) obviously have to be investigated.

Having underlying models for the variables in which we are interested clearly provides a mechanism for developing more well-constructed questionnaires. For example, if we use causal mapping to represent relationships between the variables, this gives a natural structure for the questionnaire required to quantify the data. If we return to the classic example in Section 4.7, there we said that "Many of the variables required some degree of subjectivity in their quantification. So the qualitative model was used to define what was meant by specific variables in the quantitative model, and small subsets of the map used as a framework to collect data on the variables." In that case, if we had

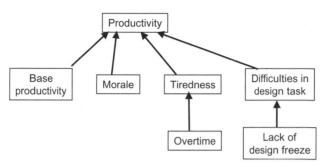

Figure 7.4 Causal map

developed a causal map in which "productivity" was defined according to Figure 7.4, then we would try to quantify this relationship by asking project participants their estimates of productivity, perhaps at a particularly memorable point of time, and their estimation of the relative contribution of these four factors (using where necessary subsequent levels of the map as explanation – e.g. "tiredness due to overtime" and "difficulties in design task due to lack of system freeze"). This will also help to validate the model – or sometimes reveal some lack of coherence in or disagreement with the model, which will enable further development of the model.

This latter use of questionnaires might be not only to individuals but also to groups, and we do need to recognize the fact that collection of "soft" data is often a social practice. As well as the interaction between analyst and interviewee, there are also the social and political effects within the organization. This is particularly the case when workshops are used to collect data, and considerable care needs to be taken in such forums to take into account (and mitigate) these effects. One effect is "groupthink", sometimes used as a simple way of referring to the way that people think when they are in a group and their efforts to achieve unanimity override their ability to think clearly. As Janis (1973) defines groupthink, though, it is a complex and multi-layered phenomenon which causes groups to think and act in quite different ways than the individuals (he talks, for example, about "an illusion of invulnerability . . . which creates excessive optimism and encourages taking extreme risks; collective efforts to rationalize in order to discount warnings . . . an unquestioned belief in the group's inherent morality . . . stereotyped views of enemy leaders . . . direct pressure on any member who expresses strong arguments against any of the group's stereotypes, illusions, or commitments . . . self-censorship of deviations from the apparent group consensus . . . a shared

illusion of unanimity . . . the emergence of self-appointed 'mindguards' ' ").
Other types of bias caused by the social environment are discussed in the next
section, such as "expert bias", "management bias", and so on. This all leads
to the conclusion that, where possible, we should take advice from those
experienced in running workshops to collect data; Eden and Ackermann
(1998), for example, offer practical wisdom in this area.

Open questions from questionnaires provide some soft data. But one of the
key types of data within an organization is "stories" or "narratives". Perhaps
the best-known work in this area is Gabriel's (2000) book, *Storytelling in
Organisations: Facts, Fictions and Fantasies*. He looks at how stories are used
in organizations, and how important narratives are in providing the memory
of the organization. He describes how stories invite us to engage with the
meaning as stories describe the experience of the teller, distinguishing between
reports (facts-as-description) and stories (facts-as-experience), but talks about
both. "Story work involves the transformation of everyday experience into
meaningful stories. In doing so, the storytellers neither accept nor reject
'reality.' Instead, they seek to mold it, shape it, and infuse it with meaning,
each in a distinct and individual way through the use of poetic tropes"
(Gabriel, 2000). (He describes eight of these 'poetic tropes', including attribution of motive, attribution of causal connection, attribution of responsibility
(blame/credit), attribution of agency and so on.) In line with our discussion
of the need for a multi-methodological view of management situations, Gabriel
does not view narratives as the entire answer to how to learn lessons: "researchers who want to use stories as a research instrument must be prepared to sacrifice at least temporarily some of the core values of their craft . . . they must
rid themselves of the assumption that quality data must be objective, reliable,
accurate etc. . . . at the same time researchers must not lose sight of the relation
between stories and facts: facts are not dissolved by stories but recreated
through them." Here again we come up against the issue of *triangulating* the
various types of data, which we will discuss shortly. But the use of stories,
carrying with them their complex organizational context (Connell, Klein &
Meyer, 2004), and showing how actual practice often differs from company
procedures or norms (Brown & Duguid, 1991) can be of vital importance in
seeing how events occur and effects happen within the causality of a particular
event. This, for example, is why they are important in learning lessons from
complex projects (Williams, 2007).

All of the discussion in the last two sections has probably appeared to put
our data on a much less certain footing than simple measurement of "hard"

well-defined variables. "Reliable data about organizational life is predominately qualitative, situational, and is collected as the opportunity arises. Traditional tests of validity, therefore, cannot be used when data is collected in this manner. This, systematic method, as well as critical reflection and triangulation becomes particularly important" (Eden & Huxham, 2006). The topic of triangulation is one we mentioned in Chapter 4, when we discussed how there are often multiple perceptions of different aspects of the situation, each with different interpretations, rather than a single "real" "truth". We said there that we should check the validity of any results or data by approaching a question from as many different angles as possible (Denzin, 1989), using different data to cross-check or, more generally, using different methods or different analysts or participants, or particularly different methodological stances – or any different way of attacking the same question.

Interestingly, when Eden and Huxham (2006) discuss "action research" (an intervention mode we mentioned in Chapter 2 and will discuss in Chapter 13), while emphasizing the importance of triangulation to ensure data validity, they say that: "action research provides also a uniquely different interpretation of the concept of triangulation". They discuss the different understandings that can come from different types of data collection and different settings, and say that:

> These different perspectives are not competing but provide alternative meanings to the data that nevertheless need to be triangulated with respect to emerging insights. Exceptionally therefore action research provides an opportunity to seek out triangulation between i) *observation* of events and social processes, ii) the *accounts* each participant offers in different settings and iii) the changes in these accounts and interpretation of events *as time passes* (Haré and Secord, 1976). From *these* three perspectives *the data are not expected to triangulate* (agree). Indeed we may be more surprised if they do agree than if they do not given the deliberate attempts at discovering multiple views. . . . Importantly a lack of triangulation acts as an effective dialectic for the generation of new concepts (Eden & Huxham, 2006).

Therefore, as we attempt to triangulate perceptions and understandings, our use of different approaches, methodologies, assumptions and interviewees will lead us to contradictions or differences, which we then need to explore with the participants – and this is part of the creative dynamic that enables us to develop models that more properly reflect the situations that we are trying to represent.

> Collection of soft data is an important part of our role as Management Scientists. We need to take a multi-methodological stance as well as take a multi-lensed view of the situation. Questionnaires, workshops, interviews, storytelling; all these have an important role, with care needed to ensure they are used methodologically correctly. Triangulation helps to pull these together, with disagreements between them and the dialectic following providing an important creative dynamic to model-building.

7.6 Subjective probability

There is one particular type of aspect we often wish to measure that is worth considering specifically, and that is the need to measure or estimate probabilities. One main reason to look at this specifically is that many of our management science problems involve inherent uncertainties, and we need to try to estimate these in order to understand appropriate ways of modelling the future. The other reason, however, is that this is a well-developed field that can illustrate some of the issues involved in collecting "soft" data, and it provides a useful specific example with which to look at those issues.

In some cases, there might be historical evidence on which we can base our projections. But even in such cases, we need to use judgement in considering whether that evidence gives a good guide to the future. Pugh (1987), for example, illustrates an example looking at the duration of military-aircraft development projects between 1950 and 1980. Plotting the durations by start of development – which implies a small but steady increase in project durations – gives quite a different forecast to plotting the durations by the end of development – which shows a rapid rise in project durations, then, starting again with very short-duration projects and again rapidly rising, this hiatus being due to a fundamental change in aircraft technology.

So, in nearly all cases, assessing a probability requires an element of judgement – Shafer (1994), indeed, goes as far as to say that "subjectivity is an aspect of all applications of probability". And we usually need to depend on the judgement of our clients and experts in assessing probabilities. So, we need to consider what we are doing when we ask someone to estimate a probability, and what are the traps of which we need to be wary. Let's consider first what the idea of "subjective probability" actually means in practice – a fundamentally difficult concept treated in depth by Wright and Ayton (1994).

We use various ideas of probability in a variety of ways in everyday life: "The next throw of this die is *unlikely* to produce a six" . . . "Smoking reduces the *chances* of healthy life" . . . "We will *surely* have a good harvest". These are quite different terms and quite different uses of the idea. There has been much research on the question of what we mean by such probability statements, but much of it comes essentially to a separation of two types of statement. Shafer (1976) defines these two types as: *aleatoric*, relating to intrinsically uncertain situations (Latin *alea*, a dice), and *epistemic*, relating to a measure of belief, or more generally to a lack of complete knowledge. (Oakes (1986) discusses this in much more detail.) For example, a machine that makes castings will cast a different amount of material each time, and we will often see a recognizable distribution, such as a normal distribution, of amounts building up over time (*aleatoric*); but ask how much material a *new* machine will cast, about which you have little underlying knowledge, and you have to express a certain uncertainty (*epistemic*).

Some authors expand this idea to the idea of "ambiguity" – often used as a term for a middle point where we feel we know the model underlying the phenomenon, so it is essentially an aleatoric uncertainty, but we do not know the values of the parameters involved, so there is some epistemic uncertainty. This type of situation was famously expounded by Ellsberg (1961), who claimed that people generally preferred an unambiguous gamble to an apparently equivalent ambiguous one. Ellsberg's example compared gambles based on drawing a ball at random from an urn containing 100 balls, and you win if the marble is of a colour that you have pre-chosen, where:

- in Gamble 1, the urn contains 50 black balls and the remainder are white balls, and
- in Gamble 2, the urn contains between 0 and 100 black balls and the remainder are white.

It was found that many people preferred the first gamble.

One key problem we have, though, is that most thinking about statistics, and in particular most experiments, have been based around simple aleatoric situations. The Ellsberg experiment above is an obvious example: in all of these experiments, the experimenter is able to estimate what the probabilities ought to be, and the epistemic uncertainty is effectively zero – and the experimental subject is aware of that. Unlike these experiments, the real world is hugely complex, and the ability that humans have to think about the world and come to assessments is similarly complex, and as yet ill-understood. Indeed, some feel that the very language of probability is inadequate to describe this: "The structure of the world is prodigiously complex, and this is mirrored in the heterogeneity and complexity of our knowledge of it. . . . Indeed, the subjective features of 'belief' itself appear to be quite complex. . . . Insistence that the laws of objective and subjective belief must be axiomatized in the same way (via the laws of probability) blurs a distinction between what is a useful technical device and common experience" (Fox, 1994).

If we accept for now that the idea of a subjective probability is simply a device for conceptualizing an idea and using it in our models, how can we go about enabling an expert to quantify his or her subjective feelings about a probability in a robust, coherent, consistent way? A literature of formal methods has been built up, particularly in the late 1980s (Kahneman, Slovic & Tversky, 1986; Keeney & Winterfeldt, 1989). The classic paper, however, is by Merkhover (1987). This describes perhaps the best-known methodology for assessing a probability, sometimes called the "SRI encoding process". It is a six-stage process, summarized below. This is a long process aiming to achieve some level of rigour. In practice, it is rarely worth carrying out this methodology in full – although for situations where quantifying a small number of probabilities is central to the problem, it is very useful (e.g. the risks of an earthquake when assessing where to site a nuclear waste repository). The methodology is summarized here because it highlights the main biases that can occur in such elicitation. It is these biases that we have to watch out for when we are quantifying our models, and this can give us some useful pointers.

- Stage 1 is called "motivating the subject", to establish rapport with the subject. The aim of the exercise is explained: namely to measure the subject's knowledge and best judgement concerning the quantity, not to predict the quantity. This distinction may be important if the analyst detects in the subject either *management bias* or *expert bias*. The first of these is when the subject views the quantity as a goal rather than an uncertainty – "if the boss wants me to minimize cost, I'll estimate it as low as I possibly can". The second, expert bias, is where the subject feels that as an "expert" he or she should down-play his or her uncertainty – a question such as "you're the expert in estimating this parameter, what is the uncertainty in its forecast?" is likely to result in an underestimate of the possible deviation. An important goal in this stage is also to explore the potential for *motivational bias* – that is, for a conscious or unconscious adjustment in the subject's probability assignments motivated by a perceived system of personal rewards.

- Stage 2 is called "structuring the variable" and has two purposes. The first is to structure the uncertain quantity into one or more logically related well-defined variables suitable for quantification. The second is to explore how the subject thinks about the quantity, which helps to indicate the likelihood of various *cognitive biases* (i.e. distortions associated with the simplified rules that research suggests people use to reduce the complex task of assigning probabilities to events). Having said that, as we mentioned in Chapter 2, more recent work such as by Gigerenzer *et al.* (2000) looked further into these rules and found humans are actually good in practice at "fast and frugal" decision-making, based on heuristics that we develop to assess uncertainties – so we should not be too hasty in discounting our clients' own mental processes. The elements are then precisely defined so as to remove all possible ambiguities in its definition, then the analyst explores the usefulness of disaggregating the variable into more elemental variables (which can help to combat motivational bias by producing a level of detail that disguises the connection between the subject's judgements and personal interests). The final step is to list all the assumptions the subject is making in thinking about the variable.

- Stage 3 is "conditioning the subject" and aims at drawing out, into the subject's immediate consciousness, all relevant knowledge relating to the uncertain variable. This is to avoid technical errors in judgement that are found commonly to occur, such as underweighting distribution information and regression toward the mean. Then the analyst seeks to counteract *anchoring bias* (the tendency to produce estimates by starting with an initial value) and *availability bias* (giving a higher probability to occasions that are easier to recall).

- Stage 4, "encoding the judgement" quantifies the uncertainty. Merkhover describes various methods available, mostly related to presenting the subject with options which are given probabilities, or options which are equated in probability (e.g. by using a "probability wheel").

- In Stage 5, "verifying the result", the judgements obtained are tested to see whether they agree with what the subject really believes, by checking that the subject is comfortable with certain aspects, such as shape or implied results.

- And finally in Stage 6, "resolving expert differences", it is often desirable to obtain probabilistic judgements from more than one individual. Merkhover discusses how these might be aggregated into a single distribution – a particular area which has received much interest in later work such as by Cooke (1991).

7.7 Conclusion

In any modelling science, the collection of data to populate those models is of fundamental importance. In any quantitative modelling science, this also involves characterization of aspects as variables and measurement of those variables.

We have taken a very limited view in this chapter, looking solely at issues in the collection of that data. There are many practical issues we have not touched on – such as how to store and re-access data; how to ensure data stay up-to-date (how often to re-collect data to maintain models); how to maintain the confidentiality of data; or how to delve into large data-sets to look for useful information. Indeed, we haven't touched on how "useful" the data are at all (precise, well-collected data might actually be irrelevant to our study!).

For Management Scientists, there are some particular issues in the collection of data to populate our models as we move into the complex "wicked" world that we described in Chapters 1–4. However, these issues can be a creative impulse to generating innovative and effective models that represent the situations we study, including the perceptions and understandings of our clients and our own observations. This is an exciting area and, rather than the ivory tower of the "Glass Bead Game", it is one where the Management Scientist comes face to face with the reality of his or her discipline.

8

Appropriate Modelling

8.1 Models

As well as collecting data, a key part of any Management Science intervention is creating a model – indeed, some would say that this is the fundamental distinction between a Management Science or Operational Research intervention and other forms of consultancy. But what constitutes a "good" model? What are the issues the professional modeller needs to consider? What decisions need to be made? Of course, this chapter does not stand alone, but will be set within the context of our first seven chapters. We will look at what types of model there are, and what is the most appropriate model in a given situation, and some aspects of the process of modelling. We will illustrate all these aspects with an example.

We discussed what a Management Science model is in Section 1.4. The conclusion there was that it represents or describes perceptions of a real situation, simplified, using a formal, theoretically based language of concepts and their relationships (that enables manipulation of these entities), in order to facilitate management, control, understanding or some other manipulation of that situation. All of those words were important, and represent ideas that will recur during this chapter.

8.2 What types of model are there?

In order to consider what the most appropriate model is in a given situation, we need to characterize what sorts of model there are. And as we look at all of these characteristics of models, we will cover many of the issues that we need to include in our consideration of an 'appropriate' model. There are seven key questions that we need to answer, and these are addressed below.

An interesting set of characteristics is also given by Mitchell (1983), who provides seven sets of dimensions on which we can place a model. The first of these is the level of abstraction (i.e. whether the real system is experimented on), which as he says really distinguishes Management Science models from others; where the other dimensions come into our structure is shown below by referencing the Mitchell (1983) dimensions with a "#".

(1) Why is the model being built?

Some models are useful to predict outcomes, some to explore different options (Dimension #2b). We can of course widen this to all the different purposes of modelling which formed the basis of our taxonomy in Chapter 5, and, as we said there, we choose our methods to match our underlying aims:

- Are we trying to structure a problem-situation?
- Are we trying to derive some attribute of a system?
- Are we trying to find the optimum action to take?

and so on. But, as we have discussed (e.g. in Chapter 2), our purpose should colour the whole modelling process and define the shape of the model.

(2) For whom are we building the model?

As we discussed in Chapters 2 and 3, who the client is, and our relationship with the client, is fundamental to the modelling process. But there are two particular generic ways in which models differ:

- One is accessibility. Mitchell (#6) distinguishes between a "private" model (accessible only to specific people, such as client users) and a "public" model (open to all). A more extreme end of this dimension is the model built solely for the analyst, which is not even revealed to the client. There are clearly issues here about confidentiality, about revealing conflicts or compromises in views of the problem situation, and so on.

- Another is transparency. If the client (where s/he does see the models) can understand the working of the model and its internal processes, s/he is likely to buy-in more to the output; this is the aim of methodological ideas such as the mapping/System Dynamics structure outlined in the example in Section 4.7 (see Figure 4.4). (This is related to, but not the same as, Mitchell's #2a below).

(3)   How much of the system is to be modelled?

A key set of decisions is in the area of the extent of the 'real' situation that the model is trying to represent, which we can think of roughly as the breadth and depth of our viewpoint:

- *Scope:* that is, how much of the system are we trying to model – part of a system or the whole system (#7)? As we discussed in our exposition of Soft Systems Methodology (Section 3.2), this is a key question and answering this is fundamental to the skill of a Management Scientist.
- *Resolution:* that is, the level of detail that the model tries to represent ("micro" or "macro", #2d). This affects the level of effort required of the modeller, but in earlier times was strongly influenced by limitations in computing power (#2e), when a detailed simulation could take many hours to run. This is increasingly less relevant to modellers, although still sometimes an issue. This question is also influenced by the fifth question below.

(4)   How general is the model to be?

Mitchell (#4) distinguishes between "absolute" models (valid anywhere at any time) and "relative" models (situation-dependent), but makes the point that "almost all models are relative ones, or at least more relative than absolute". But it is still necessary to consider the extent to which (say) client values and perceptions of reality are built into the model, or the extent to which the modelling is valid under conditions other than those that the modeller assumed, if the model is likely to have a life beyond a one-off decision limited to a single group of clients. (This can also affect the extent to which the model will be purpose-built rather than standard, #3.)

Following our discussion of the type of problems Management Scientists try to model in Chapter 1 – wicked messes (see Figure 1.2) – there are two generic aspects that we need to think how to model.

(5) How is causality to be modelled?

Looking at the dynamic complexity axis of Figure 1.2, we need to consider how to model this underlying complexity. Mitchell distinguishes (#2a) between "structural" models, in which the underlying mechanisms in a system are modelled, and "black box" models, in which patterns are looked for (without necessarily any search for the causality of these patterns) and it is assumed that the patterns will persist. There are issues of credibility, sensitivity and validity here. Will a client trust a "black box" without understanding what goes on inside the model? How can you be sure that the combination of the causal effects will act as the model implies (remembering that dynamic complexity implies that "the whole is greater than the sum of the parts"). How sensitive is the model behaviour to the structural assumptions? And so on. (Mitchell (#2c) also distinguishes the dimension of "instrumental" versus "realistic" models – the latter built from "refutable theories about the system modeled"; the former "works but no one quite knows why").

(6) How is behaviour to be modelled?

We must also look at the behavioural complexity axis of Figure 1.2. As we discussed in Chapter 1, Management Scientists have moved from simply modelling physical systems to trying to represent human behaviour within that system. Thus, we need to consider:

- Firstly, does the model need to represent behaviour at all (#5a)? Care must be taken to ensure that the model does not assume behaviour implicitly. For example, we might assume members of an organization follow the espoused procedures or processes, whereas in reality they may well exhibit "non-canonical" behaviour. Or, we might assume that behaviour aims towards what we modellers see as an "optimum", but where our criteria might be quite different from the participants'.

- Sometimes, modelling of the behaviour of the humans in the system simply seems too difficult. One way round this is to use interactive models (#5c), where the human intelligence of the entities in the model is supplied by real humans interacting with the system. In some circumstances, this can be used as part of a structure to capture the behavioural aspects of a system and include a simulation of them in an overall model, as described in the example in Section 8.3.

There is one other way of looking at how we model the complexity of the model, and that is the question of how complex or how simple a model should be. This is the seventh question that needs to be answered.

(7) How complex or how simple should the model be?

There are two key balancing principles generally accepted in modelling. The first is known as "Occam's razor". There are various verbalizations of this principle, which in its essence dates back to the fourteenth century. Essentially, it expresses the idea that if a few entities or reasons are sufficient to explain a phenomenon, this is a preferable explanation to one using many entities or reasons. (The idea of "parsimony" used in statistical analysis is similar.)

The decision about whether an element of a model is necessary to explain the phenomena being modelled is often not easy, and will depend on many issues, including the purpose of the model, the intended closeness by which the model must replicate actuality, and so on. But the general application of Occam's razor to our analysis and modelling will lead us to using the simplest models appropriate to our task. The error from which Occams' razor tries to keep us is that of needlessly over-complicated models: if we fail to define our system tightly enough (thus try to model the whole system around our problem-situation), or include every possible interaction, whether or not it is significant, we lay ourselves open to many problems – needless work, possible emergence of false or misleading results, unrobust models, accusations of "fiddling". Morgan and Henrion (1990, ch. 11) give some useful examples of problems that have arisen due to over-complex models being constructed and (mis-) used. Salt (2007) gives as one of his "seven habits of highly defective simulation projects" the problem of "Trifle-worship", which he describes as "the habit of unrelenting pursuit of detail, and of proliferating entities beyond necessity; the apparent worship of mere trifles", based on the belief that "the more detailed the model, the better". He goes on to say that "Trifle-worshippers confuse detail with realism. Although one very frequently hears people talk of 'realistic models', it should be recalled that 'realism' is a term that comes from the world of art and theatre, not from mathematics. . . . The function of simulation models (at least, those used for decision support, rather than for training) should not be to get users to suspend their disbelief, but rather to assist them in understanding the system under study." One motivation for over-detailed models he suggests might be "in order to reassure oneself one is leaving nothing out. This is a fool's errand, for simplification is the essence of modelling, and if it were possible to create a full-fidelity model of a system it would presumably be no easier to study than the original."

All of this, however, must be balanced by the second principle: "requisite variety". This idea, from Ashby (1956), derives from the world of cybernetics. A model must be able to represent the features in the system that the modeller needs to be interested in; thus, it must have sufficient variety. Thus, again, requisite variety is not an intrinsic feature of the phenomena being modelled; rather, it is a function of the phenomena when considered with the purpose of the model and so on.

The error that we must try to avoid here, of course, is the creation of over-simplistic models. A model of a complex situation which does *not* have requisite variety, in other words, does not represent sufficient features of the situation and will not display the essential features of complexity – where the whole acts in a way beyond simple combination of the parts. We remember Simon's (1982) definition of complexity quoted in Chapter 1, which included the words: "the whole is more than the sum of the parts . . . [such that] . . . it is not a trivial matter to infer the properties of the whole." So, actually it is not the model on its own that must exhibit "requisite variety", it is the model and its user together that must be able to match the complexity of the system being studied. Phillips (1984) describes a theory of the development of "requisite decision models", describing an iterative process of analysing a model representing the shared understanding of the situation, which facilitates the emergence of "new intuitions" about the problem, so that the model can be developed further and re-analysed until no new intuitions arise. Our models, then, must represent sufficient variety as we use them to replicate adequately the complexity of the situation.

It must be emphasized that the judgement of simplicity versus complexity requires consideration of the purpose of the model, as we discussed in question (1), which will also imply the desired degree of replication of actuality.

> We need to consider what the most appropriate model is in a given situation. That means we need to consider the seven questions in this chapter: Why is the model being built? For whom are we building the model? How much of the system is to be modelled and to how much detail? How generally applicable is the model to be? How is causality to be modelled? How is behaviour to be modelled? And, how complex or simple should the model be?

8.3 Example

Let's look at an example and see how the different questions pertained to it. The example involves "Replenishment at sea" (RAS), and is described fully in Williams, Gittins and Burke (1989). RAS represents the replenishment of fighting warships by vessels of the Royal Fleet Auxiliary (RFA) at sea and is a vital factor in naval operations. These RFAs vary widely in purpose and size. Collectively these vessels supply everything that may be required in peacetime or war, from fuel and lubricants to munitions, food, spare parts, rope and grey paint – about 760 000 different items in all – as well as supporting helicopter operations and maintenance. The RFAs that carry the stores were, at the time of the study, front-line tankers, larger tankers, and carriers of solid goods (ammunition, food and so on). The start of the study was prompted by three factors:

- A class of "one-stop" ships was being built, which would carry both liquid and solid stocks. In particular, this posed questions about how the new ship should be used, and how the RFA fleet should be balanced between these vessels and conventional RFAs.
- A new class of anti-submarine frigate was being built. To operate properly, these had to stand some way off from other naval vessels; this required consideration of the replenishment implications for its mode of operation.
- The accumulation of operational RAS data from a recent conflict, which had also served to underscore the strategic importance of RAS.

The overall aim of the study was to examine the effect on RAS performance of support, warship capacities, RFA speeds and tactics. For simplicity, at this point, the action of an enemy force was not considered, nor were the effects of attrition – an early decision to limit the problem being studied.

Since the complexity of the movement and decision-rules involved in the scenarios under investigation precluded an analytical optimization, a discrete-event simulation model was built. The model used as input details of ship design parameters, such as liquids and solids capacities and maximum speeds, as well as force disposition, warship duties, consumption rates and RFA supply capabilities. The model then at each event updated a dynamic database, giving details of the ships' speeds, fuel and stock levels, current duties etc.; typical events might be "warship puts out request", "ships meet each other for RAS", "end of RAS" etc. The model was to be used for a variety of warship dispositions, so a generalized format was defined to describe these dispositions, covering various search areas, screen sectors and ship patrol tactics.

But a simulation can't operate just with that – a "force controller" was required to interrogate the dynamic database and give the ships instructions based on the information received, including such considerations as how conflicting requests are prioritized, or whether warships travel to RFAs or vice versa.

The development of this part of the model came in three natural stages. The model as described above simply took in data, and required the user to instruct the RFAs (and, if necessary, warships) about their every movement. While this was useful for model-development purposes, it was much too time- and thought-consuming for any other purpose.

In actual operations, the force commander would gather status reports from his task-group each day, and issue the next day's orders. This was imitated in the model by designing a "daily order scheduler", which worked as follows. The user was presented with:

- a map of the ship positions;
- a "tote" that gives details, for each ship, of status, position, heading, speed and stocks (levels, usages and requests);
- for each RFA, details of deliveries and stocks.

The user could then issue "orders" to be carried out over the next day. These orders could be in simple forms, such as "go to position X at time T", or "ship A goes to ship B to RAS", or (more usefully) they can be in more generalized forms, derived from discussions with naval commanders and observing them using the model, such as:

- "milk runs": the RFA visits each of a series of ships in turn;
- "withdrawals": ships or pairs of ships withdraw in turn to an RFA, which stays stationary relative to the task-group;
- "rendezvous": a series of rendezvous between an RFA and withdrawing ships or pairs.

At the end of the simulated mission, results were output on such statistics as stock-levels at replenishment, times between requests and satisfaction, and proportion of time spent off-task by warships.

A second form of the model was thus produced which enabled the user to input a day's orders at one time. This Visual Interactive Simulation could run complete missions, but human input was still required, the results were dependent on the user, and the results were not statistically significant. For example, if the ships gradually all ran out of fuel, it was impossible to tell whether this was due to a user incompetent at commanding fleet replenishment operations, or to the group of ships having intrinsically insufficient RFA resources for that speed of advance. So, this was useful step, but still wasn't giving useful results (although it did provide a lot of fun and had some educational benefit!).

Therefore, experienced commanders were observed using the system on complete simulated missions and specific pre-prepared problems, in order to elicit the rules by which ships were scheduled. A rule-base was thus generated covering issues such as methods for partitioning a task-group, the effect of perceived capacity constraints and threat assessment, stock-levels at which demands become urgent etc., allowing decisions to be characterized by a small set of data which defined the relative priorities of competing requests (e.g. if an RFA has a request for torpedoes from a frigate due east, which only has X left in stock, and a request for fuel from an aircraft-carrier due west which only has Y tonnes of fuel left, which request is more important, all other things being equal?). Now the model could be run for complete missions automatically, without human input, requiring only the extra small input of the priority data. (The model thus represented the type of scheduling that would happen in practice, and scheduled well on this basis. Although it begs the question as to whether more "optimal" rules were possible, that was actually never raised in the project.)

This third form of the model could be used to assess the effects of varying model inputs (task-group disposition, task-group speed of advance, fuel capacities etc.) on performance statistics (e.g. stock-levels, time to supply, time warships spend off-task etc.). In an extended form (see Holder & Gittins (1989) for initial indications of the extension), this was used in MoD support planning, and was quoted as playing a part in a reduction in fuel-holdings.

We therefore followed a sequence of methods. First a Visual Interactive Simulation was made that an intelligent user could control, then archetypal user-decisions were defined so that a user could simulate a reasonable period of time without having to model every action; expert users were observed and their knowledge of the task captured; this enabled an expert system to be created, which was embedded in the simulation to provide an intelligent, automatically run simulation. Having developed the base (first form) model, the development of a model that was useful thus required three stages, each stage giving individual extra side-benefits:

- *Elicitation:* during elicitation, problems were identified, clarified and structured, forcing decision-makers to think. This gave side-benefits of providing structure to the problem and added to the domain knowledge. Indeed, the model included new problems, in that "one-stop" ships were included, so aiding more the development of domain knowledge. (During this phase, the second form of the model was built.)
- *Emulation:* the study built an "expert system" which could also be used self-standing; for example, the system could be used as an operational aid, or perhaps more likely as a training aid.
- *Embedding:* providing a realistic simulation (giving the third form of the model).

Having seen the project, let's have a look at our seven questions – how was the choice of model influenced by the answers to these questions?

(1) *Why is the model being built?* Was it (say) to predict outcomes, or to explore different options? Well, there were multiple purposes. There was a main need to predict outcomes (how fast can the fleet go?). But there was also a need to explore options for different sizes of the RFAs, different numbers of the RFAs and how to replenish the fleet (requiring

parameterizing the different methods of manoeuvring). This was reflected both in the simple, automatic form of the model but also the way it was built. A later purpose became a very simple question – "can we lower our fuel stocks around the world?" – and this model became a part of a billion-pound decision.

(2) *For whom are we building the model?* This was a little clearer; there was effectively a single client group (part of the Ministry of Defence), but the work needed to be clearly understood by the client, so requiring transparency of both modelling of the system and modelling of the behaviour. The immediate client had clear requirements to supply summary results to his client-group.

(3) *How much of the system is to be modelled?* Consideration of the scope of the model was defined by the client at the start, then grew later. It was initially confined to the operations of a single warship group, in order to give a bounded well-defined situation that could be conceptualized and start to be modelled, although widened slightly to represent a few additional features (such as tankers that plied to and from main ports). (In Section 8.4, we'll see a real change to the breadth in incorporating enemy action into the model, making quite a different model – but that comes later.) Evaluating the resolution of the model was a little less easy. Results on overall behaviour were needed, so it was clear that it wasn't necessary to model 760 000 stock items; rather, only the main categories. Study of other warship-manoeuvring work gave some helpful leads in modelling this.

(4) *How general is the model to be?* This too was defined by the client-group. The model was to cover a number of warship groups, but naval planning at that point used a specific set of pre-set scenarios to be modelled. The model was only to relate to this particular navy. (A later attempt to provide the work to a foreign defence ministry was not particularly successful.)

(5) *How is causality to be modelled?* We were trying to investigate how a ship-group might behave. So, clearly here we needed a structural model, in which the underlying movements and behaviours were modelled. A "black box" model was not possible, even apart from the lack of client credibility there would be. We could build a structural model from some physical rules that were fairly unarguable and some behaviours that we had to impute. The latter meant that we would need to look at the sensitivity of the model behaviour to the modelling of those behaviours. Simulation was needed as the issue was too complex to solve analytically.

(6) *How is behaviour to be modelled?* Behaviour was key – how do RFAs move around the fleet? Our discussion of question (1) showed that an automatic model was needed to give statistically sound results (independent of any particular commander), particularly as multiple runs were needed to look at different ship-size options. So, clearly the behaviour of the commander had to be modelled. We assumed that the fleet did as the commander instructed, so it was considered that no other behaviour needed to be modelled. In looking at *how* the commander behaviour was to be modelled, the concept of day-long instructions was taken from actual behaviour. But because the behaviour wasn't obvious, and anyway the system being modelled was new in a number of ways so there was no actual evidence, interactivity was needed to investigate how real commanders would behave in different circumstances, and decision-rules were modelled to mimic this.

(7) *How complex or how simple should the model be?* The model was developed until the combination of modeller, client and model did not feel that omissions were having a significant effect. On the other hand, it was felt that little was included in the model that was not necessary: a simpler model would not have been able to model the complex behaviour of the RFAs and so would be unlikely to give insight into the problem. The results were quite sensitive to the "speed of advance" of the fleet (with this sort of system, a fleet can only go so fast; when it tries to go a little faster, the RFAs cannot keep up). Therefore, a reasonable level of accuracy was important here, and the modelling reflected this.

8.4 Aspects of the process of modelling

As well as identifying the particular type of model that is most appropriate, there are six further aspects of modelling that we're going to touch upon in this section.

(1) The relationship with the client

We have already stressed in Chapter 2 that, to be successful, we must have a continuous relationship with the client, throughout the modelling process – as we can see in Figure 2.3. Indeed, while this is particularly true of the client, we also said in Chapter 2 that, for our intervention to succeed, we need to comprehend the whole range of stakeholders, their interest and power, and the systemic structure of power/interest relationships. This is for many reasons. To pick a few up, look at our definition of a model in Section 1.4:

- A model represents "perceptions of a real situation" – and so we have to relate thoroughly with those whose perceptions are to be modelled.
- One of the purposes of modelling is to help the client understand the situation – and that understanding will come much more effectively if s/he has been led through a modelling process rather than presented with "the answer".
- We are modelling "in order to facilitate management, control, . . ." etc., so we need the client to feel ownership of the model so that s/he will rely on the model and use it. We mentioned this in Section 2.5, and will return to it in Chapter 11.

(2) A messy process

We have said that we are modelling "messes" in the real world, but often our modelling process seems like a "mess"! This is quite unlike the clean, well-defined process offered by some writers. Gass (1987, 1990), for example, has a multi-stage process covering initiation, feasibility, formulation, data, design, verification, validation, training/education, installation, implementation, maintenance/update: a good check-list for delivering the computer implementation of a well-defined, entirely specified model, but much too neat for the practical intervention in a complex "mess". "Model building" says Pidd (2003), as one of six fundamental principles about modelling, "may feel like muddling through" (we'll see the other five later!) As we discussed in Chapter 2, our modelling often doesn't even have a clear end point, and our modelling can finish in various ways, such as when we have reached a "satisficing" point or the client's understanding of the situation has sufficiently increased. There has actually been little work done in the area to assess how experts carry out the modelling process in practice (Willemain (1994, 1995) is one of the few studies, the first giving some interesting insights into modellers' thoughts as they worked through, and the latter trying to quantify times spent but in an artificial situation that perhaps does not relate well to modelling real-world "messes"). However, it is known that it is a process that in no way follows a clear direct route. We'll discuss this further in Chapter 9.

(3)   The meaning of data

The next issue is the status and meaning of data we use to populate our models. We have already discussed the ontological and epistemological basis of our data, particularly that we are generally modelling not the objective world but our client's perceptions of the world. We rely on our clients for data, and if those data are filtered before they get to the client, or if the client takes underlying data and interprets them or overlays additional understanding, then we must seek to understand these processes in order to understand the degree of validity of the data. So, we must understand what our data represent, and whether they represent what they purport to represent, as we discussed in Chapter 7. This can be simple, such as figures of customer demand taken from a company's database will often actually be customer deliveries (so ignoring instances where customers ordered different items, or didn't bother coming to that particular company at all), but more subtle misrepresentations can occur where what is being measured is not the same as what is thought of as being measured. And, of course, we discussed in Chapter 7 that any data collected is only a sample, and then only from a particular time period.

Some of Eden and Huxham's (1996) discussion of "action research" applies also here: "A high degree of systematic method and orderliness is required in reflecting about, and holding on to, the research data and the emergent theoretical outcomes of each episode or cycle of involvement in the organization". "The processes of exploration of the data – rather than collection of the data – . . . must either be replicable or, at least, capable of being explained to others." And critically, as we discussed in Chapters 4 and 7, "the opportunities for triangulation that do not offer themselves with other methods should be exploited fully and reported" – our research methods must allow triangulation to provide cyclical data collection, where points at which data do not triangulate provide a dialectical opportunity for exploration and development of the modeller's and client's understanding.

There is a question here as to whether the data should drive the modelling process, or vice versa. Pidd (2003) (as a second of his six fundamental principles) warns against the danger of "data-junkies" "falling in love with data", and he states categorically that "the model should drive the data, not vice versa". His warning here is that the modeller should think about the underlying model, and what would be the most appropriate model – just as we were discussing in Section 8.2 – before going on to large data-collection exercises.

And this is clearly a good warning. However, as Pidd also admits, as in the "messy process" we've just been discussing, this isn't a simple "model then collect data", but rather there's an iterative procedure. If we reflect on the various figures in Chapter 4 (Figures 4.1, 4.2 and 4.4), we can see that the data informs how we build the model, which makes us think differently about how we might collect data.

(4) Gradually build up models

We have discussed the gradual way we build up models, interacting with the client-group and its perception of the world and the problem, moving from modelling to data collection and back, and so on. It will not be surprising, then, that most Management Scientists recommend that models are built up gradually rather than in a single "big bang". In Pidd's (2003) six "principles of modelling", there are three on this subject, which say:

- "Model simple, think complicated". In other words, we should try to capture our analysis in simple models – as far as the balancing act between "Occam's razor" and "requisite variety" we described above (in Section 8.2 (7)) allows – but we should think critically and rigorously about these models.
- "Be parsimonious: start small and add". In other words, begin with a model we can understand and manage, even if it has rather unrealistic assumptions, and gradually refine it to nearer match our problem situation. Similar advice is given by Chapman and Ward (2002 and others) when they espouse a "constructively simple" approach to modelling and estimating. When a simple model has been built, the modeller can then concentrate on improving those areas most clearly deficient. (Salt's (2007) discussion of "Trifle-worship" claims that: "It is usually easier to add detail to a model than it is to subtract it out once added, so erring on the side of too little detail is easier to correct than too much.")
- "Divide and conquer; avoid mega-models". In other words, don't try to model everything at once, but build working models of areas that can then be put together. Pidd quotes Raiffa thus: "Beware of general purpose, grandiose models that try to incorporate practically everything. Such models are difficult to validate, to interpret, to calibrate statistically and most importantly to explain. You may be better off not with one big model but with a set of simpler models" (Raiffa, 1982, quoted in Pidd, 1995). Of course, as we've discussed earlier in the book, complex systems are

complex because of the interactions between the elements of the system, and you have to be aware of missing key interactions when you divide models into parts.

There is another reason for following this advice. Modellers need to be *agile*, so as to be able to react to a changing situation. If the modeller has gone away for many months to build a model and comes back to find parameters or options have changed, and the model is not able to deal with the changed question, then the model will be ignored. Eisenhardt (1990), for example, discusses how some managers make strategic decisions quickly and says that this is the need, mentioning models that can be run weekly to look at the possibilities of different decisions. This is, of course, part of the reason for the ongoing client relationship implied in Figure 1.5. Ward (1989) quotes agility as a key reason for using constructive simplicity.

Building up models is not the same as joining different models together. There is a danger in assuming we can take many small models and simply join them up. Salt (2007) says that "Models can seldom be joined up meaningfully. To do so requires that they share substantially the same *Weltanschauung*. Sterman (1991) points out that the simplified nature of models requires details to be left out, and 'the purpose of the model acts as the logical knife'. Models that are designed for different purposes are probably missing some of the elements needed to be usefully joined to one another." However, "seldom" does not mean "never": in our example of replenishment ships in Section 8.3 above, one of the essential inputs needed to be data on weapons and ammunition usage; a separate exercise was ongoing modelling warship battles, which showed how such supplies were needed, and because the models had been developed from similar ideas, with (not insignificant) effort they could be combined to enable consideration of much wider issues (given that the questions of "what is the best way to replenish my ships?" and "is a battle going on or not?" are obviously related to each other!).

(5) Validation and verification

We need to look at *validation*, checking that the model is a good representation of reality. As well as being critical to achieving a useful model, it is at this point that often the credibility problem occurs with models – if the client doesn't think your model represents the actuality s/he perceives, s/he won't be interested either in using your model, or in the results from that model.

Yin (1994) offers four types of validation relating to his concept of "Case Study" research. We can adapt three of these to give us the basic types of validation of the elements of modelling:

- *Construct validity.* Looking at the individual elements or concepts in the model, are we really using the correct operational measures for the concepts we claim to be measuring? This covers the issues we discussed in Chapter 7.
- *Internal validity.* Turning from the individual elements or concepts in the model to the relationships between them, are these relationships true and correctly specified? Clearly if we posit an incorrect relationship between an input and a model variable, our model will again give incorrect results.
- *Reliability.* Again, this was covered in Chapter 7, but it essentially asks, could the procedures for establishing the above two – identifying the concepts, measuring them, establishing and quantifying the relationships between them – be repeated by another analyst, and get the same results?

Yin's fourth type, sometimes relevant to validating our models, is:

- *External validity.* Looking at the following question: how far away from the domain for which we generated the model can the model's results be generalized?

These are ideas we can use to validate the *elements* of a model. But once we've combined these elements into a whole model of a complex mess, we now need to validate this whole model.

If we compare model predictions with actual system performance, and there is a mismatch, then we can often learn, and modify the model. Let's suppose that we have been through that loop and there is now a good match. Then we are happy to accept the model; but even now there are problems. Firstly there is always a possibility that the model gives good predictions for old sets of values of parameters (which were used to formulate the model) but will give bad predictions for new sets of parameter values.

But we have also identified a dilemma, pointed out for example by Wahlström (1994). If a model generates only accepted results, then there is often not a lot of information in the results, and they provide little value; on the other hand, if the results are very different from what is expected, they will not be believed. Wahlström goes on to suggest that "a model, when it is at its best, should therefore generate only mild surprises, which can be believed or at least supported with commonsense reasoning from the model assumptions".

Workers in one particular method of modelling described in Chapter 5, System Dynamics, have studied the issues of validation in some detail. Their work is based on the ideas of Forrester and Senge (1980), who set out a list of "Confidence Tests", with the idea that as a model passes these tests we gain confidence in its validity. These tests consist of "Tests of model structure", "Tests of model behaviour", and "Tests of policy implications", and it is the second of these sets from which we want to draw to look at the validity of overall models. The key test within this set is:

- *Behaviour reproduction.* How well does the behaviour of the model match behaviour that can be observed in the real system?

Subsidiary to this come four particular aspects of checking that the model behaves similarly to the real system:

- *Symptom generation.* Where the building of the model has been motivated by particular problems or difficulties within a project, the model should reproduce the symptoms of the problem – otherwise it clearly will not be much use in diagnosis or assessing proposed corrective actions.
- *Behaviour characteristics.* The model should reproduce typical characteristics of the real system behaviour.
- *Behaviour prediction.* The model should predict patterns of behaviour in the future which appear qualitatively reasonable.
- *Surprise tests for behaviour anomaly.* If a model generates behaviour that is unexpected, surprising, or different from what has been experienced to date within the real system, then the causes of this behaviour should be traced, and if possible the real system checked to see whether it would also produce this type of behaviour under these conditions.

Finally, if the model is run under a variety of conditions two further technical tests can be carried out:

- *Extreme-value testing.* This is when the model is run under extreme conditions, to check that the behaviour is sensible and consistent with what is considered would actually occur in the real system.

- *Sensitivity tests.* This is where the sensitive parameters in the model are identified, and considers whether the real system would be similarly sensitive.

This can give us a set of ideas that we can use to increase confidence in the validity of our models.

Validation needs to be distinguished from another task, that of verification, which covers ensuring that we have actually modelled what we intended to model; that is, having decided on our model, have we operationally carried out that decision and formulated the model that we think we have, in terms of writing equations and computer modelling. Or, to put it another way, having decided on the model, and validated it, if we handed the plan over to an assistant to code up in a computer program, verification would mean checking that the instructions had been carried out as we intended. This is clearly a conceptually easier task, but still important, and not always easy. "Verification is defined for computer-based models by Gass as 'the process of demonstrating that the computer program "runs as intended"'. Thus verification would help towards establishing the level of confidence of the modeller, whilst validation would establish the level of confidence of the client" (Finlay & Wilson, 1987).

(6) How much information?

As one final comment, it can be useful to look at how much information needs to be presented to the client – looking at how much information the managers actually want or need to make their decision or even how much they use. A detailed model will often provide a great deal of information, much of which is useless to the client: what do they actually want to know? One difficulty here is often that clients ask for much more information than is useful. It is well-known in the literature that managers often don't need the information they want (Ackoff, 1967) and that organizations systematically gather more information than they use, yet continue to ask for more (Feldman & March, 1981). And this can be complicated by the intertwining between formal analysis activities and social interactions in decision-making within organizations (Langley, 1989) – some of which we'll discuss in Chapter 11. So, it is worth establishing what decisions are to be made, and what needs to be supplied back to the different elements of the client to enable that element to make the necessary decisions.

Revisiting the Example

Let's briefly go through these six points, and see how they operated in the example described in Section 8.3.

(1) *The relationship with the client.* Well, as always, there isn't a clear-cut answer as to who "the client" is. The immediate client was an analyst, who was interested in the modelling, and kept an interest all the way through. The senior decision-makers were only interested in the final result, as they had an ongoing relationship with the part of the client-body in which the immediate client sat. But extra interest was gained by the commanders who used the model and helped to form the rule-base.

(2) *A messy process.* In the early days of the project, while it was clear what we wanted to achieve, it certainly wasn't clear how we were going to achieve it. The initial simulation was built without the three-fold plan laid out neatly above. And the move towards including the model of enemy action (which had been produced by a different consultancy) was not thought of until the end of the project. So, although there was extensive planning and careful thought, model-building did not take a predictable path.

(3) *The meaning of data.* One of the prompts to carry out this study was the existence of a large data-source from a recent major conflict in which RAS had shown itself critically important. In fact, while this gave a creative boost to the modelling, it's not clear that it affected the model greatly. The model was built on a number of planning data which were accepted as authoritative within the MoD – but it had to be remembered that these were envisaged scenarios, and not fact.

(4) *Gradually build up models.* It is clear above that this was true at the high level of this project: the simulation model was built, then the daily scheduler, then the rule-base, then separately the enemy-action model was incorporated. It was also true at the micro-level of this modelling project, as models were slowly developed of ship movements, and so on.

(5) *Validation.* Validation was perhaps not well carried out on the simulation model. And since a new situation was being modelled, it was difficult to validate the behaviour against the real situation. But discussions with the client gave good confidence in the three Yin (1994) constructs about the model elements. But study of the behaviour-replication modelling suggested it mimicked "real" behaviour (i.e. in the laboratory, with

real commanders). And the use of the experienced commanders gave good confidence in the behaviour of the model as a whole. This allowed something like the tests that come under the heading behaviour reproduction above to be carried out; and, separately, extreme-value testing and sensitivity analyses were carried out as part of normal simulation model testing.

(6)   *How much information?* Finally, while the immediate client wanted all details of the modelling, it was clear that this information was distilled and distilled as it went up, until all that were left were details of how many ships were required and (perhaps – this was confidential within the client) how fast task groups could move.

Of course, this all looks neat and tidy now – as reports of projects after the event often seem. But in the midst of the project, often it does seem, as Pidd (2003) said above, just like "muddling through".

> The process of modelling also has important characteristics that we need to keep in mind when modelling. We need to consider the ongoing relationship with the client throughout the process, we need to be aware of the frequently messy nature of the modelling process, we need to understand the meaning of our data, we need to be aware of the need to build up models gradually and to validate them, and we should also consider how much information the client actually needs.

The last of Pidd's (2003) six principles, by the way, as I'm sure you'll ask, is to "use metaphors, analogies and similarities" – a help in the creative process and a different subject, for the next chapter.

9

Creativity

9.1 Introduction

OR/MS is sometimes represented as a set of tools, from which the analyst chooses the most appropriate for a given situation. Much of the common OR/MS teaching consists of explaining the tools in detail and how they work, and then how to apply them in fictitious or simplified situations. And, indeed, the analyst does need to understand his or her toolbox: that's why we had Chapter 5 in this book, laying out some of the landscape of OR/MS tools.

However, the early chapters of this book hopefully gave a start to a description of the real world that we're trying to analyse – or at least to which we're trying to bring some order. This description was exemplified in the "wicked messes" described in Chapter 1. This description should make it obvious that OR/MS is much more than simply mechanistically applying given tools. In his book *The Craft of Decision Making*, Rivett (1994) talks about knowing how to use our tools sensitively, appropriately and rigorously, rather than simply assuming that we can make the problem-situation fit our model or our tool. But the expert OR/MS modeller has something more than that: s/he can see the structure of models in a problem-situation, can identify where the problem lies and where he or she can contribute to the situation. This type of analyst can see beyond the obvious to the "big picture", and see how solving a problem tells us more about the system. S/he can "see more than what is apparent on the surface, and implicates not simply the physical world but also the human component that interfaces with goals, criteria, stakeholders, people affected, objectives of people, potential scenarios, and time horizons in the framework of planning" (Saaty, 1998). S/he has a creative spark which takes the work beyond the routine application of tools – indeed, that is necessary to understand how to apply the tools in a real situation. It is this that we shall be talking about as "creativity" in this chapter – and it is this creative spark that is essential in good OR/MS analysis work.

This is not a new topic. If we go right back to the very foundations of OR/MS, to Blackett (1950), he considered that OR's "novelty lies not so much in the material to which the scientific method is applied as in the level at which the work is done, in the comparative freedom of the investigators to seek out their own problems, and in the direct relation of the work to the possibilities of executive action. . . . The really big successes of OR groups are often achieved by the discovery of problems which had not hitherto been recognized as significant. In fact, the most fertile tasks are often found by the groups themselves rather than given to them. That this is so is only to be expected, since any problem which is clearly recognized by the executives is likely, in an efficient organization, to be already a matter of study. . . . During the war, OR workers attended the regular staff meetings at many operational headquarters and so learned the type of problems facing the executive."

Such creativity is undoubtedly intangible, and is equally undoubtedly difficult to define, let alone discuss. Students can be trained to a certain extent such as by use of unstructured problems and mini-projects (e.g. Williams & Dickson, 2000). And creativity is no doubt developed as an analyst gains experience and confidence in his or her analysis – this is all part of our tacit knowledge that we develop as analysts as we reflect on our practice (which will be the subject of Chapter 13). This current chapter will simply look at a few ways in which a start can be made to creative thinking, to help get the beginner analyst over the hurdle of "where do I start?", and hopefully the reader will be able to use some of these ideas in his or her practice.

But what is creativity? There has been research on the creative process in general, in the arts and as general inventiveness in science and engineering (such as Csiksznetmihalyi, 1996). In these latter fields, it is sometimes taken as read that we know what creativity is, but it is difficult to define let alone measure. The editors of *Creativity Plus*, after exploring the issue in depth, simply come up with the remark that: "Creativity may be a bit like pornography was to Supreme Court Justice Potter Stewart. He said roughly, 'I cannot measure pornography, but I know it when I see it, and I think it ought to be decreased'. We may not be able to measure creativity, but we sort of know it when we see it, and it ought to be increased" (C+ Editors, 2000). Torrance comes nearer to giving a definition in his classic (and, to some extent, standard) assessment of creativity as "the process of becoming sensitive to problems, deficiencies, gaps in knowledge, missing elements, disharmonies and so on . . ." (Torrance, 1974). Herbert Simon, the Nobel Prize winner, however, felt that "creativity" is simply the normal exercising of thought patterns that any expert uses (Simon, 2001) – and it is clearly so embedded within the OR/MS analysis process that it must form part of any analysis. So, we do not take it here to be a "special" attribute of an analyst – rather, it is something that should be nurtured and developed in all analysts; and perhaps we can give some hints here for starting the analyst off.

> Some degree of OR/MS creativity is an essential part of all OR/MS analysis. But a high level of creativity is the spark that marks out good, effective OR/MS from the mundane application of tools.

Researchers who have studied OR/MS creativity have differentiated aspects of the individual, in some circumstances his or her environment, and the process followed (e.g. see Evans, 1993). In this chapter we'll have a brief look at the individual, but since this is a book to help all OR/MS analysts, we'll concentrate on the process, which will include looking for generic underlying structures in different analyses, and also aspects of OR/MS analysis as a social process.

9.2 The individual

There is no doubt that OR/MS in practice is heavily dependent on the individual analysts. Rivett (1994) describes OR/MS as "an intensely personal activity". Cropper (1990) (quoted by Keys, 2000) says that "there are significant differences in practice between consultants using ostensibly the same methods" and notes that individuals use "a varied repertoire of methods according to personal rules of choice". Keys (2000) goes on to say that: "Underlying these rules and choices is the particular combination of technologies available in an individual's repertoire and the way an individual sees their role and way of working with those technologies. There should be a degree of mutual support between this 'personal philosophy' and how an individual chooses to combine tools, concepts and techniques of analysis when faced with a specific situation. The picture is therefore one of the analyst as designer; using knowledge and experience to create ways of working from a set of available approaches and personal preferences to move a situation forward."

Two reasons clearly make modelling very personal in analysing wicked messes in practice. One is that the analyst is dealing with intangible, sometimes nebulous, entities or ideas that, as we saw in Chapter 7, are often difficult or even impossible to measure directly, let alone for that measure to be unambiguously quantitative. The second reason, which we discussed in Chapter 2, and which will be key in our discussion later, is that the OR/MS process is a social process involving both the client-group and the analyst – so the analyst clearly has a personal impact on the process.

The actual attributes that promote (OR/MS) creativeness in an individual, however, are not at all clear. Evans says that: "Researchers have often looked at the characteristics of the individual who creates. Factors such as temperament, personal attitudes, and habits influence creativity. Creative thinking is largely a function of divergent thinking – the discovery and identification of many alternatives. Psychologists have performed considerable research on the characteristics of creative individuals that promote divergent thinking. These include knowledge, imagination, evaluative skills, awareness and problem sensitivity, memory, fluency, flexibility, originality, self-discipline and persistence, adaptability, intellectual playfulness, humor, nonconformity, tolerance for ambiguity, self-confidence, and skepticism" (Evans, 1993). Quite a list of attributes to live up to! But all of them are useful for enhancing our creativeness, even (especially?) those we might think of stifling, such as "intellectual playfulness" in the "serious" business of analysis.

Furthermore, some of the attributes that contribute to creativeness are dependent on the circumstances of the individual. For example, I once tested a set of OR MSc students and a set of art students as they came up to their final examinations, looking at their levels of anxiety and their levels of performance.

For ordinary examination testing the application of OR tools, which required little creativity, levels of anxiety were unrelated to performance. However, for an unstructured examination requiring a high level of creativity to see the underlying problems and a solution path (Williams & Dickson, 2000), there was a strong direct correlation – those students who got emotionally charged could bring creative ideas (out of their unconscious?), while those more relaxed and passive did less well. A similar result, incidentally, applied to the art students looking at the final "creative" element in their degrees, except interestingly these students had a far greater range of (Spielburger, 1983) anxiety scores, both extremely relaxed and extremely anxious, and beyond a 'normal' range of anxiety, not surprisingly, a disbeneficial effect set in, and the students became too anxious to be creative.

But much of what we think of as creativity comes from our tacit (internal and personal) knowledge as analysts – it develops from our feelings and commitments within the creative act (as we mentioned in Chapter 2 when looking at ideas developed by Polanyi (1962)). And to develop this, a key attribute that individuals need to have we are leaving until Chapter 13: that is, the ability to reflect on our practice and see how the situation "talks back" to us – having what are sometimes called "reflective conversations" with a situation. This is central to our development as creative individuals.

All of the above has said something about ourselves as individuals, some of which is not really under our control, some of which might give you ideas about self-development, and some of which we will discuss developing in Chapter 13. But this current chapter is looking at ways of carrying out the OR/MS process that will help us to be more creative in approaching a problem-situation – whoever we are. This chapter, then, is about processes and techniques.

9.3   The process: underlying structures

Of course, blindly following a pre-set process can never provide creativity, and there is an immediate trap in looking for a process to answer every situation. Salt (2007) points to such a danger in simulation modelling, believing that: "If only we follow the method assiduously enough, everything will be all right." He suggests that: "Given the essentially creative nature of decision-support modelling, the obvious mistake here is to imagine that there can be a fixed drill for thinking about new things. Related to this is perhaps the belief that the people who wrote the method are more knowledgeable than you are – which they might be in general, but almost certainly are not about the situation you are in right now. . . . Recognizing problem patterns and having a bag of thinking tricks to get you started are both good things, but they become harmful when they turn into unthinking adherence to a fixed process."

If we want to look at how a process might help the analyst, then that process will need to be based on what we see are the underlying structures within OR/MS problem-situations. The key difficulty the new analyst faces is the thought of starting an analysis from a "blank sheet of paper" with nothing as a foundation – if there were generic ideas from which to start, this could take the analyst over that first hurdle. It might appear that each problem we face is unique; however, Schön (1983), whose work about reflective practitioners generally we'll look at in Chapter 13, said that: "faced with some phenomenon that he finds unique, the inquirer nevertheless draws on some element of his familiar repertoire which he treats as exemplar or as generative metaphor for the new phenomenon". But are there any such structures for the Management Scientist? Of course, we would be sceptical of any claims to universal applicability, but this chapter has three ideas that have proved useful. These can help to get the analyst started on the OR/MS process and surface issues, questions, problems and ideas that can help the analyst construct a methodology for a full analysis.

9.3.1 Causality

Perhaps the most useful generic theme in OR/MS modelling is the description of the underlying structure of causality. For Saaty (1998), this is at the heart of looking at creativity in modelling. "The unifying principle or force in OR/MS is the flow and impact of influence of interaction. . . . The concept of influence occurs in all fields of knowledge – from physics, with its gravitational and electromagnetic influences, to sociology with it societal, political, economic, and technological influences. We argue that influence, a sensed, perceived or inferred stimulus, is the single most central concept for analyzing causal relations in OR/MS problems. Problem solving is contextual and focuses on the distribution of influence in allocation, queuing, inventory, and similar problems by manipulating measurable quantities. Because most influences are abstract and intangible, emphasis on creating structures to represent and measure the flow of influence of intangibles and their propagation is critical for the development of a general scientific theory for OR/MS" (Saaty, 1998).

Of course, the idea of tracing and mapping the underlying causality within a system was the basic idea behind the mapping/SODA problem-structuring method we described in Section 3.3. It is a useful and well-proven process for considering how a system operates and why. It can also be useful for exploring with a client-group where the problems lie, and what would be useful avenues of analysis.

Much OR/MS work is called on because a client-group finds it difficult to comprehend a complex system ("complex" in the Simon sense – see Chapter 1) – which suggests that causal mapping can be a good start to understanding the system. Much more than this, in practice much of the difficulty comes because a considerable subset of the system consists of intangible or human-based entities, and the influences between them are difficult to establish or are socially constructed. The use of cognitive mapping first, to explore the participants' thinking on the entities and influences, is thus clearly a good weapon to get an initial understanding of a problem-situation. And, again, building such maps helps the analyst in developing a reflective conversation with the situation, as we will discuss in Chapter 13. In addition, Saaty's analysis of creativity in OR/MS also places a key emphasis on the areas of decision-making and feedback (Saaty, 1998), and the cognitive/causal mapping chain not only encourages modelling of decision-making, it is ideally set up to help analysis of areas of feedback; these are not only difficult to perceive intuitively, but can often be important determinants of system behaviour.

> The use of cognitive and then causal mapping is a good first weapon to facilitate reflection on the situation in a structured way, to help bring understanding and some creativity to the start of an intervention.

9.3.2 System thinking

To Saaty (1998), again, part of creativity comes from system thinking. "Concern with the general system will force one to look back at the whole picture rather than to beat the problem to death by increasing the detail of analysis."

Again, system thinking is the basis of the Soft Systems Methodology (SSM) that we covered in Section 3.2. It clearly gives a good framework to start thinking about an OR/MS problem-situation where neither the situation nor the client-group's thinking about its problematic aspects are clear. Although SSM is specifically *not* a "recipe" for how to do OR/MS analysis – and Checkland modified his presentation of the methodology to avoid analysts blindly following a seven-step predefined process – it does appear that even those who find it difficult to think creatively about how to approach a problem-situation can use SSM specifically as a guide to start attacking a problem. While it is designed as an all-encompassing methodology for problem structuring, it can also be used as good first stage to get analysts over the initial problem of how or where to start.

How does system thinking help improve the OR/MS process? Doyle (1997) looks at the claims of how system thinking interventions affect behaviour and organizational performance, and four areas in his analysis are relevant here:

- *Analogical transfer.* "The identification by system dynamics researchers of structural similarities among systems in widely different fields has led to speculation that systems thinking interventions can improve participants' ability to transfer problem-solving insights from one context to another (see, for example, Forrester 1993 and Senge 1990)" (Doyle, 1997). And we have already mentioned in Section 4.6 the "total systems intervention" methodology, in which the first phase is "creativity", taking a series of "system metaphors" intended to encourage creative thinking about the organization and the issues confronting the managers.
- *Mental models.* It is felt by systems thinkers, particularly system dynamicists, that such methods help to improve participants' mental models, and to help participants understand the structure of systems.
- The systems literature suggests that such interventions help improve decision-making processes (e.g. Doyle quotes Park *et al.*, 1996). Much of this appears to be helping participants appreciate the feedback within systems, so the methods in Section 9.3.1 will give similar benefits here.
- System thinking also appears to help knowledge retention, although Doyle points out that almost any sensible framework of knowledge organization will aid memory.

However, it should be noted that the point of Doyle's (1997) paper is specifically that, while there is anecdotal evidence to support these claims of benefits, there is not yet firm reliable evidence. One very good example of an attempt to justify some of these claims is Caveleri and Sterman (1997), who carried out a systems intervention and tried to monitor managers' thinking, behaviour, and business results to see the effects of the intervention. The results of this example are somewhat mixed: managers did appear to "experience a shift in their mental models towards a more systemic understanding of the . . . system and its dynamics" (other participants, who received less training, did not); behaviour also changed among managers; however, it was difficult to see measurable improvements in business performance after the intervention.

> Looking at a problem-situation with a system perspective gives help in creatively approaching it in a way that does indeed comprehend the complexity. SSM, in particular, is a useful way to begin the analysis process and give the analyst an initial route to follow.

9.3.3 Values and goals

Another starting point for the OR/MS process is echoed again in Saaty's (1998) call to look at the "big picture": "Goals determine outcomes, and outcomes modify goals". A fair amount of OR/MS work is geared towards identifying different alternative actions in a decision situation, and evaluating them to find a "good" action. But Keeney says that

> Focusing on alternatives is a limited way to think through decision situations. It is reactive, not proac-tive. . . . Almost all the literature on decision making is based on alternative-focused thinking. It concerns what to do after the crucial activities of identifying the decision problem, creating alternatives, and specifying objectives. But where do these decision problems, alternatives, and objectives come from? More importantly, where should they come from? It is values that are fundamentally important in any decision situation. Alternatives are relevant only because they are means to achieving your values. Thus your thinking should focus first on values and later on alternatives that might achieve them (Keeney, 1993).

Literature (such as operations management literature) has moved over the past 20 years from looking at the tactics of how we achieve our stated aims, to thinking about what those aims should be. Techniques such as the famous Balanced Score Card (described recently in Kaplan & Norton, 2005) and much subsequent work has focused attention on: what are our values? What are our goals?

Often, an assignment given to an analyst will appear to be partly predefined – the client knows what s/he wants, and the analyst is there to establish how to make it happen. Keeney's point is that moving the dialogue up to a higher level to look at the overall goals gives a much more creative look at the problem. Keeney (1996) outlines a simple process of identifying objectives, structuring objectives, creating alternatives and identifying decision opportunities. The second of these reflects the complexity of the situation: causal mapping can be useful to trace means–ends relationships and ask the question "why is this particular objective important?", which will also help the analyst to "ladder up" to the fundamental objectives.

> Looking at the underlying values and goals of the client-group, and the structure of subsidiary goals, can be a useful start to an analysis.

9.4   Creativity in the social process of OR

We have been exploring ways of helping an analyst think creatively when faced with a new intervention situation. The picture we've perhaps painted is of an analyst, on his or her own, looking at a situation and trying to think creatively about the nature of the problem, the type of intervention required, and the types of analysis that might be useful. But, of course, OR/MS is not like this at all. As we described in Chapter 3, analysts approach a situation in collaboration with a client-group, they seek to understand the clients' perceptions of the situation, they explore the issues with the client and try to bring structure to the clients' views in partnership with those clients. The OR/MS intervention described in Chapter 3 is a journey undertaken by client and analyst together in partnership, to a point where the client has been moved on in the situation. This means, of course, that analysis is not a lone process, but the analyst's creativity can be provoked and stimulated by the interaction and dialogue with the client. Indeed, experience shows that it is the interaction with the client that is one of the main founts of creative thought.

A major part of the need for creativity, but at the same time a main source of creativity, comes from the fact that many of the problems that we seek to approach are socially constructed. Keys says that

> Tsoukas and Papoulias (1996) argue that analysts '... have no unique access to the nature of a problem, nor does the problem have a given, predefined nature ...' and consequently '... build creativity into the process of enquiry ...' in order to reveal how situations may be usefully

understood by those involved with them. This leads to the conclusion that creative MS/OR proactive has the '. . . basic epistemological premise . . . that most of the problems MS/OR analysts encounter are, partially at least, socially constructed' (Tsoukas and Papoulias, 1996). It is in the process of social construction that analysts, and other participants, are able to act creatively to bring about their preferred view of the world (Keys, 2000).

Exploring these constructions with the client-group is integral to the creativity of the process.

This also, of course, means that problems will never be defined unambiguously – and certainly not if the client is represented by more than one human being. Keys (2000) claims that: "It is argued that the most effective MS/OR practice is realised when all of the elements brought together by an analyst are mutually supportive and have no dissonance between them, thus achieving closure for the analyst for a given piece of analysis." But this is generally quite unrealistic in practice, as there will always be disagreements and dissonances. However, the very dialogue as conflicts and differing perceptions are aired and discussed is a source of creative development for the analysis.

Problems embedded within a real-life client situation are such a rich source of interaction that our creativity will naturally be promoted, however we interact. Simply having meetings and discussions with the client can help to raise new thoughts in our minds or suggest new lines of research. But it makes sense to design our analysis process to make the most of the opportunity for creative development. Of course, all of our interventions should be designed – that, after all, was one of the aims of Chapter 6, where we discussed the initial phases of an intervention. But we could design a process that is rigid and predetermined, which can limit or even stifle creative thought; or we could try to maximize the creativity arising from the dialogue with the client-group and the problem-situation (e.g. see the discussion in Ormerod, 1997).

As an example, the case discussed in Section 8.3 (the "RAS" example) was not at all predetermined. But development of the original simulation model in collaboration with the client (in the spirit of Figure 2.3) led to discussions about the nature of the new vessels involved and their use (as described in the case, the warships were new anti-submarine frigates that operated much further away from their mother group than previously, and the replenishment ships were for the first time carriers of both fuel and weapons). This led to development of a wide range of work (covering both the use of the ships and also some commenting on ship design), and the rule-base described in Section

8.3. And as we mentioned in Section 8.4, discussion of the data on weapons usage led to integration of the work with a separate exercise modelling warship battles, which was then able to look at a much wider range of issues.

Designing such interventions clearly requires the plan to be highly flexible, and here we are back to the dichotomy we discussed in Section 6.5. Our plans need to be built on the interaction with the client, and thus need to flow from the client–analyst dialectic with the flexibility and contingency this implies. But we also need to design firm plans, particularly if we are in a fixed-price environment, and sign a contract to carry them out. This forms a constant tension within OR/MS analysis. Phasing the work can be a help, particularly where early phases are small (preferably cost-plus) pieces of work often called something like "scoping", "problem structuring" or "problem definition", but this does not remove the problem entirely as the client–analyst dialectic continues and develops throughout the intervention.

Keys, in looking at real, practical OR/MS approaches (what he calls "practice-led" approaches as opposed to those that are "theory-led"), says that such approaches "seek to explore how a practitioner undertakes their work in a manner informed by their experience and particular view of the world. These *private methodologies* are seen to encompass *social actions* that relate the analyst to the situation of concern. Such approaches concentrate on *role paradigms* that express how an analyst presents themselves during a piece of work" (Keys, 2000). Interestingly, he goes on to say that: "The placing of situations in a wider context means that they are viewed as part of a stream of activity and may be seen as *longitudinal* rather than immediate. The emphasis here tends to be upon the practice of MS/OR captured by the social actions relating an analyst to longitudinal situation." In other words, work on a problem-situation with the client develops a relationship that often goes beyond the immediate problem. In particular, problems are rarely isolated within the client organization, but are related to other issues and situations, and the work can spill over to these areas as the relationship develops. If we look at the examples that have been noted in the book so far, the RAS work we described above (Section 8.3) started as a small simulation assignment, and developed into a seven-year relationship covering a range of related issues. The "*Shuttle* wagon" example of causal mapping/system dynamics described in Sections 3.3.5 and 4.7 started as a well-defined, bounded assignment (working on a dispute related to a specific train-building project), but developed into a number of similar assignments and then, finally, as relationships developed, became a research contract to use all of the ideas and data developed in these assignments throughout this one (global) client organization, in order to help manage the risk of large projects within that organization more effectively (the story is told in Williams *et al.*, 2005). Various statistics are quoted for how much OR/MS analysis work is "repeat" business (i.e. work for clients following on from previous assignments). Whatever the true proportion, the figure is certainly high.

> The collaboration and dialogue with the client which forms the basis of an analysis intervention also provides the creative dynamic for the analysis. And this can outlive the immediate assignment as part of an ongoing relationship with the client.

10

Ancillary Practical Skills

An OR/MS analyst needs to be competent in the fundamental skills of OR/MS. S/he needs to be able to look at a problem, relate to the client, comprehend the social geography of the client body, creatively identify opportunities for analysis, structure a problem, model it, analyse the model, relate the results to the real situation, and so on.

But there are other, supporting, skills that are needed as part of the practice of Management Science, and we touch on some of these very briefly in this chapter – more to show what is needed to develop as an OR/MS analyst than to treat any of them fully. The main area we will deal with is formal communicating with the client and reporting. Before that, we'll talk about two other areas which are required before an OR/MS assignment: marketing and selling. And after these, we will look at two areas that are essential in carrying out an assignment: the area of workshops and facilitation, which will include some of the personal skills that you require as an analyst, then a note about computing.

Of course, sometimes a Management Scientist will act as part of a team, and it may be that some of these tasks can be given to those in the team most capable of carrying out those tasks – something we'll touch on again in Section 11.6.

10.1 Marketing

Marketing represents the activity of putting your OR/MS offering into public view – or, rather, into the view of possible clients. It is not really similar to the type of marketing that goes on in companies selling consumer goods because OR/MS analysts rarely market their services to the general public. Instead, our marketing is aimed at individuals (and maybe organizations) we think might use our services. Since our whole practice is based around the client–analyst relationship, clearly our marketing has to focus on potential clients, and particularly

* look at their needs and wants;
* consider how we could best meet those needs and wants;
* such that delighting the client and achieving our own business goals are aligned as far as possible.

This is true whether we are working in an external company trying to sell into organizations or an internal group trying to sell within its parent organization – although of course the marketing is different.

Your marketing strategy should naturally follow from your business strategy. What type of company or organization are you aiming to be? What unique experience do you have? What unique skills or competencies can you offer? OR/MS analysts often have the problem that they are offering a generic skill rather than a niche product, and this is difficult to sell. You therefore need to make a clear differentiation between your "product" and that of your competitors.

In planning your marketing, you need to have made some clear strategic decisions on what you are aiming to do:

* What type of client are you seeking? From which sectors?
* How important is keeping your current clients? We have already said that "repeat" business is a very large part of most consulting practices, and it is certainly many times more expensive to win a new customer than it is to gain a repeat contract. But our past customers cannot be taken for granted – they need to be continuously "kept warm" by observing and acting on their needs and wants.
* How important is generating new "products" to sell? Developing skills, knowledge or, particularly, software is time-consuming and generally gives

no immediate revenue. How much of your effort should be put into development?

- Are you looking for many small contracts, or a small number of major contracts?

But, at its heart, the OR/MS analysis offering is not a product but a service. Indeed, this is true for all management consultancy: "Consultancy is a business, but it is also a professional service, and, as such, it is inherently personal. The consultant sells their own skills and knowledge, but these attributes come bundled together with the consultant's personality, interests, values, creativity and will. It is these human extras that create differentiation between consultants" (Pollecoff, 1998). So, it is the development of the relationship with clients that is at the heart of our marketing.

Different consultancies have different approaches to their business. Tonkin (2002) looked at the different ways in which consultancies market themselves – their claimed "unique selling propositions" – and came up with eight: four were to do with ability (experience, creativity, product/technology and innovation) but four were to do with want she termed "affability" (collaboration/skill-sharing, listening, people and practicality). Tonkin (2002) quotes many actual advertisements from the business press – mainly the *Harvard Business Review* – such as for Ernst and Young "highlighting their capacity for listening. A double page spread shows a line drawing a pair of spectacles. On the left page, in the left hand spectacle lens are the words 'Hearing improves vision'. On the right hand page in the right lens: 'Solutions that are individually designed to fit your growing needs can only come from people who listen better'. And see farther. Together, we can think and do more. Let's talk."

To whom do we market? Well, we market both to past and potential customers – but this statement has been refined by Raphael, who divides possible clients into a "ladder of loyalty", represented in Pollecoff (1998) as shown in Figure 10.1.

"Suspects" here are those you suspect may be able to use your services – the pool of all possible clients; "prospects" you have identified as those worth marketing to (i.e. they definitely could use your services); "customers" have used your services already. At the next level, "clients" are those who "naturally call you when they have a need for your type of service" and

Figure 10.1 Raphael's "ladder of loyalty". From Pollecoff. Copyright 1998 Kogan Page: London. Reproduced with permission.

"advocates" are clients who like what you do and tell others about you. Obviously, you want to try to move organizations up the ladder. For small consultancies (although it's obviously true for larger organizations too), the clients and advocates are particularly valuable – especially the latter, who can extend your pool of actual clients. (One client in the "*Shuttle*" team mentioned in Section 9.4 became an advocate, and initiated a relationship which led to a major piece of work undertaken for a paper mill.) Equally obviously, the quality of our work, and particularly the quality of our relationship with the client, is what helps move the "customers" up to those two higher levels.

Marketing methods are many and varied, and very much subject to your circumstances, but here are a few ideas of mechanisms that various people have found useful in the past.

- A website, with links from as many other organizations as possible, and using strategies to get as high up on the search-engine listings as possible.
- A regular company newsletter – in paper, or perhaps better via email. If this contains useful tit-bits or advice, people will read it and maybe come to accept you as "the expert"; similarly, online articles of general interest that show that you are "the expert".
- Talks at conferences (also sponsorship of events, such as parts of conferences).

- Workshops or seminars, maybe for a small fee.
- Targeted research and reporting of it, either in the trade press or in peer-reviewed academic journals (the former better for reaching clients, the latter for establishing credibility as an accepted expert).
- Publicly noticed "pro bono" work, not only to show your skills but also provide a useful social service.

Marketing is a time-consuming businesses, which does not bring in immediate revenue. It therefore has to be carefully managed and a realistic view taken as to what is useful. Different circumstances require different strategies, but practical experience is a very useful guide – so talk to fellow Management Scientists. In the literature, Beam (2004) gives an account of developing a business "through cold-calling, networking, paying referral fees, and teaching. To transform contacts into new business, I fill and manage a pipeline, ask for and follow sales advice only from successful salespeople, and never write a proposal until I have both a budget and a deadline. As a sole proprietor, my time is my money, and I have learned to manage it carefully, especially because much of my time is not billable – including the hours I spend drumming up business." A pithy summary of one (successful) man's experience of marketing OR is given by Gene Woolsey in Woolsey and Hewitt (2003).

10.2 Selling

Having identified a potential client, and identified a need, we still need to finalize a contract. There is a wide range of circumstances under which we might find ourselves selling: it could be a new client, or repeat business; we might be bidding as the result of a proactive approach by us to a client, or reacting to a call for proposals; we could be the sole bidder (e.g. because the client has approached us alone or because we have identified a need that others haven't), or we could be bidding in competition with others; there might have been a general enquiry or a formal contractual announcement of an invitation to tender. These all require subtly different approaches. But we can make some general points.

We looked at the approach phase of a relationship in Chapter 6 and discussed there what we needed to do to get a good proposal prepared. The key points are worth repeating:

(i) We have to show that we have come to an understanding of what the problem actually is.
(ii) We have to convince the client that our approach and view of the problem is a good match with the way the client sees the problem.
(iii) It must be clear to the client why s/he should take up this proposal.
(iv) We have to convince the client that we are able to do the work.
(v) We will have to convince the client that we are the most suitable candidate for the work.
(vi) We need to help the direct client convince others in his/her organization that we are the best.

So, what do we need to do to satisfy the above points and to sell ourselves? The first two points require a number of skills:

• Interpersonal skills in active listening and empathizing with the client, or "wearing your clients' shoes" as Flowers (2000) puts it: being able to see the situation as the client does, questioning in a structured and analytic way, and demonstrating insight.
• Analytical skills: an ability to conceptualize situations and identify key problem-areas.
• Knowledge: knowledge of the way business operates generally, domain knowledge of this problem area if possible, and knowledge of the different analytical approaches available.

Point (iii) above requires clarity in our presentation, which we discussed in Chapter 6. But it also, along with the last three points (iv)–(vi), is helped by strong personal relationships with the client. As the relationship grows, and trust builds up, so we help the client to have faith in our proposal. It is this interpersonal aspect that is key to the selling phase, as it is to the whole intervention. The selling phase reflects the type of approach we take to the whole intervention, and if we are to adopt Eden and Sims' (1979) "negotiative approach" (as we discussed in Chapter 2) throughout the intervention, then we will want to take a negotiative stance in the selling phase, to set up the relationship in the way we wish it to continue. Management Science proposals for the "messy" type of projects we are discussing in this book are never clear-cut and are always to some extent asking the client to take a leap of faith in us and our proposal. Hence the personal relationship and the trust underlying this relationship is key, as is careful management of expectations. We must make sure that we do not promise what can't be delivered, and that the client is not expecting more than we can deliver (and thus will be disappointed when s/he sees the result of our work). That is one reason why "deliverables" must be clearly spelled out in our proposal.

There are also slightly more pragmatic issues to consider. When we sell to an individual within an organization, have we identified the right individual? Does s/he have ownership of the problem? Does s/he have budgetary authority to let a contract? With whom are we competing, if anyone, and do we need to modify how we pitch our offering because of our competitors? And we must include all of the issues we identified in Chapter 6. However, it is the interpersonal effects that are at the heart of our selling.

> Marketing needs to be carefully thought out and targeted. Remember that you are selling not a product but a personal service. Of particular value are customers with whom you have already established a relationship, particularly those that become advocates for your services. When we have got a potential sale, we need to work at closing the deal, where again the interpersonal relationship is key. Marketing and selling are time-consuming activities, and require a realistic and pragmatic approach.

10.3 Formal communicating and reporting

We have said often that at the heart of our practice is our relationship with the client and so communication with the client is obviously an absolutely key factor. In a study by Forder (2007) of how senior decision-makers can be engaged, he reports that: "It is hardly surprising that all those surveyed put great emphasis on the way in which the results of analysis are communicated."

Different modes of communication are appropriate at different junctures in our relationship, depending on the timing and the status of the project, and on pragmatic aspects such as how busy our client is. Our first communications may well come under the heading of marketing or selling as above; we will communicate throughout any intervention, and there will be formal and sometimes informal reporting at the end of any contract. Saunders and Jones (1990) carried out an interesting study of how managers acquire information as decision-making processes unfold, and of suitable sources and media that can be used throughout the decision-making process. Discussing the "increasingly complex and turbulent environments" within which modern management has to make decisions, the paper gives interesting insights into the fast pace of such decisions – a pace that the analyst needs to keep up with if s/he's going to make the analysis "reactive and timely" (a condition for success, as we will discuss in the next chapter). They suggest that various sources and media are more appropriate at different points in the decision-making process, and although some of the points are fairly obvious (e.g. decision-makers working on a number of high-priority decisions simultaneously will be more likely to use electronic media, even almost 20 years ago), ensuring our mode and style of communication is appropriate is important as we try to give our client what s/he needs at any particular point.

Also, different modes of communication suit different clients. In Forder's (2007) study, he reports that several of those he interviewed "stressed the importance of tailoring reporting methods to the preferences of individual decision-makers – senior people are used to things being done their way. Some were very happy to be presented with overtly quantitative material – graphs and diagrams – while for others this would be an obstacle to understanding and straightforward prose was preferred. Others, again, preferred the material to be encapsulated on a small number of *PowerPoint* slides. And while for some the idea of engaging interactively with a simple model . . . would be attractive, for others it would be a non-starter."

10.3.1 Written communication

The key medium will be the written form – we'll mention presentations later in this section. There are various forms of written reports, some more formal and some less so. We mentioned in Chapter 6 that we might expect to write interim reports to describe progress, and there might be papers for other purposes during the intervention. At the end of a study there is likely to be at least one report (and more probably two): nearly always a formal complete end-of-project report, that is kept as the deliverable from the contract, and often a briefer summary report that is what is actually used in the organization (sometimes the executive summary from the formal report serves this purpose). Indeed, Forder (2007) reported from his discussions that: "Very little use now seems to be made of the traditional, full report. Typical quotes were: 'The two-page summary report is very important and can take as long to write as a full report'; 'Papers should pass the 10-minute test – they must be readable and understandable within 10 minutes'."

We clearly need to consider at any particular reporting point how much information should be presented to the client. How much information does the client need? We have already discussed in part (6) of Section 8.4 (page 209) that managers often don't need the information they want – organizations systematically gather more information than they use, yet continue to ask for more. So we need to think carefully about how much information to present. At a final, formal reporting stage, perhaps a lot of information needs to be reported and archived; in the midst of an intervention, perhaps only a sparse amount of information will be absorbed – so long, of course, as the analyst is there ready with explanation and justification if either are wanted (as well as perhaps an explanation of why information not presented is not needed at that point).

There isn't scope for a full discussion on how to write a report here, but some lessons are well-known.

The first point is to structure the report from the outset. Although the product you need to produce at the end is a linear document, that is often not the best way to write a document. The structure is a primary element that gives an impression to the client, and a busy client uses the structure to navigate around the document in an efficient way. But more than that, structuring the document facilitates structuring the argument of the document, and this is key to making sure the report is well-received. The logical flow of the reasoning throughout a document is as important as the individual pieces of content – and while a reader might be uncomfortable with individual statements, a particularly frequent reason for a reader feeling discomfited is if one section of a document doesn't logically follow from previous sections, or the reader doesn't know why s/he is reading a particular part. If a reader comes across a heading or a line that starts discussing a particular subject and says to him or herself "why are we discussing this subject now?" (or, worse, "gosh, that heading was a surprise, I've lost the thread of the discussion now"), then you will lose the reader. Similarly, if the document makes assertions without the logical reasoning up to that assertion, you will also lose the confidence of the reader.

A good technique to use to help avoid an ill-structured document is to use a "storyboard". This is a term with a variety of meanings, but here we mean a brief document with the main headings and subheadings, and a brief summary of each section. In this way, you can prepare a two- or three-page summary of a document – without worrying about exact wording or phrasing – which shows the logic and the essential content. A colleague (or client) can look through this to see whether it is understandable by another reader and the logic can be followed. Then, when you have written the actual content, you have the confidence that the logical argument will flow well throughout the document. (Indeed, this technique can be useful when two or more authors are preparing different parts of the same document.) This is akin to the old idea of "top–down" computer programming. In a study of novice writers and expert writers by Bereiter and Scardamalia (1987), it was observed that novice writers adopted a linear style, whereas expert writers kept a mental map of the finished product and could move in and out of the various parts of the writing process – and a storyboard can be a visible statement of that mental map.

It is not possible to give a generic structure that will be suitable for all reporting documents. But in general:

- There should be an executive summary, which gives all the information needed for a busy executive to understand what is in the document, so s/he can decide whether or not the detail needs to be read.
- Information or data that would interrupt the flow of the argument and is not necessary to understanding the main thrust of the document should be put into appendices.
- Remember that the reader may be distant from the project, so you need to consider carefully how much background information to put in (that may be known and boring to the direct client). In particular, for a final report it is often a good idea to include the original brief or terms of reference.

Remember in your document writing, too, to make sure that:

- The report is kept simple where possible, without unnecessary jargon or qualification.
- The work should be sensitive to considerations of organizational politics, and to the culture of the client and national organization (so, for example, a report for a UK civil service body may be different to one written for, say, a young IT company).
- When writing in a group, take care with version control of the documents (i.e. take care that you all know which is the master version of the document and who can amend the document at any particular time). "Change-tracking" is a useful tool for members of a team to review proposed changes and see whether they agree.

- Proof-read carefully. This includes not only spelling, punctuation and grammar, but also checking cross-referencing, ensuring all references are in the reference list, and ensuring that any appendices referred to are included. Think about whether acronyms are defined and whether a glossary is needed.

10.3.2 Presentations

Of equal importance to the written report – even if not such a permanent legacy – is the face-to-face presentation. Indeed, one quote reported in Forder's paper (2007) went: " 'We put more effort into the presentation than the analysis' ". He continues,

> [this quote] was not intended to be cynical, but reflected both the potential power of simple analysis and the realization that it is wasted if the message is not conveyed effectively. The point was made that, frequently, there are just one or two key relationships which analysis has uncovered – or merely, perhaps, thrown into sharper relief – and the presentation should focus on getting the decision-maker to understand these. In the right circumstances . . . across-the-desk interaction using a simple, or superficially simple, what-if? model was seen as effective in illuminating key issues exposed by the analysis. Such models may be a simple spreadsheet or a more elaborate model but with simple input and well-visualized output.

Again, there is not scope in this book to give detailed instructions on presentations – there are good training courses, and personal training is valuable in this area. However, a few simple points would include:

- All of the remarks above about the logical flow of reports apply equally here, if not more so. The audience has to follow your talk in the order in which you give it, so it must follow logically from step to step.
- Face the audience, and try to make eye contact with them.
- Think carefully about the length of the presentation – what is an appropriate length? What is the attention span of your audience? Shorter is normally better than longer; if the presentation is long, can it be broken up with different speakers, rest periods, or interaction with the audience?
- Think about what the appropriate format is for this presentation – is it to be a small seminar, or a large formal talk?
- Don't simply read notes verbatim – this makes audiences lose attention. And if you are showing *PowerPoint* slides, don't simply read out the words

on the slides – this wastes the audience's time as they can read the slides just as well as you!

- Be sensitive to the culture of the organization. Is this an appropriate format to make jokes? Humour can be a huge boon to a presentation, but in inappropriate circumstances can be enormously counter-productive. You also need to be sensitive to the national culture of your audience.
- Rehearse your presentation, so you can give it freely and easily.

The use of *PowerPoint* as a back-drop to presentations has become fairly ubiquitous, and indeed it can be a useful tool. However, the use of any tool has to be a considered decision, and you shouldn't use *PowerPoint* automatically; some situations might be better served simply with a personal presentation without technological help. Plus, there are pitfalls in the use of *PowerPoint*, so much so that the phrase "Death by *PowerPoint*" has become commonly used. There is a wealth of advice available on how to use *PowerPoint* effectively, including advice on keeping slides simple and "clean", avoiding the overuse of different fonts and *PowerPoint* "effects", and concentrating on content. Key here is knowing your audience. A most interesting presentation available on the Internet is by Karl Kapp, Professor of Instructional Technology at the Bloomsburg University of Pennsylvania (Kapp, 2008). He shows a number of apparently rather good slides and explains how they can be made much better by providing animation and various effects. Some readers might watch this and feel that the slides have been made less effective – but these presentations are for a particular type of (particularly, young and American) audience, and are there to support interaction with that audience. A presentation is not a self-standing item, but it is a vehicle to help you as the presenter interact with the audience and to help to bring them with you as you deliver your message. Kapp's methods are superb for his type of audience; you will have to judge your audience and adjust your style accordingly. What is appropriate to some organizations, or some national cultures, is not appropriate to others.

It is easy to become overly didactic in presentations. The use of stories in presentations has been found to be a valuable device for bringing along an audience and guiding their sense-making, which to some extent gets around this problem. Klein, Connell and Meyer (2007) describe how stories are used in OR/MS practice, both telling the story of the content of a model and telling the story of the intervention that generated the model (of which they say the content story can be seen as a "sub-plot"), and give lots of examples of how stories have been used to help the intervention.

10.3.3 Presenting complex information visually

One particular issue that will arise both in many OR/MS reports and in presentations is the need to present complex information visually – or, at least, there will often be obvious advantages in doing so. Figures and diagrams can often present information very much more powerfully than using text and numbers. However, there are numerous traps to avoid, in which diagrams can mislead, and poor presentation can make complex ideas even more difficult to understand.

The simplest form of presentation of numerical data is the table. Even here there are important things to remember:

- Remember to title the table and (where relevant) the columns and rows – it may be obvious to you what the columns are but the reader might have a different interpretation.
- Remember to include units for numbers, including currencies for monetary numbers.
- Choose the format to make the presentation most understandable as well as most appealing; this includes not just borders but also subtotals, subsections and so on.

In drawing graphs, writers can sometimes unwittingly mislead (or, perhaps, sometimes not unwittingly!). You should beware of:

- breaks in the scale, making differences appear more extreme than they are;
- using areas to represent changes in linear measurements;
- making small parts of time-series out of context.

These are fairly obvious ways in which we can mislead. Figure 10.2 shows an example, giving the UK retail price index between 1987 and 2006, first as it is, then with a carefully selected scale, and then representing the doubling of the index by an illustration that doubles in both width and height.

Visual presentation is an additional complexity that causes many Management Scientists to fall down – you need to ask yourself, can the reader understand this graphic? Is there more information here than can be absorbed visually? What about different forms of graphic – heat-maps, or tornado graphs, or some other method? Popular, academic and technical literature around us

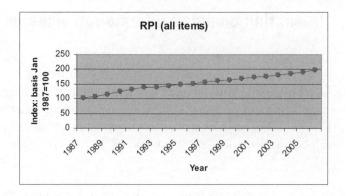

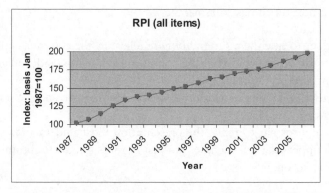

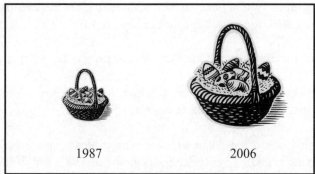

Figure 10.2 The UK retail price index (all items) for 1987–2006 (National Statistics, 2007)

abounds with poor graphics that inhibit the reader from understanding the underlying message.

The leading author on such presentation is Edward Tufte. His first book, *The Visual Display of Quantitative Information* (the current edition is Tufte, 2001) talks about visual representation of numerical data, and deals with statistical charts, graphs, and tables. His second book, *Envisioning Information* (Tufte, 1990), deals with putting more complex – often three-dimensional or even more dimensional – information into two-dimensional space: "The world is complex, dynamic, multidimensional; the paper is static, flat." He gives many examples of how to present information effectively (charts, maps, diagrams, timetables and so on).

> Our work will only be accepted if we present it effectively. The medium must be chosen carefully. Reports need to be carefully structured and written. "Storyboards" are useful for planning out the logical flow. Presentations need to be attractive and effective. Both reports and presentations need to be professionally done. Care must be taken to ensure graphs are clear and do not muddle or, worse, mislead the reader.

10.4 Skills in interacting with the client, and facilitation

Since we have been saying that at the heart of our practice is our relationship with the client, then it is almost a truism to say that the skills involved in interacting with the client personally are vital. In order to build the interpersonal relationship, we must be personable and friendly. We must be able to relate to the client outside the specific work assignment. We should bring in the appropriate level (as we've said above, we need to be sensitive to the culture of the organization) of humour into the relationship, and we should be energetic and show enthusiasm. The first meetings particularly are important in setting up that relationship and building *trust* and *credibility* – lose either of these and they are very difficult to recover. Ease in moving within a client body and navigating the internal politics of an organization is also important – this perhaps comes with practice and with experience, generating confidence.

In many – or maybe even most – interventions, domain-specific knowledge will be important. While Management Science is thought of as a generic discipline, some domain experience is important for a modeller to gain and maintain credibility with a client, so an analyst working within an engineering domain should be comfortable with the engineering discourse, or an analyst working within the financial sector should have a basic knowledge of how finance works. This is true of most advisory domains (a key project risk analysis standard, for example, says that: "It is unlikely, for instance, that a risk analyst fundamentally trained in software engineering will readily be accepted by a team who are building a bridge" (Simon, Hillson and Newland, 1997)). This is perhaps why many successful OR/MS analysts were originally trained in other disciplines. Even if you are not fully familiar with the domain, it is useful to get to know the ways the organization thinks and any "jargon" it uses – having constantly to define terms and ideas for a consultant gives the impression that s/he is an "outsider".

A key need for interaction with the client body is obviously to gain information or data from them – often their subjective views or arguable data. So, we'll look now at some of the skills necessary to hold workshops with groups of clients (to "facilitate" workshops) and gain the required output. Many of these points apply equally when you are interviewing individual clients. This section will look at the skills you need for this type of activity over and above the procedures of the actual technique used, and so would apply if you were using any of the techniques of Chapter 3, or simply carrying out a workshop to gain data. This discussion is very brief – an excellent and very practical guide to facilitation is in Eden and Ackermann (1998), and they give some further useful references also.

As in many such areas, preparation is key. But before preparing the actual workshop, you need to first prepare the client-group. Setting expectations is vital. If the participants feel that the exercise is pointless, then it is likely to fail; but over-expectation can be just as bad, with discouragement setting in when it becomes clear what is actually going to be achieved. And while you will have an aim in the workshop, the client also needs to keep some sense of control. S/he needs to be aware of the aims of the workshop, and – continuing our theme when we looked at problem-definition in Chapter 2 – you need to negotiate what's going to happen during the workshop. Which brings us onto planning the workshop itself.

Experience again shows that meticulous planning is important to the success of a workshop. This means:

- Planning who should attend. Usually, you will be looking for a heterogeneous group, covering various parts of the organization, both to capture the variety of perceptions within the organization and gain the different knowledge that different groups will have, but also to prompt creativity, as different ways of thinking come together and feed off each other. And think about what size group would be appropriate for the tasks you are expecting.
- While planning who should attend, this is a good opportunity to think about how you might form any sub-groups if you are thinking of breaking into smaller groups in the workshop.
- Planning where the event will be. Despite the bad reputation office "away days" sometimes have, getting participants away from the interruptions of their normal jobs can be valuable if the task warrants it in terms of importance and the duration of the workshop (although if they keep their mobile phones on, sometimes the benefit is lost!). Of course, if they are likely to want to return to their desks to refer to data or documents, then the workshop has to be on-site.
- Making sure the workshop is physically pleasant. Tea, coffee or whatever is culturally appropriate is important. Walls are needed if you need to put up flip-chart paper and/or use "Post-its". If you are using technology such as a computer and projector, then this needs be carefully tested beforehand – nothing annoys a workshop more than keeping them waiting for half-an-hour while you struggle with technology!
- Preparing a memo or email to invite participants, which should be sufficiently short but informative, give all the information necessary (maybe including a little expectation-setting and perhaps a preliminary summary agenda), and generally be attractive.

In terms of actually carrying out the workshop, it is a skilled task and training is very valuable. But here are a few pointers.

- Remember that you are there to manage both the *process* and the collection of the *content*. This can be a daunting task, but don't be frightened to ask the group to pause while you catch up occasionally. It can be a very good idea to work with two facilitators, one leading the group and running the workshop (i.e. looking after the process) while the other captures the content, giving any indications to his/her colleague if the workshop needs to be nudged in a particular direction.
- Introduce the workshop carefully. Explain the aim of the workshop, what is going to happen, and the role of the participants, and try to engender a

feeling of shared ownership throughout the group in the workshop and its outcomes.

- Remember that each member of the group will have their own opinions. Encourage openness and allow opinions to come out. In particular, *you* should be open to alternative views – after all, if you've followed Chapter 2, you won't be in "coercive" mode, imposing your views.
- Remember that you have a group – and usually a heterogeneous group at that – for a purpose. Look for interdependencies between views so that the overall output is more valuable than it would have been by interviewing the individuals separately.
- Look out for members who are not participating and encourage them. Watch out for the different roles people might have in the group. (We'll talk a bit about types of group-involvement when we look at Belbin's work in the next chapter.) Take note both of what is said and non-verbal signals that might indicate restlessness or a lack of engagement.
- Occasionally summarize to the group where the workshop has got up to, to show that the group is achieving progress.
- Watch out for a "blame culture" inhibiting discussion (e.g. Busby, 1999) or any particular topics with which participants appear particularly uncomfortable.

Finally, don't forget to feed back the output to the group, if for no other reason than courtesy – it is the result of a joint effort!

> Fostering a good relationship with the client is vital. It is important to build trust and credibility. An important part of the interaction with the client is in facilitating workshops. This is a difficult task, and training is valuable, but it is an important part of the Management Scientist's skill-set, and there are many practical lessons to be learned.

10.5 Computing

One additional particular area of competence needed by most OR/MS analysts is in the use of computing. There is a range of skills needed, including for example the following:

- The analyst needs the ability to pick up new software packages very quickly. Different techniques often are realized within particular software packages – an analyst using System Dynamics, for example, will generally produce the work in a standard package such as *Powersim* or *Vensim*. Just as a Management Science analyst needs to be able to learn a new technique relevant to the particular situation and apply it quickly, so s/he needs to be able to pick up a relevant software package and use it very quickly indeed. This is an important skill in the life of an analyst.

- It is difficult to generalize about which particular computing tools are most useful. However, the ubiquity of standard Microsoft packages such as *Excel* and *Access*, as well as the interfaces to common OR/MS tools (e.g. the discrete-event simulation package SIMUL8), means that *VBA* has become a very useful tool for the modern analyst. This enables the modeller to modify the standard use of the tools and shape them to his or her particular circumstance, taking the tool from a standard package to which the situation must be shaped, to a more general tool that can be shaped to fit the situation.

- The analyst must also be comfortable collecting data from a variety of information systems – although it is helpful if a client will supply all the data we need, often we need to hunt for the data ourselves, particularly if we are not entirely certain of what information we actually need, and so the ability to navigate a client's information system is very valuable.

- The analyst should also have an analysis facility ready to hand that s/he can use for quick data analysis – some will use a package such as *SPSS*, or *SAS*, or *S-plus*; others will rely simply on a good capacity in *Excel*; others will use a programming language such as "*C*" or even *Pascal*. The important issue here is whether the analyst feels comfortable with the facility and can use it quickly and easily without it getting in the way of the creative process.

- The analyst also needs to be able to work at two different levels: s/he needs to be able to rustle up a computer program quickly to satisfy an analytical need of his or her own – which may not look pretty but is robust and does the job. But often a client will want software delivered in order that that work can carry on after the analyst's intervention. The supply of user-friendly software is a subject beyond the scope of this book, but it needs to be taken on with great caution, whether it is a purpose-built package or simply a realization of an existing package (such as a simulation model).

One particular area which is often lacking within OR/MS analysts is the proper engineering approach to building software programs – or, particularly, model with software. This perhaps harks back to the early amateur beginnings of Operational Research, and the natural tendency of analysts to "play" with models. And all OR/MS is to some extent an exploration into the unknown, without a clear path. But when preparing a model within a software package, it is essential to be disciplined and systematic (all the attributes in fact of the software engineer). Programs must be documented so that others can understand and follow them up. Crucially, all parameters and relationships should have a good audit-trail, so that they can be justified if called to account. (Sometimes, of course, a variable might be "just my guess" – but this needs to be recognized and identified, not just put into the software.) Remember that not only others may wish to follow your work, you may also have to revisit it months or even years later, when you won't remember what you've done! This is all *as well as* the issues of validation and verification that we covered in Chapter 8.

10.6　A final note

Of course there are other skills needed by anyone in a similar consulting role, not necessarily just OR/MS, but mundane skills such as the ability to:

- *Keep files effectively:* a remarkably useful skill but if you look at an OR/MS analyst's files, it is surprising how often they are a mess! File keeping is essential to be able to keep an audit-trail of data and meetings, as well as simply keeping track of all the information that flows through a Management Science study. Some interventions can take months or years, so memory cannot be relied upon to find pieces of documentation.
- *Take notes of meetings.*
- *Fast read* (or *"skim read"*) documents to be able to track down crucial information quickly in amongst the mass of unimportant details.

This chapter has tried to outline some of the skills which are required by the well-rounded specialist Management Scientist.

> The OR/MS analyst needs to have many skills. As well as being an analyst, s/he needs to be an excellent communicator – with good presence in personal communications and good style in written communications, and the ability to communicate complex quantitative and qualitative ideas in as straightforward a way as possible; s/he needs to be a marketer, a programmer, a salesperson, a software engineer; s/he needs to be able to engage interpersonally, interview and facilitate, and able to absorb large quantities of divergent material. . . . A well-rounded professional indeed.

Part IV
Practice

11

What Makes for Successful OR?

11.1 OR/MS in the past and today

In this chapter, we're going to look into what makes an OR/MS group or individual successful in OR/MS. We'll identify a set of reasons which should give the professional OR/MS worker a set of areas on which to concentrate. These areas will come from work that has looked at the success and failure of OR/MS over the years. We'll first put this into context by looking very briefly at the history of the subject and its current status – where we are now, and how we got there. (The first few pages of this book mentioned the change in nature of OR/MS over its history – here we're looking at its success, or otherwise.) Being written by a UK author, this chapter will naturally be rather UK-centric (after all, the UK was the birthplace of the discipline!), but other countries will feature also and hopefully the comments will be useful generically.

The development and rise of OR/MS over the past 60 years or so has been well documented. Kirby and Capey (1998) give a long history of OR from 1945 to 1970, which led to the well-known and authoritative book by Kirby (2002): *Operational Research in War and Peace: The British Experience from the 1930s to 1970*. Following the powerful influence of Blackett (whose work on this period we quoted at the start of Chapter 9), OR had undoubted successes in the war – making, as Kirby and Capey (1998) put it, "decisive contributions to the allied war effort in a number of theatres". This gave OR an impetus to seek applications after the war in peace-time activity. After a period of political problems (see also Rosenhead, 1989), there followed for OR a period of being very influential in the corporate sector in the 1950s and 1960s, with the groups in the National Coal Board and also the steel industry being particularly prominent, then joined by well-known groups in Cadbury's and then in the oil industry. Goodeve and Ridley (1953) looked at the 160 large corporations in the UK and found that 45 had "OR-type groups" (not all of which used that name).

Where did this success come from? Kirby and Capey (1998) report that: "It seems likely that the introduction of OR into the corporate sector was not so much in conscious recognition of OR's wartime achievements, but in response to personal advocacy at a level high enough in the managerial structure to ensure serious consideration" (citing those such as Goodeve) . . . "Once introduced, OR's survival was guaranteed by its success in dealing with a sequence of tactical problems . . .". Similar success was in civil government following the Fulton report of 1968, in which the proposal from the OR Society for an OR group had already noted that "the level of contact within various ministries would have to be carefully established in order to sustain a high enough profile for OR" (Kirby & Capey, 1998). They also point to OR/MS workers' role as "credible gatekeepers" to the rising influence of computers, and, again, "the prevailing belief in rational scientific progress as a means of alleviating the human condition".

The story of OR during the 1970s, however, was one of mixed success. One positive influence was a change in attitude towards scientific methods generally. Locke (1981), for example, talks about a paradigm shift in the US in business education, from being based solely on practical experience to being based on what were seen as scientific-based ideas, including statistical and OR methods and the beginnings of what was to become computing. This influence in the US has continued through to today, and can be seen in the more "hard" mathematical flavour of OR/MS as practised in the US.

The progress of OR groups through the 1970s, 1980s and 1990s, particularly in the UK, is picked up by Fildes and Ranyard (1997). "Apparently well-established groups were closed down during the recessions of the early 1970s and 1980s in both the US (Geoffrion, 1992) and the UK." Various references are given for the UK but the most important one is perhaps the

Commission on the Future Practice of OR (Mitchell, 1986), which however concluded that, in the UK, "where O.R. is practised, it is in a reasonably healthy state" and which (considering three possible futures, including "absorption", "continuous change" and "stability") looked to a future of OR changing in response to the changing environment but remaining, and contributing, in a similar organizational context. Shortly afterwards the CONDOR (Committee On the Next Decade of OR) report came out in the US (CONDOR, 1988), which took a similar view of the future of OR but was criticized (e.g. by Wagner *et al.*, 1989) as not representing the changes in practice that would come about because of the technical innovations discussed in the report. In the later 1970s and early 1980s, OR/MS went through a lot of heart searching, particularly following Ackoff's work, which we discussed in the first few pages of this book. In the UK, "the recession of the late 1980s to early 1990s again saw more OR groups being closed," say Fildes and Ranyard (1997), but they found at the end of 1994 that 17% of the Times Top 100 companies had OR groups and 48% contained at least one OR Society member (and, similarly, 54% of organizations in the Fortune 200 have one or more members of the US society, INFORMS).

So what is the current status? There are now active OR societies in over 45 countries, with a total membership of over 25,000 (from the International Federation of Operational Research Societies, IFORS, 2008), the largest being INFORMS in the US; there don't tend to be established groups in the poorest countries, but there are thriving groups within Southeast Asia (particularly Japan and Korea) and South America. Members come from universities as academics and researchers, in-house consultancies and operational units within companies, central and local government (the 380 or so analysts working in various parts of the UK central government have an umbrella organization known as GORS (GORS, 2008)), consulting organizations, the health sector, military and defence sector, as well as other areas such as non-profit organizations and so on. The UK Society has a little under 3 000 members. Many Management Scientists/Operational Researchers start by studying OR/MS at a university. Some study it as a distinct discipline at undergraduate level, usually in the UK combined with another subject such as mathematics, finance, statistics and so on. More study MS/OR at the postgraduate level, courses generally requiring students to have some quantitative basis in their first degrees, but allowing students from as diverse backgrounds as engineering, psychology and pure sciences. Such degrees, certainly most of the UK postgraduate degrees, try to instill the breadth of skills that we have discussed in this book. But it will be clear from the discussion up to here that MS/OR can be best learned with knowledge of the "real" business/industrial/commercial world, and some of the best analysts have taken degrees only after gaining initial business experience, or undertaken part-time or distance-learning degrees, or even simply learned "on the job".

Of course, this does not represent the entire community that practises OR/MS – indeed, it is really confined to those who see themselves as "Operational Researchers" rather than the more general community of Management Scientists – but gives an indication of those who feel that OR is their main role, both practitioners and academics. Abdel-Malek *et al.* (1999) give some indications of the types of groups, people and applications within the US community, and Fildes, Ranyard and Crymble (1999) similarly give some indications of the types of OR groups and applications in the UK. Pappis (1995) gives a description of OR societies throughout Europe, although if you extract the UK society, his figure indicated only 6 500 members throughout Europe, 50% of whom were academics. (This last paper, incidentally, is part of a Special Issue of the *European Journal of Operational Research* (vol. 87, issue 3) that includes summaries of OR and the OR societies in the Czech Republic, Finland, Germany, Greece, Hungary, Iceland, Portugal, South Africa (!), Spain, Switzerland and the UK.)

As we look to the success and failure of OR, we'll look mainly at the success and failure of OR *groups*, because that is what data there are, and it is much harder to track the progress of individual OR/MS workers. Having said that, it should be noted that there is a lot of evidence of a trend over the past 20 years of OR/MS being dispersed from large self-contained groups of OR/MS workers to individuals (and, to a lesser extent, small groups) working with their client-groups. As an indication, a survey of specifically OR groups in the UK in 1994 (Ranyard, 1995) looked at 111 groups, with an average of 11 in each group; this too though recognized that there were "fewer large groups, fewer in-house groups (though more external OR consultants), more dispersed OR professionals, and probably an increase in 'do it yourself' OR by managers and other non-OR specialists". Bennett (1994) describes this process of dispersion again in the UK with the title "dispersion to vanishing-point?" and warns of the dangers of groups becoming "too small to achieve a 'critical mass' of influence and competence", while feeling that this can be outweighed by the much closer client contact that can be gained from such a move.

One other notable change over the past 20–30 years is that the sectors in which OR is practised have changed radically. OR was, as we saw in the early days in the UK, strongly associated with coal and steel, and as these industries have declined so, obviously, has the OR supporting them. These sectors also had very large OR groups, so the evidence suggests that with these groups disappearing, or shrinking considerably in line with their sector, and with the production sector generally shrinking, the average size of an OR group has also declined (Bennett, 1994), although some large OR groups remain (e.g. in the defence sector). The Fildes, Ranyard and Crymble (1999) study in the UK compares the sectors of the OR groups they found with those found by the Commission a decade earlier, and while the number of workers overall has increased by 40%, and the number of OR groups within the public sector had increased slightly, and the number of consultant groups had tripled, the number of groups in the productive sector had halved – with chemicals/oil, general manufacturing/pharmaceuticals, nationalized industries and food/drink/tobacco showing particularly precipitous declines. However, we should stress again that this concerns OR groups and does not indicate the spreading dispersion of lone OR workers. Abdel-Malek *et al.*'s (1999) survey (of OR workers, not groups) shows a US picture of more OR workers in the military, but only one-fifth of those responding with a single sector replying "manufacturing" – 30% replying "military", a quarter replying "consulting", followed by "transportation" and "telecommunications".

There have also been two main changes to the wider environment within which OR works.

- One difference, which we have already noted above, is obviously the rise firstly of computing, then information systems (IS), and then the Internet. Each of these has provided challenges – for example, while OR people were sometimes initially seen as the guardians of computing, the rise of the IS professional took that role away from them to a large extent. But these developments have particularly given opportunities to the practice of OR/MS. The immense rise in the size and depth of databases has given OR techniques the source data on which to work and offered huge opportunities. The increased power of computing has, we noted in Chapter 5, enabled hugely more powerful algorithms; the increased power of the PC has enabled developments to give clients tools "on their desk"; and the virtuality provided by the Internet has provided new ways of working, both within OR teams but particularly working with dispersed clients.

- The other difference in the environment is the move from production into services, as we noted above. Indeed, Geoffrion (1992) saw the main forces shaping the OR future arising from the following: the competitiveness crisis in US industries, economic globalization, and the transition to a service and information-based economy (which picks up our first point). OR/MS has therefore had to move into the analysis of service-industry problems, which will often be more behaviourally complex and moves OR/MS more into the type of problem we discussed in Chapter 1.

Although OR has become a distinct discipline, all this needs to be set in the context of the wider profession of management consulting. If you read the definition of "management consulting" given by the Management Consultancies Association (MCA), which represents the major UK consulting firms – "The rendering of independent advice and assistance about management issues. This typically includes identifying and investigating problems and/or opportunities, recommending appropriate action and helping to implement those recommendations" (quoted in Rassam, 1998) – it reads like a general definition of Management Science! In many ways, OR/MS represents a particular analytical, rigorous flavour of management consulting. The history of OR can be seen in a small way to be intertwined in the history of management consulting (Rassam (1998) gives a brief account of the latter), with key points being the development of "Management by Objectives" in the 1960s – helping a strong analytical OR/MS community – then the oil crises of 1973 and 1978 and subsequent recessions, which prompted companies to look to their financial performance, but unfortunately led to disposal of what were seen as "non-core" activities (which sometimes included OR), then the rise of Japanese manufacturing methods (again requiring strong quantitative support), globalization (the implications of which OR/MS has perhaps been slow to pick up on) and the rise of IS, as we have discussed. The size of the management consultancy market, though, was estimated by Key Note Publications (quoted by Rassam, 1998) at the end of the twentieth century to be £116bn, with the USA representing £50bn of this and Europe £36bn. He quotes the top five consulting companies (IBM Global services, Accenture, Cap Gemini Ernst & Young, PricewaterhouseCoopers and Deloitte Consulting/Deloitte Touche Tomatsu) as having joint revenues of £40bn, and a dozen other companies not far behind. A further analysis of the European market suggests that 23% of this market is in "Operations Management" – which all suggests that the market for OR/MS services is there!

11.2 Success and failure: capturing the attention of decision-makers

So, what makes OR/MS groups succeed or fail? One key aim has to be to capture the attention of the decision-makers – particularly senior decision-makers – in the organization, so that the OR/MS group is seen to be useful and valued. Three studies illustrate how fundamental this requirement is, and will be used frequently in the discussion in this chapter:

(i)   Firstly, the UK OR Society sponsored a project in late 1993 to examine factors that seemed to be important in influencing the "success and survival" of in-house OR groups (abbreviated as "the SSOR project" below). Different aspects of this study are reported particularly in Fildes and Ranyard (1997), Fildes, Ranyard and Crymble (1999), Ranyard and Fildes (1998) and also Ranyard, Fildes and Crymble (1997). "Lack of OR champions" comes as the third most important organizational issue on a decision to close an OR group (below general staff-reduction pressures) in Ranyard and Fildes (1998). The last reference in the list concerns the death of an OR Group: major reasons identified being "lack of visibility: lack of a clear image and failure to publicize project successes, particularly at Executive Board level" as well as "marketing/selling: insufficient marketing to secure new clients". Of course, we need to consider which of these aspects are still relevant today – but many still are.

(ii)   The second source is Abdel-Malek et al.'s (1999) survey of members of the US OR society, INFORMS, which was mentioned above. In this, respondents were asked about factors leading to the success or failure of OR applications, and one of the seven "success" factors identified was "Management support/involvement", whereas one of the six "failure" factors was "Customer not sold on the project". (Having said that, it should be recognized that in this study, "success" appears almost synonymous with "successful project implementation" rather than the wider view of Section 2.5 – and as we said there, one can have valuable OR studies whose work is not implemented as such.)

(iii)   The third source is from two studies by Roger Forder, a leading member of the biggest OR group in the UK, working within the defence science/technology establishment serving the UK Ministry of Defence. He had undertaken a major overview of OR in the Ministry of Defence (Forder, 2004) (in which he notes that: "In short, then, the primary reason for the observed level of survival and success . . . is simply that OA [Operational Analysis] has been found to be useful; or, more precisely, that its benefits have been seen by a sufficient number of senior people in the Ministry to outweigh the resource costs involved."). Shortly after this, Forder also reported on his study to see how senior decision-makers can be engaged (mentioned in Chapter 10 (Forder, 2007), including the conclusion that "without the confidence in OR at senior levels that direct visibility should bring, its contribution . . . will be hampered and the OR function may, indeed, become organizationally vulnerable.").

But how do we make our OR successful? How do we capture the attention of senior decision-makers? We're going to look at four areas of issues, with clear lessons in each:

- Understanding the client
- Our relationship with the client
- What we analyse, and
- How we do the analysis.

It won't come as a surprise, knowing the approach we said we'd take in Chapters 1 and 2, that two of the areas (and two-thirds of the lessons) involve the client.

11.3　Understanding the client

If the client is so important in our work, we need to understand him or her or them, and how they work. We discussed some of this in setting the scene for our work in Chapter 2, so this will only be summarized here, but there are four key areas to which need to pay attention.

11.3.1　Understanding the social geography and politics

We said in Chapter 2 that we must understand individuals and their bounded rationality; and also understand the groups, with the group dynamics and political and social effects involved. Only then can we understand how an organization makes decisions and help them make those decisions.

We quoted Eden and Sims (1986), who say: "When we study what is going on in the process of behaving as a consultant...we see a complicated drama unfold which involves power, influence, negotiation, game playing, organization politics, complex social relationships with real people, not merely office holders." There we discussed at length the need to comprehend the politics and social geography of the client-group, and that this was fundamental to our understanding of how we intervene in management situations.

This need comes out strongly in the work looking into the success and failure of OR groups. Abdel-Malek *et al.* (1999) perhaps put it most strongly when they report on interviews with senior OR/MS practitioners and conclude that: "Socio-political aspects need to be fully addressed. In an almost universal response, the interviewees could not say enough about the need to address the socio-political side of the problem. It was as if this is the main cause of all problems brought to the OR table." In the SSOR study, Fildes and Ranyard (1997) move away from a traditional definition of OR to say that "an alternative definition could be 'intervening in a social process to facilitate feasible and desirable change', which places great importance on understanding and interacting sensitively with the employing organization's culture", and the "failure to respond proactively to the changing culture" was certainly one reason for failure in the case study of failure in Ranyard, Fildes and Crymble (1997).

11.3.2 Understanding how managers make decisions

The second area we discussed at some length in Chapter 2 was the need to understand how managers make decisions. We looked at individual decision-makers, and the fact of their "bounded rationality", as well as cognitive effects such as hindsight, overconfidence, optimism, ideology, and self-interest. But as well as the individuals, we looked at the effects of groups making decisions, since those groups will condition the decision-making; and where strong structures exist and where strong power gradients exist between members, it sometimes appears that decision-making becomes apparently less "rational" – we looked for example at the case of "Groupthink". Shared views or shared beliefs will both influence, and be influenced by, the strategic decision process of strategy formulation and implementation (Schwarz, 2003). We need to be aware of these effects as we intervene in the decision-making process.

11.3.3   Understanding how managers work

As well as the fundamental understanding of how managers make decisions, analysts undertaking client-facing interventions need to understand how managers work, to be able to fit their interaction within the main demands on managers. Figure 2.3 (page 48) is all very well but, of course, managers are embedded within the whole organization, with its culture (as we discussed above) and main demands on the managers, so the interaction is more like Figure 11.1.

So how does the way managers work affect managers? A classic text is Mintzberg's (1973) *The Nature of Managerial Work*, which talks about various aspects of managers' work – such as their long hours at an unrelenting pace, their preference for meetings/groups, their preference to be active and so on, and concludes that this makes them less likely to take notice of modelling. Abdel-Malek *et al.* (1999) put it more succinctly in a quote from one of their interviews: "The key to communication is understanding the impatience of the client." Forder (2007) gives a rather longer list: Senior decision-makers "are busy people, often working to pressing and non-negotiable deadlines on many topics simultaneously – they must take a broad view of issues, and many of the factors that they are required to take into account might be characterized as 'political' – they are able to question assumptions and constraints that others must accept as given – they acknowledge their responsibility for decisions, knowing that they are expected to use their judgement and defend it – they may well not have a technical background and may, indeed, be sceptical

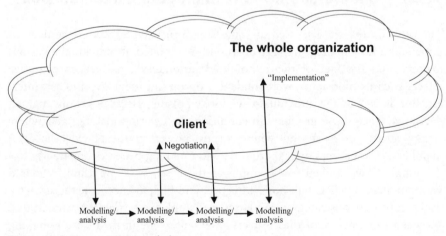

Figure 11.1 Figure 2.3 extended

about modelling and analysis – they are used to getting things done their way!" Some of these points will come up in other parts of this chapter, but we do need to relate to our clients within their modes of working – we cannot treat them as we would fellow analysts, but must modify our behaviour and relationship to fit in with the way of working with which they feel comfortable.

11.3.4   Understanding managers' attitude to analysis

As well as the context of the organization, managers also live in the wider context of the world, and there have been significant changes in the general attitude within society towards scientific and analytic decision-making over the past 50 years. There is clearly a view that the success of OR in the 1950s and 1960s was partly due to there being a "prevailing belief in rational scientific progress as a means of alleviating the human condition" (Kirby and Capey, 1998). But despite some movements in the intervening time (such as the moves in the 1970s noted by Locke (1981) referred to above), there has been a trend away from an unquestioning faith in "scientific analysis", including some of the philosophical trends we noted in Chapter 1 such as postmodernism.

We have already quoted, in Chapter 2, Rosenhead (1998), who talks of the current "anti-analytic, and indeed anti-intellectual, cast of management thought". Burrell (1989) warns that "a view of OR/MS as scientific activity may leave its practitioners stranded on the beach as the tide of public respect for science ebbs away" (quoted in Pidd, 1995). And "anti-analysis feeling" was certainly one of the organizational influences on group closure divisions identified by the SSOR study, although not a major influence (Ranyard & Fildes, 1998). And perhaps social attitudes have been hardened in recent years by public perceptions of "failures" in science, such as global warming, energy crises, nuclear waste and so on. These wider social attitudes towards analysis are referred to in the SSOR report in Fildes and Ranyard (1997). They note Drucker, saying he "quickly revised his 1955 opinion as to the possible contribution of management science to successful management . . . describing OR in 1974 as 'already a disappointment' (Drucker, 1974). . . . The trend in popular management culture re-enforced by an academic critique of scientific management, in general, and OR, in particular . . . has left the set of ideas that lie at the core of OR, in particular that of rational decision analysis, with little support within the managerial culture. Pockets of interest have remained where the solution of (usually operational) technical problems offer organizations major benefits." Fildes and Ranyard (1997) go on to say: "Thirty years of changes in managerial culture have seen a move away from rational analysis towards a more intuitive, holistic view of the importance of leadership driven by a purposeful ideology. Strategic planning notions within a diversified, expanding, centrally directed company have been rejected in favour of tightly monitored short-term financial objectives and the development of a set of core competencies based in the business units as embodying the organizational mission. Most of these major changes are inimical to the success of an internal OR group. However, some have the potential to be exploited by a creative OR group, rather than merely responded to reactively."

This gives probably a too gloomy (although not unmixed) view of attitudes towards OR-type analysis. Certainly Figure 11.1 ought really to be widened to include the wider society with its current attitudes to science and analysis. And if analysts take a narrow, over-positivist view of the organization, our clients will naturally be sceptical about the ability of rational scientific analysis to deal with the realities of organizational life, with its politics and complex human-centred issues. But if OR/MS is founded on the wider philosophical basis laid out in Chapters 1 and 2, then it can develop and grow, and it still has the power to influence and guide within modern society.

> We need to understand our clients and how they work. Key is understanding the social geography and politics within the client organization in which we are intervening – unless our work comprehends that, we will not effectively influence decision-making. But we also need to understand how managers make decisions, and how they are influenced by the wider social attitudes towards analysis. We also have to shape our intervention to meet managers in their current ways of working rather than expect them to adapt to the analysts.

11.4   The relationship with the client

Understanding the client is not enough, of course – the way in which we relate to the client will be crucial in managing the interaction which is at the heart of the OR/MS process shown in Figure 2.3. There are many aspects which could be explored here, but we will focus on seven that appear to be important.

11.4.1 Trust

Trust must be at the heart of the client–consultant relationship. Forder's (2007) survey of best practice explains this as follows:

> Although senior decision-makers will ask penetrating questions and insist on a clear answer, they have neither the time nor (probably) technical background to delve into all the details of the advice and submissions made to them. As a result, they have to have some measure of trust in what they are being told, and, on the whole, they find it easier to develop trust in people rather than in an abstract process. The importance of building up trust between decision-makers and individuals within the analysis function – often, of course, but not necessarily the senior people in that function – was therefore stressed. This issue seemed to be particularly pertinent in the commercial organizations surveyed. In internal groups, decision-makers have regular exposure to even quite junior analysts and will begin to trust those that give a good account of themselves.

Clearly, those that have good personal experiences of working with someone are more likely to trust that person, and this is another reason why analysts should be involved in the "social geography" of their client (Section 11.3.1 above). This relationship-building is all part of the knowledge-creation process: Swart (2006) describes how knowledge is co-created (and hence decisions are influenced) by two main processes, the socialization between parties (which essentially builds common valuations and trust – social capital) and organizational social capital (which establishes the basis on which this interaction and the co-creation of knowledge takes place). Trust is at the heart of this relationship.

This is important to carrying out a single analysis intervention – but it is even more central to establishing an ongoing relationship with a client if we want to capture "repeat" business. (The extended relationship from the "*Shuttle*" example noted at the end of Chapter 9 came about because the senior members of the client-group grew to trust the analytical team – I like to think both the quality of work and the relationship.)

Of course, the need for trust is not limited to the analyst–client relationship, but is generally true in business – although it is a more personal role in this sort of relationship, and trust in the individual analyst both as a person and as a professional are important. But looking at business in general, we need to recognize that trust is on the decline. Edelman carries out an annual trust survey called the "Edelman Trust Barometer" and the latest version of this (Edelman, 2007) shows a decline in trust particularly amongst developed countries, towards business, media, government, religion and even NGOs; the UK appeared particularly cynical. But it is not all bad news – although as the credibility of traditional figures of authority seems to be steadily declining, there appears to be a gradual increase in our trust in the "average person like me" (Edelman, 2006), so perhaps the scope of the individual analyst to develop a trust-relationship is still strong.

11.4.2   Keeping reactivity and timeliness

It is important to keep the work with the client up-to-date and not let it become too late to be useful. There are a number of separate but related issues here.

Firstly, within any one project, it is important to stay reactive to the client and keep the results timely. Large studies that report after the situation has moved on are rarely any use to a client. "Analysis delivered too late for the decision-making process, or which misses the key issues, is worthless. Analysts wishing to engage successfully with senior decision-makers must therefore be ruthless in matching the focus, approach and tempo of their work to decision-making timescales. Quite apart from any external pressures, if the issue is of genuine importance to top management, then they will be impatient for an answer," says Forder (2007).

This can be particularly important – but particularly difficult – where the commissioning client is not the decision-maker. One type of analysis that prompted Forder's study was looking at work to support UK defence procurement – but that was work that is given to one level of official, summarized for the next level, and so on until, when it gets to the final level, time has passed and sometimes the work is out of date – certainly, it cannot react instantly to requests from the client in the spirit of the relationship in Figure 2.3. Therefore, often a snap analysis which covers the main points of the situation and is delivered quickly, is much more useful than a full report delivered too late – particularly if we are trying to enhance our client's understanding rather than giving "the answer".

This is not to say that all OR/MS work should be "quick and dirty" – a mode of working we've mentioned in previous chapters. And besides, the direction of studies cannot be changed every day, otherwise they achieve nothing. But it is easy to think of all OR/MS study as being pre-planned extensive and exhaustive studies. As we discussed in Chapter 6, the key here is to be able to judge the best level of effort to put into a study, and the best level of reactivity to the client's requests and requirements. Sometimes a planned stream of work is appropriate, during which results and other communications help the client during the work.

The second aspect in this area, though, is being reactive to the organization in seeing new issues. This is obviously somewhat easier for internal OR groups, and indeed is perhaps one of the main benefits of having an in-house group. Forder (2007), though, says that: "The obvious prerequisite for effective analytical support to senior decision-makers is to address the right issues at the right time. For internal OR groups, many issues will be identified as part of established tasking processes, but this will not always be the case, especially when they are out of the normal run of the group's work or arise unexpectedly. . . . Senior analysts themselves must . . . be agile in identifying opportunities for analytical intervention, capturing requirements and allocating resources quickly." External groups do not have this type of access to the decision-makers or the decision-situations, which is why it is so important to develop the social networking with the client-group in order to discuss strategic and day-to-day issues and be able to identify useful opportunities for analytical support for decisions.

Finally, there is a point about our models here: once they have been established, they immediately start to go out of date. Horner (1991) gives five lessons for the success of OR at FedEx, one of which is that models were considered "living", not "cast in stone". This is well captured by Salt (2007), with another of his "seven habits of highly defective simulation projects" (which we quoted in Chapters 8 and 9). This is his "dead fish fallacy": "What makes simulation models interesting and worthwhile is the way they capture the dynamic behaviour of systems. Live systems cannot usefully be studied using dead models. . . . This fallacy consists in thinking that one can successfully model dynamic systems using a static model."

(Actually, while this last point is a general truth about models, there is also a rather technical point being made in addition here: if we develop a model of the steady state of a system, we are often missing the main, most interesting aspects of the situation, which is in the system's dynamic behaviour. This may be a trap more often fallen into by users of discrete-event simulation than, say, system dynamics, which is more interested in dynamic behaviour, but the established wisdom of letting a simulation "run-in" and settle down to steady-state can sometimes miss the interesting "transient" behaviour of the system.)

> Our advice to our client is key to the OR/MS process. Trust between the client and consultant needs to develop as the relationship grows, otherwise the advice will not prosper. And our work needs to react to the needs of the client and be timely – both within a project and as the ongoing relationship develops – otherwise we will not be seen as useful. This sometimes needs a mature judgement to balance "quick-and-dirty" reactions to a need, against careful reflective investigations of a situation.

11.4.3 Both enhancing understanding and giving results

We have emphasized throughout this book that it is important that we work with clients and bring them along with us, so that they understand what is done and why. Forder's (2007) discussion of how to engage senior decision-makers says that one of their characteristics "is that 'they acknowledge their responsibility for decisions, knowing that they are expected to use their judgement and defend it'. In other words, when they come to a view and must defend it to their peers and superiors, they themselves will need to be convinced of its justification and will not base their position on a simple faith in 'what came out of the model'." This means that clients must be involved with the analyst in the learning process, and we emphasized in Chapter 2 that our way of engaging with clients was to work with them throughout an intervention – after all, that was why we do not necessarily "solve" a problem, but often arrive at a "satisficing" point or a point when the client's understanding of the situation has sufficiently increased.

However, there is a balancing truth here. OR/MS groups need to be able to point to measurable benefits to their clients/organizations, otherwise they will not be seen to be offering any advantage, and may not even survive. We have already quoted Forder (2007) above when he said that "In short, then, the primary reason for the observed level of survival and success . . . is simply that OA has been found to be useful; or, more precisely, that its benefits have been seen by a sufficient number of senior people in the Ministry to outweigh the resource costs involved." Abdel-Malek's list of seven factors affecting project success includes "verifiable and useful results" and "economic benefits/business results" (Abdel-Malek *et al.*, 1999). "Failure to demonstrate value for money" was one of the organizational influences on group closure decisions identified in the SSOR study (both in Ranyard and Fildes' (1998) general paper, and the case study of a group's closure in Ranyard, Fildes and Crymble (1997) mentioned above). If we're not seen to give benefits to "the bottom line", our position will be difficult to justify.

So, we again need to have a balanced view of what we bring to the organization. We aim to enhance the organization's understanding and bring it with us, and in doing so we aim to build relationships and trust. But at the same time we also need to establish a visible auditable track-record of useful work that we can point to with parts of the client organization with whom we have not had personal contact.

11.4.4 Ensuring our understanding of the problem

Once we have started our relationship with the client, we should emphasize again the importance of the step we started discussing in Chapter 3 – understanding what the problem is, and what the client wants from the study. This is vital to whether OR work succeeds or fails. Abdel-Malek *et al.*'s (1999) table of "Factors affecting success or failure of OR application" lists as one of seven factors for success "Understanding true spirit of request" and one of six factors for failure as "Poor problem definition/planning". Forder (2007) identifies "Capturing requirements" as an important requirement for success. This has been the topic of a lot of this book, so won't be discussed further here.

But we should remember that as well as an understanding of the problem itself, we need to understand the social geography and politics around the situation – all that we discussed in Section 11.3, in fact – and also the reasons why the client commissioned the particular piece of work we are undertaking – which again does not always have a simple explanation. Hartley (1989) looked at the reasons why formal analysis is commissioned within an organization, and categorized what he found into four main groups: firstly, to obtain information, to gain a better understanding of issues; secondly, to communicate a conviction of what somebody thinks is clearly the right thing to do or to bring other people over to this point of view; thirdly, to solve a specific problem or detail and implement a particular decision (that is, for direction and control to focus subordinates' attention); or fourthly analysis may be commissioned for purely symbolic reasons – to "impress others within or outside the organization or to hide another less laudable motive". Discussing this work specifically, Forder (2007) says: "The lesson for analysts is that an understanding of the underlying motives which led to the commissioning of a piece of analysis is one of the keys to an effective engagement process. In a large and complex organization, different stakeholders may well have different perceptions as to where any given piece of analysis lies in the above categorization."

> We need to understand both the particular assignment on which we're working, and the environment within which it lies. We also need to ensure we not only carry our clients with us in our investigation, advancing their understanding as ours advances, but also provide concrete results that can be attributed to the study.

11.4.5   Reporting and fitting into the organization

Where an OR group sits within an organization, and in particular the level to which it reports, is likely to influence the view taken of it. If we look back to the first days of OR, Blackett's tone "was very much that the OR worker should have unconstrained access to the highest levels of the organization and a roving brief to help in defining as yet unidentified problem areas for study. The role envisaged could be described as 'ranger' where the authority to get involved, thereby identifying and solving problems across almost all aspects of organizational activity, has been conferred at the highest levels of management. As organizational OR matured and became more widely diffused, this attitude changed however. The admirable aspirations of Blackett, Ackoff and others, founded on a wartime model of a roving brief, where strategy and tactics were closely interwoven, did not become widely established in either private industry or the public sector. As Dando and Sharp (1978) document, the evidence up to 1978 was that this view of OR was a myth based primarily on aspiration" (Fildes & Ranyard (1997), reporting on Blackett (1950), a founder of modern OR).

So, while OR might have had access to the top of an organization at its birth, over the past few decades, it has tended to report into middle management.

Eilon's (1980) view was that while there is a "conviction that [OR/MS] can and should make a contribution at the top decision-making stratum of the organization . . . [and] that the dispassionate analysis of data, which is the trade mark of the true scientist, must elevate OR/MS above the politics of power and make it acceptable to any sought after by the senior executives . . . [however] . . . reality is rather different from this rosy picture. The OR/MS group reports at a level well below the Board; its work concentrates on tactical problems." Moving forward two decades, in the survey for the SSOR, half of groups were located three levels down from the board. The closest any group got to board level was two levels down; furthermore, groups were located one level lower in the organization than the Commission study a decade earlier (Fildes, Ranyard & Crymble, 1999).

However, it seems likely that the situation is changing. One reason is that OR/MS is moving into areas of more strategic significance for a company (see Section 11.5.1 below). Another is the move towards flatter structures: "Heads of internal OR groups can exploit the fact that they work in day-to-day contact with their policy-making or executive colleagues, and, to at least a useful extent, sit on the same committees, attend the same ad hoc meetings, see the same e-mails and share the same gossip. Especially in today's relatively flat management structures, quite senior decision-makers may typically be only one layer above the heads of OR groups, so access can be relatively straightforward even where there is no direct line management relationship" (Forder, 2007).

It is accepted wisdom that, to succeed, an OR group – at least, an external consultancy – needs the attention of the top level of the organization, preferably the CEO. But attachment only at a high level is not necessarily the best for an OR group, and they may need grounding within lower management also. Miser (1998), talking about the US Air Force, advises that "the principal analysts [should] be at levels sufficiently senior to command respect on this basis alone" but goes on to warn that

> Attachment at a very high level may seem to be the ideal for ambitious analysts who dream of exerting influence on the great strategic issues but a high executive may be too busy to offer the day-to-day support that an OR group needs, and, in spite of the group's principle about reporting its findings only to the problem-owning client, experience shows that lower-level staff hesitate to expose their problems to such a high-level group until they have had a chance to solve or at least ameliorate them. On the other hand, experience shows that a middle-level attachment for administration is not a bar to working on important strategic problems;

the headquarters office in which I served in the fifties did work that extended to cabinet and even White House levels (Miser, 1998).

A common piece of advice is to find a "champion" at the top of the organization. To take a last piece of evidence, in the UK Ministry of Defence (MoD) for example, "The institutionalisation of OA [Operational Analysis] as part of the scientific capabilities of the MoD has brought it an enduring champion within the MoD hierarchy, in the form of the CSA [Chief Scientific Advisor]. The CSA operates at the most senior official level in the MoD and is able, directly and through his staff, to ensure that OA (as well as other scientific inputs) are given due weight in the Ministry's decision-making processes" (Forder, 2004). If that is not available, or the organization is smaller, Eilon's (1998) preferred solution is to constitute the OR/MS group as a think-tank reporting directly to the chief executive officer (CEO) or his/her deputy.

OR/MS is also naturally tied to the information function within an organization. Much OR/MS requires the information system to provide data – for some data, this will be their "window" into the client company. And information systems require OR/MS to make sense of the data they hold and make them useful – and help the function to move from information management to include knowledge management. Information systems functions are normally represented at a high level in the organization – most companies now as part of their so-called "C-suite" have a chief information officer as well as a CEO and chief operating and finance officers (COO and CFO) – albeit different countries will use different names. So, this liaison can be useful both practically and politically.

11.4.6   Maintaining engagement

As well as capturing the attention and engagement of the client-group, it is important to maintain that engagement throughout the intervention, as indeed Figures 2.3 and 11.1 would imply. Sometimes that happens naturally but generally it has to be planned, either as part of the particular project or in the case of an internal group carrying out interventions with the same clients as a regular routine: "an iterative way of working – discussing results and responding to "what if?" questions – is often crucial to get the best out of analysis" (Forder, 2007). "User support/involvement" is one of Abdel-Malek *et al.*'s (1999) seven factors affecting the success of an OR application.

We have already discussed, Mintzberg's (1973) classic statements about the nature of management work, and we need to understand the managerial mind-set and keep attention and engagement through regular, face-to-face meetings. While this might be obvious from previous chapters of this book, remembering or forgetting this simple aspect can be critical to the success or failure of an OR/MS study or even an OR/MS group.

11.4.7   How information is presented to the client

We have already discussed in Chapter 10 that effective communication is a vital part of OR/MS, and Abdel-Malek *et al.*'s (1999) short list of factors affecting an OR application's success includes "well organized/communicated/ presented" and "too technical/abstract approach". This is not simply so that the client understands our message, it is part of what we discussed in Section 11.4.3 above – the need both to give results and to enhance clients' understanding. Clients will "need to be able to integrate analytical input with their own judgement and intuition, modifying these latter as appropriate. To do this they need to understand why what is being told to them is as it is, rather than it simply being presented as an 'answer'. . . . The need to be able to transfer understanding and not just answers is . . . essential, and this leads naturally to the importance of effective communication" (Forder, 2007). We need to remember all of the lessons of Section 10.3 about choice of medium, and about clarity, structure, presentation of appropriate information and careful use of graphics, whether presenting in spoken or written form.

> The mode of our relationship is also important. It is vital to keep the clients' engagement. Information must be reported in a mode and format appropriate to the use that will be made of the work. Reporting into a high level in the client organization will give the work more visibility, although care must be taken not to become detached from lower levels of the organization.

11.5   What we analyse

The third set of pointers moves the focus away from the client to the actual content of our analysis: what should we actually be investigating? Two aspects need consideration – for neither of these is there really a "right answer" as there was for most of the above (such as "trust" is better than "lack of trust").

But these are aspects in which the balance of our work needs to be considered, and there are lessons to be learned from the success-and-failure studies that have been carried out.

11.5.1 Level of analysis – both strategic and tactical

If we loosely define the term "tactics" to be the actual operational means used to gain an objective, while "strategy" is the generation of the overall plan itself which defines those objectives, then over the 1960s and 1970s, some feel that OR/MS concentrated on tactical – perhaps more easily quantified – issues, neglecting the more important – but perhaps harder to model – strategic issues. Although the evidence (e.g. from the SSOR study) is mixed as to whether this is true, there are certainly calls that OR needs to move into supporting strategic decisions. Respondents to the Abdel-Malek *et al.* (1999) survey "felt that the true power of operational research is at the corporate level assisting strategic decisions. . . . Some individuals felt that operational research needs to grow beyond its operational focus to become strategically oriented." Ranyard, Fildes and Crymble's (1997) case study about the failure of an OR group cites "failure to broaden the role of the Group and gain involvement in strategic issues" as a cause. The evidence in the early 1990s is that while MS/OR had the potential to be used for high-level strategic analysis, it wasn't being used in that way (Clark & Scott, 1995). Bell (1998) saw this potential and called for OR to operate at the strategic level, claiming that: " 'Strategic operational research' is not an oxymoron . . . it is time for OR to start seeking senior management's attention as a critical component of strategic IT." For him, this is defined by private-sector competitive-advantage ideas: that is, if there is a key strategy for the company, OR that attacks that issue is "strategic". Examples he gives include yield management in airlines ("I believe that yield management is the single most important technical development in transportation management . . . ," (Smith, Leimkuhler & Darrow, 1992)) and in car rentals ("OR basically saved National Car Rental," (Greenfield, 1996)).

How do we move into the area of strategic analysis? Bell (1998) finds that most firms that have strategic OR started with some event or need that initiated the development of an OR capability, then the OR group "has to capture CEO attention. Those that have done this have successfully addressed one or more very large and significant problems facing the firm, and in doing so have changed the culture of the firm. This cultural change has required senior management commitment and attention. . . . Eventually, the OR Group has become institutionalized in the corporate policy, either through the head of OR reporting directly and often to the corporate CEO, or through OR appointments to key committees, or by written policy." This capturing of the attention of senior decision-makers replays one of our themes from this chapter. Indeed, one sign Bell used for how "strategic" was the OR, was "evidence that the CEO of the firm knows about the OR activities and their importance", and he gives recent examples of this, such as "OR plays a big role in the five-year . . . approximately $1bn . . . program" (president of San Miguel Corporation, from Del Rosario, 1994). Bell expects "an OR group that scores a strategic success may be expected to have gained significant credibility within its parent organization. As such, it is expected that the opinions of the group should be regularly sought on important decision issues."

But it is not necessarily the case that we as a profession should be doing "strategic" OR *instead* of "tactical" OR. One of Tomlinson's "six principles for effective OR" (Tomlinson, 1998) is "The balance principle: the programme of an OR group should be balanced in a number of important ways – between long and short projects, between tactical and strategic, between old and new work." Much of the award-winning work we'll look at in the following section looks at tactical work, which can be vitally important as we'll see when we address the second question of balance.

11.5.2 Supporting both one-off and recurrent decision-making

As computers and information systems developed, OR found an important role in providing the underlying algorithms for computerized decision-support systems. This meant that as well as providing support for one-off decisions, it could provide the basis for recurrent decisions that were made many times over – sometimes many times a day: stock-control decisions, revenue pricing decisions, scheduling containers in a terminal, planning production, scheduling rolling-stock, and so on. While these are certainly "tactical" decisions, getting them right (or wrong) becomes important at a strategic level for the organization simply because they are made so many times – indeed, some are fundamental to the organization's *raison d'être*.

In Chapter 1 we looked at the OR work that has won recognized prizes in the success in application of OR/MS work. The most well-known of these is the US INFORMS "Edelmann" prize (described for 2004 in Spencer & Graves,

2005), and we said there that of the last 12 winners or runners up, all but one describes an ongoing process, with regular incremental decisions, for which the task of the OR/MS group was to supply a decision-support system to enable these decisions to be taken, including a user-friendly computer program. The same is true of the winners of the European "EURO Excellence in Practice" awards (see Euro, 2005). This work involves large numbers of decisions, which therefore involve large amounts of money when added together. This area of work illustrates the close relationship OR/MS has to have with information systems – the work can hardly exist without being fed data by, and supplying results to, a corporate information system. One study involved operations on the Canadian Pacific railway with "dramatic improvements in its costs and service levels . . . catching the attention of . . . [the] current CEO" (Ireland *et al.*, 2004). In many of the cases, the organization was geared mainly towards a particular activity, and creating an algorithm for that activity was core to the organization's success, such as developing an algorithm for direct-marketing application, at the core of the company's business (and some sort of algorithm would be essential), or developing an algorithm for manufacturing scheduling application (in work at Bridgestone/Firestone, "top management was particularly happy with the additional revenue that was generated that day" (Degraeve & Schrage, 1998)). Perhaps the most telling example is from an analysis of pricing at Merrill Lynch (Altschuler *et al.*, 2002), where the company president is quoted thus: "Management Science and Strategic Pricing provided the modelling and analyses that enabled me and my executive management team to better understand the revenue risks", pointing out how important the nature of the topic is to upper management by continuing "This is the kind of thing that kept me up at nights!".

So, again, the balance principle is relevant here: OR/MS clearly has a role contributing to the recurrent small decisions, whose importance stems from the many times such decisions are made. We have also seen how OR/MS should be playing a role in the major one-off decisions. The flavour of OR/MS used might be different, but the same principles apply to each, and we as a profession should be seen to be contributing to both.

Of course, both of the divisions above (strategic/tactical and one-off/recurrent) are slightly simplistic, and there are many types of decision process within a company. Kriger and Barnes (1992), for example, look at eight long-term complex decision processes in big heavy manufacturing companies, and define a six-level framework of decision complexity: instantaneous decision choices, and what he calls decision actions, decision events, mini-decision processes, decision processes and decision theatres. For each of these, the role of OR/MS would be different, from small aids to enabling better minor decisions, to establishing well-founded bases for major decisions. The key is to shape our intervention to suit the type of decision – and to consider at the start what type of decision it is, to be able to intervene with a suitable level of depth, timeliness and repeatability.

> Supporting different types of decision requires different types of intervention, and the analyst needs to judge the type of intervention at the start. OR/MS has an important role in contributing to strategic and tactical decision-making; it also has an important role in contributing to recurrent decision-making algorithms and to major one-off decisions. OR/MS as a profession should make sure it works at all of these types of intervention. A good OR/MS group will need to consider carefully where its appropriate balance of work lies.

11.6 How we carry out the work

Finally, we must look at how we actually carry out our work. We'll touch on four points only briefly, as we they have been dealt with earlier in the book.

11.6.1 Avoiding putting theory before the problem

There can be a tendency amongst some Management Scientists to take to particular techniques, and "see" the world through that technique's particular "glasses", trying to solve all problems with that one technique – or, at least, to choose the technique before fully studying the problem situation. It is proper to work with the techniques we know (as we'll discuss in Chapter 12), and we often have to think of possible solution routes before knowing all about the problem (as we discussed in Chapter 6); however, pre-choosing the technique is a trap into which analysts can fall and can blind them to much better modelling techniques that would be more natural for that particular situation. "The tendency of OR practitioners to superimpose inappropriate theoretical structures on business problems, one of Ackoff's reasons for pessimism, continues to be a major inhibitor to successful application. The answers given in the survey regarding the identification of factors leading to project failure support this viewpoint," report Abdel-Malek *et al.* (1999).

11.6.2   Mixing hard and soft techniques

This was covered in detail in Chapters 2–4, and so will only be noted here. Most interventions, where OR/MS is called upon, require some element of quantitative analysis, which must take into account the qualitative issues if it is to be appropriate. So, it is a general point that OR/MS should be looking more towards the integration of these halves of its toolbox in order to make an impact on the management world. This is not a new – nor a UK-only – viewpoint, but it has increased in urgency over the years, and the UK seems to have taken a lead in this. OR/MS analysis which neglects the "soft" factors loses credibility, as we have discussed in earlier chapters; analysis which is non-quantitative finds it more difficult generally to be seen to contribute to the "bottom line" (see Section 11.4.3), and so is more difficult to justify. We need to bring both to bear with an integrated methodology.

11.6.3   Maintaining professionalism

Perhaps because of the nature of its birth, OR/MS has sometimes had a slight flavour of amateurism about it – and an amateur discipline cannot survive in the business environment of today. (The tendency of some academics to carry out "academic" OR may have exacerbated this.) Abdel-Malek *et al.* (1999) report "lack of professional competence" as a key reason leading to project failure, and that, "Among the reasons respondents often attributed failure were the highly theoretical approaches taken, and the lack of professional competency stemming from the inability to properly model the problem."

Modern Management Science calls for professionals – with expertise not only in modelling, but also in the skills that surround the OR/MS process, many of which we've discussed in this book. Abdel-Malek *et al.*'s (1999) table of six factors affecting failure of OR applications includes "over budget, not timely" and "poor problem definition/planning" – both of which are indications that the task is not being carried out professionally. The case study we've quoted above of the failure of a group (Ranyard, Fildes & Crymble, 1997) contained many reasons suggesting a failure in the professional management of the group, including lack of regular post-project reviews, the failure to enhance consultancy skills quickly enough, and so on. Looking at successful groups (we've already quoted the FedEx example), however, we see one of the reasons for their success was that "the OR team conducted itself as a learning organization" (Horner, 1991), becoming both ever more knowledgeable about the parent organization and skilled at their craft. We need to be professional at our task – planning well, meticulous in our work, knowledgeable and skilled in modelling and the ancillary skills, maintaining the highest level of integrity in our relationship with clients. This also means, of course, not only carrying out each intervention well, but also reflecting on each intervention and learning for the next – indeed, reflecting on our practice during each intervention – and we will look at this area in Chapter 13 (particularly relying on the work of Schön (1983)).

11.6.4 Team-work

Having said that we need to be professional, we have already mentioned in Chapter 10 that not all members of the team need take on all tasks. We have tried to set out in this book the picture of the well-rounded Management Science professional, but some teams will operate with individual members playing to their strengths. It can be, for example, the case that more client-friendly consultants, perhaps happier in the facilitation role than some of their colleagues, will perform the client-facing tasks, while the more technically skilled will perform the "back-room" analytical tasks. In this way, the Janus effect of Figure 4.1 (page 83) is dealt with by having two analysts facing different ways; then, the communication task is to ensure that the knowledge flows between these two analysts. Having said that, there are clear dangers in allowing analysts to stay in the "back-room", as they will then lose the sense of the "real" problems they are trying to solve, and so a definitive division of responsibility has its dangers.

But there is a lot of work that has been done to suggest that we are happier taking different roles in our organization. The most well-known of this work is that by Belbin (1993), who described quite distinct roles within the team (a summary is available on the Internet at Belbin, 2008). She defined nine roles including, for example, the *plant*, who is creative and unorthodox but tends to ignore incidentals; the *co-ordinator*, mature and confident, promoting decision-making, but can be seen as manipulative; the *monitor-evaluator*, sober, strategic and discerning, but not inspiring others; the *completer-finisher*, painstaking and conscientious but worrying unduly and not delegating, and so on. Sorting out where you naturally fit within a team can help you feel comfortable, although all of us need to be stretched and developed. And different personalities help for different aspects of the project and at different stages of a project, from the plant, who may well be more appropriate for the problem-solving part of a project, through to the completer-finisher, who is needed to ensure that the final product is properly supplied.

Such knowledge can help the team organize itself with each member "playing to his/her strengths". But MS/OR is a creative discipline, and the interaction of a good team can pay great dividends. Some of the best MS/OR work has been done by teams working together, particularly where those teams have mixed skills, and these teams need to reflect together on the effectiveness (or otherwise) of their practice.

> As well as all the aspects surrounding our practice, we need to do good Management Science as well! We should be open to appropriate techniques, mixing hard and soft where necessary, and above all be professional in our practice, whether as individuals or as part of a team.

These are all aspects that the evidence suggests will influence whether or not our OR/MS work is successful, and as such all need attention in our practice.

12
Ethics

12.1 Why ethics?

An important part of any profession is the notion of acting "ethically". All of the traditional professions – doctors, lawyers, engineers, priests – have an understanding of what it means for their profession to act ethically. So, what does it mean for the Management Scientist?

Of course, the question of how to act ethically is not confined to our professional life but is part of all our lives, and each of our lives are full of ethical dilemmas (what do I do when the husband/wife of a friend of mine tells me in confidence that he/she is having an affair?). So this chapter does not attempt to deal with the whole question of "what is ethical" – that would take a lot more than one chapter, even if I did have any special wisdom to impart (and I don't think I do!). This chapter deals solely with the question, "What does it mean for a Management Scientist's professional practice to be ethical?"

The most obvious question to ask is, "is working for this particular client ethical?" – or, more particularly, "is helping this client achieve this particular aim ethical". We can all think of examples of carrying out good, effective OR/MS for clients with whose aims we would strongly disagree. An oft-quoted hypothetical example is the scheduling of railroad trucks destined for the death camps in World War II to improve efficiency – the technical work might be just right, but we would not approve of the aim of the work. Similarly, planning crop planting/harvesting and subsequent manufacture to optimize illicit heroin production might be an interesting piece of work technically but again we would not approve ethically of the aim of the client. A suggested Code of Ethics for Policy Scientists includes the statement: "a policy scientist should not work for a client whose goals and values, in the opinion of the policy scientist, contradict basic values of democracy and human rights" (Quade, cited in Barabba, 1994). But, of course, this could apply to any client–contractor relationship, and for the remainder of this chapter we will take it as read that there are no ethical problems of this nature with our particular assignment.

There have always been important issues of ethics for Management Science practitioners as they build models for clients. Section 12.2 below will look at some of these issues about behaving professionally and ethically in the limited terms of model-building.

But ethics is an area that has come to the fore more within the last couple of decades or so, for reasons that can be seen if we look back to the discussion in Chapter 1 about the types of situation in which Management Science seeks to intervene. If we look back 20 years ago, say, we can see Management Science/Operational Research starting to move into areas beyond problems that have only dynamic complexity to those which have also behavioural complexity, and because of the complexity of a human-based situation, then ethical issues starting to increase. Commentators then started to see weaknesses in the practice of OR/MS: for example, in 1990, a plenary paper at the triennial IFORS conference stated:

> Broadly, Operational Research handles issues which are, at most, only loosely linked to outside interests. Our successes, therefore, have concerned matters which do not touch crucially the organization's identity, strategic posture, survival. . . . [It is unclear] what factors have promoted and maintained this narrowness of focus. Elsewhere, I have speculated that OR's natural science origins may be partially responsible. . . . With much which was of value in this scientific tradition, we also acquired, uncritically, a belief in the possibility of value-free knowledge, and the importance of finding the one right answer. This translated too easily into an assumption that there is only one perspective on a problem situation, and that the operational

researcher's task is to find the corresponding unique optimal solution. . . . Mainstream OR's ultimately simplistic assumptions about the nature of social life have weakened its contribution in areas where these human and social aspects of systems are of the essence (Rosenhead, 1990).

As OR/MS moved more into problems with a social dimension, so ethical issues increasingly emerged.

At the heart of the matter is the growing importance of how we (and our models) relate to the client and the client-group, particularly in these behaviourally complex problem areas. Section 12.3 will therefore look at this area, with Section 12.4 asking the specific question of whether these issues can (or should) be dealt with in a Code of Ethics as is the case with many professions. Section 12.5 will then widen the discussion out further (as Rosenhead foresaw) to the implications of our work beyond the immediate client-group.

12.2 The model

If we leave aside the questions of modelling "soft" human-oriented issues, and consider simply building a model of an objective system, it might appear at first glance as if there are few ethical considerations. However, even in this traditional Operational Research arena, there are important areas in which we need to consider our practice.

Chapter 8 dealt with good practice in modelling, including a discussion of how to build and check a "good" model. An ethical Management Scientist will clearly be carrying out such rules of good practice. A model should be capable of evaluation by other parties, and include good documentation, be transparent about its data and intentions, and be able demonstrate adequate data validation and validation of the operations of the model and model verification (see the discussion in Section 8.4, part (5)). There are areas here where complete standards do not exist – such as the verification, and particularly the validation, of simulation models. However, the effort has to be put into making the models transparent and validated, and particularly into ensuring that the underlying assumptions of the model are made clear and have been tested as far as is reasonable. "Any model is based on particular *assumptions* (for example, it may assume linear equations, or Poisson processes with specific parameter values). Hence, the model results apply if those assumptions apply. But, what happens if these assumptions do not hold? This is often not known – because the modellers did not investigate this issue – or it is not emphasized enough – because the users did not want to be bothered by 'all these technicalities'. Yet I think that this . . . meaning of ethical is of great practical importance!" says Kleijnen (2001) – although, again, he does go on to point out the problems in this under certain circumstances, such as in disaster risk analysis, which might model unique events.

A useful aid for looking through a model and its presentation is provided by a check-list of questions that a model-user might want to ask of a model-builder, given by Barabba (1994) – who is also credited with Barabba's law: "Never say the model says" (i.e. simply because a model gives a result does not mean that that is sufficient basis for making a decision! – we'll return to this below). Barabba's check-list is reproduced in Figure 12.1. If the model-builder can give a good account on all or most of these questions, s/he is well on the way to demonstrating good modelling practice.

It was to cover this sort of area that the then-called OR Society of America (ORSA, which later became part of INFORMS) drew up some guidelines for professional practice. In 1969, the US government was considering deploying a missile system, called the anti-ballistic missile system or ABM, to shoot down enemy intercontinental ballistic missiles (ICBMs). This was a highly contro-versial issue, and a series of hearings were held in the US Congress between supporters of the ABM and its opponents. The evidence on both sides relied heavily on evidence of an Operational Research type – which was contradic-tory between the two sides. A key issue, for example, was whether the propor-tion of US ICBMs left after the enemy's first strike would be sufficient to form a credible deterrent against the enemy. Two eminent experts, in particular, quoted a proportion respectively of 25% (Prof. George Rathjens of MIT) and 5% (Prof. Albert Wohlstetter of the University of Chicago). The first was considered to represent leaving a credible deterrent, while the latter was not. In the hearings, and in an exchange of letters in the press afterwards, they each insisted that their OR analysis was correct, and that the other was wrong. There was a lot of heart-searching in the US OR community over this public disagreement, and when Prof. Wohlstetter wrote to the President of ORSA to appoint a panel to consider the professional conduct and ethics of the debate, a committee of six highly regarded experts in OR/MS was set up. This com-mittee drew up a report, which was influential for many years, and still remains pertinent in the area we are investigating here. (The Report is given in ORSA, 1971, and its story is told and reflected upon a decade later by Machol (1982).) The report covers quite a few pages, but its main section "Guidelines for Professional Practice" covers in summary the following:

- General points:
  - An OR analyst should "apply the scientific spirit (open, explicit and objective)"
  - An OR analyst should "take a broad and disinterested view, free of parochialism, inflexibility, or prior prejudice, that includes a lively sense

---

Questions for the model-builder

Several of the following questions were originally posed by Barbara Richardson and her colleagues at the University of Michigan in 1979 (Richardson, Joscelyn & Saalberg 1979).

1. How well does the model perform?
2. Has the model been analysed by someone other than the model authors?
3. Is documentation adequate for the users' needs?
4. What assumptions and data were used in producing model output?
5. Why is the selected model appropriate to use in a given application?
6. Will the model be run directly and specifically for the present purpose?
7. What is the accuracy of the model output?
8. Does the structure of the model resemble the system being modelled?
9. Is the model sensitive to the inputs being varied?

In addition, the model-builder could introspectively ask the following questions when preparing the model:

1. Do I understand the problem?
2. Are the assumptions reasonable?
3. Is the method I have selected the best? Are there other possible ways to do it?
4. Can I get this done within the time frame available?
5. Are the data I am using to build and run the model correct?

Figure 12.1 Questions a model-user would want to ask a model-builder. From Barabba, pp. 153–4. Copyright 1994 Elsevier Science Ltd. Reproduced with permission.

of the public interest, as well as of the narrower interests of the organization involved".

– Instructions to be technically competent and considering alternative tools.

– Instructions to become fully familiar with the situation and be open to evidence, and being aware that a study might cover only a part of a complex situation.

– Various instructions about confidentiality and keeping the client informed.

• Beginning a study: *"in close cooperation with the client throughout this step"* (emphasis in the ORSA report) collecting data, considering alternatives, understanding subjective and objective issues and so on.

• Conducting a study: using the best methods, verifying data and checking accuracy and sensitivity.

• Reporting a study: reviewing a study and following-up studies. (All from ORSA, 1971)

> Preparing any model for a client should be done in a professional and ethical manner. This covers many areas, including ensuring that the model is transparent and verified, assumptions and data are validated, and the modelling uses appropriate techniques.

All this concerns good professional conduct in preparing a model for a client. It generally applies even in the hypothetical situation when a "hard" objective model is being prepared for a single, rational decision-maker. But even in this hypothetical situation, mathematical techniques are not value-free: for example, if we use a mathematical programming model and assume an objective-function that optimizes, we are making assumptions about the motivations of the client (particularly that that objective, often cost-minimization or profit-maximization, is the sole motivation).

In real practice, of course, we are rarely in this idealized situation. We are not modelling entirely "hard" physical systems – our modelling generally involves systems in which humans are involved, and many of our parameters involve "soft" factors or human perceptions. That is why we discussed the nature of reality and knowledge (ontology and epistemology) in Chapter 1. Our models, therefore, are not a definitive statement of the structure of the real world and a definition of what a rational decision-maker should decide; rather, they should be regarded as accounts of reality that provide aids to decision-making. There is, therefore, an obvious ethical problem if we present our models to our client as objective truth or we let our client regard them as such (hence Barabba's law above, for example). But it also leads to other ethical issues, in particular the ease with which such models can be manipulated: "With subjective OR models, it is easier to construct a model that legitimizes ex-post the selection of a solution identified ex-ante. The distortion of the model takes place in the choice of the weights and is difficult to detect. For someone else than the decision-maker and the builder of the model, it may be impossible to appreciate a possible manipulation" (Le Menestrel and van Wassenhove, 2004).

Furthermore, our clients are not single, rational decision-makers – that is why we discussed the nature of rationality and how groups of decision-makers make decisions in Chapter 2, and we need to consider the nature of the client when we think about how to behave ethically.

The next section therefore will look at the client relationship and ask what "ethics" means to our practice here.

12.3 The client relationship

The relationship with the client is at the core of our practice. Even if we look just beyond the model, we need to bring our client relationship into our ethical consideration. Mason (1994) says: "At a minimum, a model builder is obliged to do at least three things: (1) to represent reality to clients adequately, (2) to understand and to incorporate the clients' values into the model in an effective way, and (3) to insure [sic] that actions the client takes based on the model have the desired effect. These are the three major covenants a management scientist or operations researcher has with clients, and they comprise the core of the ethics of the profession."

This implies two levels at which we need act ethically. The first is that we must act competently and professionally, to represent the situation as closely as is appropriate, so that the client can trust our work. Indeed, we have already said in Section 11.4.1 that client trust is essential to the success of OR/MS work, both practically, as the client does not have time to go into all the details of the modelling, and also in order to have any chance that our analysis will be acted upon. We assert in providing a model that it is an appropriately suitable representation of reality, and our client trusts us that we have used our particular OR/MS skills to provide this – and indeed trusts us that we have the requisite skills and knowledge within this particular area of OR/MS (taking on work which we are not competent to carry out is a particularly unethical act). However, because we are not modelling only physical objective systems, we also need to incorporate our understanding of the goals of our clients, and their values and visions, and incorporate their perceptions of the situation, and we need to act ethically in this second arena in attending to what our client wants from the study. Part of our OR/MS skill is to assess the client's aims (such as in an objective function) and values in our models – and that can, of course, imply uncovering and representing a heterogeneity of aims and values within the client. "So", continues Mason, "the management scientist qua professional enters into two major implied covenants that define his or her primary fiduciary responsibilities. These are: (1) the covenant of reality, in which the model builder is entrusted with understanding things as they actually exist in the problem area and representing their salient features as accurately as possible, and (2) the covenant of values, in which the model builder is entrusted with the visions, goals, and objectives of the client and pledges to serve those values as loyally as possible. For the most part, management scientists have little difficulty adhering simultaneously to these two covenants. Sometimes, however," claims Mason, "they come into conflict. When they do, a management scientist is faced with a moral dilemma" (Mason, 1994). Well, you might feel that these conflicts should always be avoidable by a consultant whose relationship is based on giving open, honest and truthful advice – but certainly issues arise in this area which need careful consideration.

Some find it helpful to divide these two areas of our work: the building of the model, and the discourse with the client about the model that enables the trust relationship. In this view, conventional modellers seek to gain as much objectivity in their model as possible. Le Menestrel and van Wassenhove (2004) quote Wallace thus: "One of the ethical responsibilities that was agreed upon is that the goal of any model building process is objectivity with clear assumptions, reproducible results, and no advocacy," but they then go on to point out that this (perhaps naïve) view cannot be held to completely in modelling the types of situation which Management Scientists are now called upon to model: "The main criticism is that objective OR models are based on a conception of scientific methodology that does not properly reflect the specificity of social sciences with respect to natural sciences, i.e. the fact that human beings have values which are evolving and are local."

So, while it is useful to consider these two parts of our work separately, in practice they are intimately bound together, and we need "a methodological approach that links OR models to a rational and open discourse on the limitations of these models" (again, Le Menestrel and van Wassenhove, 2004) – the type of approach that this book has been seeking to lay out. This, of course, does assume that there is a relationship with the client such as that shown in Figure 2.3 – or, rather, that there is a relationship with the client-group such as that shown in Figure 11.1, so that the whole client-group is brought into the model-building process – so that the client-group gains in understanding about the model and how it was built during the development (as we discussed in Section 11.4.3). But if we have this relationship, this facilitates the ethical development of models along with the client.

Not only can we never be a perfectly "neutral" analyst, but some situations specifically require an analyst to take on an advocacy role (despite Wallace's comment above) – as indeed in the "*Shuttle* wagon" example described in Sections 3.3.5, 4.7 and 9.4. This can be quite proper (indeed, we will see one call for recognition of the impossibility of neutral objectivity in the next section), and the ORSA Guidelines give specific guidance for the "analyst as advocate" as a particular role. This does bring its own ethical problems (such as what does the analyst do if s/he thinks the client is talking nonsense? – an issue for facilitators also!) and its own pressures (particularly the pressure to influence the model to show one type of result), but for an OR/MS analyst, using his or her skills as an advocate is not at all unethical per se, and, indeed, as we'll see in the last section of this chapter, working with powerless or unemancipated groups or "giving voice" to them can be an area of work that is particularly valuable.

We should say also that all of this so far has looked at the role of ethics in the life of the individual analyst. But many work in teams, and here we must be sensitive not only to the ethics of our client and the ethics in our individual relationship with the client, but also the ethics involved in our intra-team relationships and, particularly, the ethics of the team's or organization's relationship with the client. The latter can, in particular, cause issues for individuals if they feel that their organization is not relating to the client as they would wish to do so individually. This can be in any of the areas covered by the chapter so far – be it lack of transparency, lack of disinterestedness, keeping the client at "arm's length", manipulation of the study or the results, dishonesty (in the expertise claimed, or the analysis done), or any of the other issues. Where there is conflict between the individual's preferred client-relationship and the organizational client-relationship, sometimes the analyst has to choose between compromise, raising the issue within his or her organization, "whistle-blowing" or even parting from the organization. These are difficult issues, which there is not scope in this book to explore.

> A key aspect that marks out the ethical Management Scientist is the respect and professionalism with which s/he relates to the client group

12.4   Codes of ethics

The natural consequence of the previous discussion for a few practitioners is to look for a Management Science "Code of Ethics" by which they can judge whether a piece of work, or a fellow analyst, is "ethical" or not. The first main attempt to move towards a Code of Ethics was the ORSA Guidelines that we discussed above, whose instructions were mostly fairly unarguable as "good things to do". Years later, in 1996, the UK OR Society considered moving towards a scheme of professional membership (rather than its then open membership; a not dissimilar scheme was proposed in 1970 but rejected). As part of the discussion around this idea, one of the implications which arose was the Code of Professional Conduct to which members would have to aspire (and which would presumably be policed in some fashion). Another issue with codes of conduct is to ask, "what are the penalties for not acting ethically?", "who regulates the codes of conduct?" and "who can sit in judgement over their peers?" However, these are questions really for professional societies so we shall not discuss them here. The basic duties outlined in the proposed code were simply statements such as "a duty to be honest", "a duty to behave ethically" and so on, although these were detailed further in good practice guidelines (Operational Research Society, 1996).

Some feel that such guidelines do not really help us understand what ethical behaviour is, so, in line with many professions, look to statements of how practitioners should behave being based on principles rather than on detailed rules. This not only enables the professional to describe ethical behaviour properly, it also avoids the natural tendency for rogue analysts to try to "get round" detailed rules. The Institute of Management Consultants (the IMC), for example, is a regulatory body for management consultants whose code of professional conduct is based on three basic principles dealing with (Institute of Management Consultants, 1994, Appendix C):

- *Meeting the client's requirements:* Under this principle come rules covering issues such as keeping within the consultant's competence, formal agreements on scope, confidentiality, communication with the client and so on.
- *Integrity, independence, objectivity:* Under this principle come rules covering issues such as disclosure, conflicts of interest, inducements, privacy and objectivity.
- *Responsibility to the profession and to the Institute:* Under this principle come issues such as continuing professional development and relationships with other professionals.

Some feel that even the attempt to define a code of conduct is naïve, particularly given the complexity of real-life practice, and that our conscience can be our best guide. Certainly, as Management Scientists we do need to reflect on the ethics of our behaviour. Taket (1994) structures her ethical reflection around four elements:

- "undertaking a process of critical/ethical self-reflection";
- "recognizing subjectivity and responsibility";
- "recognizing non-neutrality" (i.e. that there is no such thing as a perfectly "neutral" analyst, there being no such thing as ideal "objectivity");
- "recognizing the pervasive nature of ethical issues" (i.e. that ethical issues come into all of our practice).

This structure helps to focus our minds on the ethics of our practice. Questions of ethics do indeed arise all the time in Management Science practice, because our work is always within a human context. Theoretical developments of techniques carried out in a "back room" (or, indeed, in the imagery of Chapter 1, playing the "Glass Bead Game") might or might not be an activity in which ethics plays no significant role. (There is, of course, an age-old issue about whether developing means for unethical behaviour is itself unethical – if gun-crime is rife, do we ban gun-*makers*? We'll return to this area at the end of the chapter.) But real Management Science practice always concerns a real situation in which there will be some ethical backdrop. Reflecting on our practice enables us to look in a personal way to decide whether we have acted ethically. For Taket, as a postmodernist, there are no fundamental truths: "This process of reflection is necessarily personal and subjective, and one for which the analyst must assume responsibility. The notion of a set of universal guidelines telling me 'what' is the ethical solution is self-contradictory, at best I can hope for guidelines as to 'how' I must decide. We must throw aside the notion that we can have an authoritative code of ethics; there is no external authority that can substitute for our own reflection, no set of absolute truths that can tell us precisely how to act, we must accept responsibility for our role as agents" (Taket, 1994). Again, we as individuals have to take our own stance depending on our own views of morals and ethics – but certainly we can see the difficulty of defining overarching rules, and we can accept the responsibility to reflect on our practice and take responsibility for deciding the ethicality of our actions.

> We can seek principles of ethical behaviour around the relationship with the client, meeting the client's needs and the need to act with integrity, independence and objectivity, but these will always be arguable to some extent. We have an individual responsibility to reflect on our practice and see how its ethicality matches up to our own personal ethics.

12.5 Wider implications

Management Science analysts have ethical responsibilities not just to the client and the profession, but also to a wider constituency. The OR/MS analyst should see each problem "as a citizen involved in a social context and then as a specialist who will insist on addressing the problem and its context together" (Koch, 2000). This is also true for the wider profession of management consultancy. Lynch (1998) says that: "Both the IMC's and MCA's [the Management Consultancy Association] codes focus on the clients. They have served these bodies and their members well up to now, but the time may be approaching when it will be necessary to widen their scope, to cover a social dimension and other ethical 'stakeholders', particularly protecting the public interest, however difficult 'public interest' is to define."

The discussion for Management Scientists here has been driven particularly by those who look to practitioners to execute an agenda of emancipation. Munro (1997) said that we need to "move from a traditional self-reflective ethics determined solely by the individual, to a discourse ethics determined by group consensus" and that enlightened Management Science "demands that the interests of all those who may be affected by a decision must be considered and not only the interests of those who are directly involved in taking the decision". But he goes beyond this simple observation: "According to [the

Critical OR] school of thought, OR professionals must not be contented to be the passive servants of powerful interests, but ought to consider the wider social implications of their work" (Munro, 1997). He looks back to Habermas' work (which we discussed in Chapter 1, on the power and dominating relationships that there are within all human relationships, and clearly within management situations) and looked for "sincere communicate speech acts" – in other words discourse unfettered by the coercive use of power. This school of thought then sees emancipation as such a situation, where citizens come together in open, non-coercive and democratic discourse, uncover hidden value judgements and realize their true interests. They will criticize a simplistic OR/MS process because of its lack of appreciation of these issues, and characterize "soft OR" as simply enabling the analyst to structure the various human issues and viewpoints to enable the optimum action to be chosen. On the other hand, this is a fairly gross simplification of the process we discussed in the first few chapters of this book, where the power relationships form part of the geography of the client organization and thus part of the analysis, and this should be part of our analysis, whatever ethical stance we take towards these power relationships. (OR/MS, of course, is not the only discipline to have this criticism – see, for example, the various discussions about the role of physicists in developing nuclear energy and nuclear weapons.)

This agenda has taken some to using their OR/MS skills for practical help to the disadvantaged. Some of this work has been referred to above. Some comes under the banner of "Community OR". As described in, for example, Midgley and Ochoa-Arias (2004), most of this latter work has dealt with complex issues in the community local to an individual OR analyst or group of analysts, with voluntary organizations, local community groups and so on. This not surprisingly has an emphasis on the use of participative types of methods. But this type of work is also starting to extend into the work on global issues such as environmental management and into developing countries. (Of course, there has been much written on the use of OR/MS in developing countries, but much of the literature doesn't take this emancipatory agenda into account – with notable exceptions, such as the work of Rosenhead (e.g. the famous paper by Bornstein & Rosenhead (1990).)

In terms of the academic debate, Ulrich (1983) has been particularly vocal in this area. He says that "experts" can have no moral authority, and we must be very wary of "expert" knowledge. Since the design of systems requires value judgements, he developed his "Critical Systems Heuristics" to facilitate a democratic reflection on which observations and which value judgements count as relevant and which others are left out or are considered less important – this is detailed further in Section 5.2.1.8. Others, such as Flood (1990), seek to extend this further and take in the work of Foucault (see Chapter 1) to try to aim for a "liberating systems" theory in which subjugated discourses are liberated and allowed to be "seen and heard".

These are important issues which we need to consider in our practice. But we need also to remember that many of these quotations are from academic papers, written by either academic authors or academic practitioners. As we move into practice, we need to take a pragmatic view of what ethical behaviour means to us – as we work with the client, as we relate to other analysts, and as we work within a complex world full of inequalities and injustices.

Ethical issues can arise because we try to separate "personal" ethics from "professional" ethics. While this chapter explicitly dealt with the question "what does it mean for a Management Scientist's professional practice to be ethical?", this is not to imply at all that our thinking about ethics can be compartmentalized in this way: the chapter merely dealt with this particular aspect of our thinking. But this has to be one aspect of our attempts to live as a holistically ethical person. These are personal judgements, on which we need to reflect, as indeed we reflect on our whole practice – which will take us nicely into our next chapter.

> Our ethical responsibilities go beyond our immediate problem and our immediate client, to the need to act ethically within a complex world. It is our responsibility to reflect on our practice in the light of our personal ethics.

13

Reflective Practice

13.1 Reflective practitioners

The idea of reflective practitioners came to prominence in 1983 with a book by Schön called *The Reflective Practitioner*. He traces the development of philosophical thought about the "useful" professions – similar to the line of thought we alluded to in the first chapters of this book – and particularly the developments around positivism and what he calls "Technical Rationality". He points to a peak of the success of the "Technical Programme" and the positivist epistemology of practice in the Second World War and the immediate years afterwards. But he then describes how the flaws were seen in the professions from the mid-1960s: "Increasingly, we have become aware of the importance to actual practice of phenomena – complexity, uncertainty, instability, uniqueness and value-conflict, which do not fit the model of Technical Rationality." And he goes on to describe how the professions such as ours have therefore had to change: "From the perspective of Technical Rationality, professional practice is a process of problem solving. Problems of choice or decision are solved through the selection, from available means, of the one best suited to established ends. But with this emphasis on problem solving, we ignore problem settings, the process by which we define the decisions to be made, the ends to be achieved, the means which may be chosen. In real-world practice, problems do not present themselves to the practitioner as givens. They must be constructed from the materials of problematic situations which are puzzling, troubling and uncertain. In order to convert a problematic situation to a problem, a practitioner must do a certain kind of work. He must make sense of an uncertain situation that initially makes no sense."

Thus Schön directs many professions to the point that we came to in Chapter 1: we have had to move out of simple problem-solving questions (as in the "Glass Bead Game") into complex views of problem-settings. Our concentration has had to move from simply solving the content of the problem to the process by which we do this: managing meaning and sense in the negotiation process, turning the emphasis from being solely on the problem-situation to being on (or at least also on) the problem-participants (see Eden, 1987). And this underlay our need to develop the problem-structuring methods in Chapter 3 that helped us make sense of a complex problem through the eyes of a client-group.

But before we turn to look at our process, the first point is that we're looking at issues within complex settings. In particular, we're looking at problems embedded within human social settings. Now, individual humans are complex in themselves. We have already looked at Simon's work on the boundedness of human rationality. Bourdieu, a sociologist, indeed developed an influential theory of how humans act (using the concept of the "habitus"), suggesting that humans develop unconscious strategies that are not rational but act at a much more fundamental bodily level, and are adapted to the requirements of the social worlds around them (Bourdieu, 1990).

But we saw in Chapter 2 that human systems involve systems of interrelationships and develop over and above the individuals within the system. Stacey (2001, 2003, amongst others), for example, developed the theories of Complex Responsive Processes of Relating, looking at complex systems of relationships as humans communicate, negotiate power, status and politics, and work in joint action towards overlapping goals; and how these relationships form part of (and are influenced by) the wider organizational system, and how organizations emerge from these human complex responsive processes of relating, and also how the individual's self-identity is influenced by them. So, we often need to include within our view of the problem setting – if not within the analysis itself – our "understanding of the actors' moral and ethical motives (practical reason) and their sense-making processes (enactment) and how their actions unfold over time and in connection with other, multiple events; the experience of emotions and feelings that drive action in complex environments; closer insight into intentions, political agendas and personal drives of individual actors; and the identification of tensions, power asymmetries and patterns of communicative relating among individuals and groups and how they are being negotiated in the context" (Cicmil *et al.*, 2006).

Indeed, a key example Schön (1983) uses to illustrate the change in the professions as a whole is, remarkably, our own profession – OR/MS. He notes briefly how OR/MS arose, and says that: "By the late 1960s, there was scarcely a described problem for which someone had not constructed a computerized model. But," he goes on, "in recent years there has been a widening consensus . . . that the early hopes were greatly inflated" and he claims that, while "formal models have been usefully employed" in the easily quantified areas, "they have generally failed to yield effective results in the more complex, less clearly defined problems of business management, housing policy, or criminal justice". A challenge to our profession, indeed! There is clearly some truth in the charge, and indeed it was reflected in some of our discussion in Chapter 11. So, how does Schön propose that we respond to such failings?

Schön concludes that the model of Technical Rationality is insufficient, and professionals in complex situations show tacit "knowing-in-action". We mentioned in Chapter 2 that Polanyi (1962) established the idea of our "knowing" being internal and personal, or "tacit" (and not necessarily easy to codify) as opposed to "explicit" knowledge, which can expressed and shared in highly specified formats, and it is clear that much of our "knowing", everyday as well as professional, is of this "tacit" variety. And we can recognize, too, that we learn from our activities and our tacit knowledge improves (think of riding a bicycle, for example). But the professional reflects in a more conscious way on his practice, as s/he comes across complex situations that are unique but of a type that will have similarities to situations the practitioner has seen – and resolved – before. "Sometimes," says Schön about practitioners, "in the relative tranquility of a postmortem, they think back on a project they have lived through, and they explore the understandings they have brought to their handling of the case." Practitioners, he says, also reflect in the midst of their practice, as surely the Management Scientist must do as s/he faces a web of interacting complex effects. Further, "a practitioner's reflection can serve as a correction to over-learning. Through reflection, he can surface and criticize the tacit understandings that have grown up around the repetitive experiences of a specialized practice and can make new sense of the situations of uncertainty or uniqueness which he may allow himself to experience." In these various ways, our reflection upon our practice leads us to understand and move forward in our practice; "practical knowledge is the 'realm of tacit knowing' that can become explicit through 'reflective inquiry'" (Lallé, 2003). (This is perhaps a fairly loose use of the word "tacit", but the point is well-made.)

We do not have space in this book for a full discussion of these ideas, but what can we conclude about the implications? We're going to look at a number of difference aspects, which can come roughly under three headings: practice, research and teaching.

13.2   The implications for practice

13.2.1   A process for self-reflection

What is the situation a practitioner finds him/herself in during an intervention? "In a practitioner's reflective conversation with a situation that he treats as unique and uncertain, he functions as an agent/experient. Through his transaction with the situation, he shapes it and makes himself a part of it. Hence, the sense he makes of the situation must include his own contribution to it. Yet he recognizes that the situation, having a life of its own distinct from his intentions, may foil his projects and reveal new meanings" Schön (1983). Therefore, says Schön in a nice phrase, the practitioner must "impose an order of his own, jumping rather than falling into his transaction with the situation" – but this is not a one-way relationship. Rather, "at the same time that the inquirer tries to shape the situation to his frame, he must hold himself open to the situation's back-talk. He must be willing to enter into new confusions and uncertainties." Following on, in a nice reflection of our Chapter 6: "he must act in accordance with the view he has adopted, but he must recognize that he can always break it open later, indeed, must break it open later in order to make new sense of his transaction with the situation."

So, as we intervene, we need to reflect on that intervention and continue that reflection as it unfolds. Indeed, the Operational Research veteran Gass (1994) would say that it is inconceivable that any OR/MS practitioner would conduct an intervention without such self-reflection. However, the reflection needs to be (a) critical and (b) systematized (Midgley, 1995). It needs to look from many angles with as few pre-conceptions as possible, evaluating the effectiveness and usefulness of the work. But we particularly need a *process* of reflection. One useful suggestion for developing a process might be from Gregory (1994), who looks at reflection in four aspects: reflection about one's own assumptions, ideology critique (about assumptions at the level of society), empirical experimental observation of the world, and hermeneutic inquiry (two-way communication with others). Key here, as we have stressed in this chapter and in Chapter 2, is reflecting not so much on the content of the problem as on the process of our intervention.

We are not specifying a pre-defined process here – but it does need to be planned and conscious. Some find it useful to involve others within the intervention: "In Ulrich's thinking [see e.g. Ulrich, 1983], the process of critical self-reflection is not wholly monological – it is not just a discussion that happens in one's own mind. It is *dialogical* – involving an exploration of relationships between one's own thinking and that of others" (Midgley, 1995).

Furthermore, the process of self-reflection does not stop at the end of an intervention, but continues between interventions as we reflect on what has happened and the "final result" (insofar that any intervention has a "final" ending). It is by such critical self-reflection that we see how our practice has operated within the problem-situation, and we learn for the next intervention.

In a complex problem-setting, interventions are not simply the smooth application of known techniques, but are rather "reflective conversations" with a situation. Reflection on our practice, looking for the "situation's back-talk", and continuous learning, can enhance our preparedness and enable us to "jump rather than fall" into the intervention.

13.2.2 The client process

"Just as reflective practice takes the form of a reflective conversation with the situation," says Schön (1983), "so the reflective practitioner's relationship with his client takes the form of a literally reflective relationship" with that client. Thus we have come to the conclusion that we reached in Chapter 2 (following the terms in Eden & Sims, 1979) – that when we intervene into a problem-situation, normally the more effective mode of engagement is a negotiative approach, in which the analyst negotiates with the participants to gain a view of reality and problem definition. As we mentioned in that chapter, Schön (1983) describes interventions by an architect and a psychoanalyst thus: "These inquirers encounter a problematic situation whose reality they must construct. As they frame the problem of the situation, they determine the features to which they will attend, the order they will attempt to impose on the situation, the directions in which they will try to change it. In this process, they identify both the ends to be sought and the means to be employed. In the ensuing inquiry, action on the situation is integral with deciding. . . ."

An analyst's claim to authority is, then, again says Schön (1983) "based on his ability to manifest his special knowledge in his interactions with the clients. He does not ask the client to have blind faith in a 'black box', but to remain open to the evidence of the practitioner's competence as it emerges." We do not face our client as an expert does to a lay-person; but nor do we act merely as a facilitator, bringing the client's expertise and knowledge out into the open. As we develop a reflective relationship with the client, as we described in Chapter 11, we act as co-producers or co-creators of the outcome of the intervention (which is why we described trust as being at the heart of this relationship in that chapter).

Indeed, the word "client" is perhaps an inappropriate word in this sort of partnership relationship. Certainly, our contractual mechanisms do seem to have difficulty describing work within such a relationship. Schön (1983) moots the idea of a "reflective contract between practitioner and client". Since this is so much at the heart of the OR/MS client relationship, perhaps our profession will lead the way in developing more appropriate contracts, to deal with the issues about preparing proposals and contracts that we dealt with in Chapter 6. Certainly the language of "strategic partnerships", "partnering contracts" and so on is more prevalent these days, but there is still a long way to go in this area.

13.2.3 Innovation

Just as the nature of OR/MS as a reflective discipline colours, indeed to some extent defines, the client relationship, it is also a useful aid to innovation for the analyst. The generic mechanisms to initiate the analytical processes, described in Chapter 9, resulted from past analysts reflecting on studies to gain generic structures that seemed useful. In reflecting on our past modelling, and our previous interventions, we can see similarities or commonalities of structure that can be utilized in our current intervention. And of course, following the last point, as we saw also in Chapter 9, the collaboration and dialogue with the client within a reflective relationship provides a vital part of the creative dynamic for the analysis, as the analyst relates his or her dialogue with the client to his or her previous experience. Then, reflecting with our client-group on our practice can provide an impetus to innovation and further development.

13.2.4 Professional development

Indeed, reflecting upon our practice does not just develop our repertoire of models, it is the basis of our development as a practitioner in many ways. To take one example, in Chapter 12 about our ethical development we discussed Taket's (1994) view based on "ethical reflection" – that being based around four elements, the first of which is "undertaking a process of critical/ethical self-reflection". It is by critically reflecting upon each intervention with our practice that we can evaluate our modelling, our problem-definition, our understanding at the proposal stage, our work-planning, our interactions with the various people within the client organization, our comprehension of the client's social geography, our professionalism, our actions in response to changes in the situation or the client's views or requirements, the benefit we've brought to the client, the effectiveness of our work, the reasons for eventual implementation (or lack of implementation) and so on.

> Management Science is a reflective practice, and this determines the nature of our relationship with the client, and our ability to act creatively in an unfamiliar situation. A planned reflection upon both individual interventions and our past history of work allows us to develop and grow as practitioners.

13.3 The implications for research

The idea in some quarters of OR/MS being simply a technical discipline that a practitioner carries out routinely leads inevitably to the idea that "research" and "practice" are two quite different arenas, and we find a division growing up between "researchers" and "practitioners". Schön (1983) sees this in many professions, and the implications are serious: "Practitioners and researchers tend increasingly to live in different worlds, pursue different enterprises, and have little to say to each other." This can happen with OR/MS – indeed we looked in Chapter 1 at the gap between the "OR community" and the "management community" (Corbett and van Wassenhove, 1993). But because real-life Management Science practice is by necessity reflective, this helps to bring research and practitioner closer together – indeed, good research and good practice are by definition brought closer together – in a number of ways.

From the point of view of the practice side of the relationship first, "on this perspective, research is an activity of practitioners. It is triggered by features of the practice situation, undertaken on the spot, and immediately linked to action" Schön (1983). Because the practitioner needs to reflect on the situation, and make sense of a complex situation, s/he is immediately undertaking research and producing innovative ideas. But perhaps even more so, practitioners can think about their interventions and reflect upon them, since the interventions are always new and unique in some aspects, and when you reflect upon a series of interventions you can often see patterns and draw out generic conclusions – often the generalized theory and insights coming serendipitously (i.e. you didn't set out to discover something general, but it arose from the study you did). One example we've discussed in this book was the series of assignments that followed the "*Shuttle* wagon" example (see Section 9.4): this was a series of pieces of professional consultancy, reflecting on which also provided a lot of research output, concerning aspects such as the nature of large projects and how to model them, hard and soft methods and their synergy, learning curves, the use of cognitive mapping as a knowledge repository, as well as a research contract (as noted previously, the story is told in Williams *et al.*, 2005). Then, reflecting at a deeper level on the implications of all this work led to interesting research in the underlying philosophy of project management (Williams, 2005).

Indeed, it is an essential part of the discipline that practitioners have to be researchers too: the "R" in "OR" is research, and true OR/MS professionals are involved in research all the time. Once a method is systemized, or original modelling work is no longer needed, the work can be handed over to a client organizer and the analyst moves on. As the Commission found in its study of 1986 (Mitchell, 1986), the practice of OR is ever-changing. The main reasons given for this continual state of transformation are the "migration of subject matter and methods to other activities and the dissemination of OR methods to other disciplines", while the envisaged future for OR is summed up by "a future of continuing change" – practitioners must research and develop new methods as part of the ongoing development of the field. Indeed, the need for the subject to develop and grow in response to client needs was one of the arguments forcibly put against professional membership in the debate within the UK OR Society in 1996.

From the point of view of the research side of the relationship, performing reflective practice implies new research if – and probably only if – we can change traditional research paradigms. These changes are discussed, for example, by Calori (2002), who wants to be involved in building theories that include understanding of moral motives, of emotions and feelings that drive behaviour, of intentions, desires and political agendas, and of tensions between the actors, and particularly of actors' sense-making before and during actions. He looks at research in which "the time-space of the researcher and the time-space of the researched overlap, and in which action and reflection are intimately connected through fusion or cooperation", involving "reflective practitioners and pragmatic researchers who get involved together in theory building" – or to put it another way, taking a phrase from the film *The Matrix*, "the researcher and the researched 'walk the path together' and try to reach a mutual understanding". This is a quite different way of researching than conventional ideas of what research is, where the researcher studies the situation from outside, and there is a distance between the researcher and the researched.

This research approach differs from the reflection on practice and serendipitous arrival at generalized insights and theory, in being a pre-planned active desire to research alongside a practical intervention. A well-known approach to this type of research is known as "action research", a well-regarded exposition of which is given by Eden and Huxham (2006). This looks at the researcher embedded within an organization, stressing (quoting from Adler & Adler, 1987) the need to be a "complete member researcher" – or, as they put it, the need for the researcher to " 'go native' in a manner that does not match the role of an action researcher as facilitator/consultant". Rather than define action research in a limiting way, in their paper they outline 15 characteristics of this type of research. In summary, such research requires both an involvement by the researcher with an organization over matters of genuine concern and a research agenda to look at implications beyond that intervention – although this agenda and the objective of the intervention might be different; it looks to incrementally developing theory emerging from the data and the experience of the intervention (rather than simply improving tools and techniques); their characteristics also include indicators of good thorough research

– orderliness, validity, replicability (or at least explicability) and triangulation (which was the context in which we discussed action research in Chapter 7).

A similar approach is contained in the concept of "Action Science" (Argyris, Putnam & Smith, 1985); a key stress here is to use the research process to encourage participants to undertake an "internal critique of [their] own practical reasoning" (Putnam, 1999). A similar, more embedded, idea is that of "actor-researchers" (Lallé, 2003), who work within an organization; here the key is for the actor-researchers to "analyse themselves in the process of acting" – raising issues of reflexivity (as the actor-researcher analyses his or her own position and actions in the organization) and complexity.

And it is this complexity that means that the reflection is so important. Cicmil *et al.*, (2006), talking about one particular management domain, say that: "In conceptualizing such an inquiry, researchers typically engage in a reflective deliberation about theoretical traditions that address the issues of management as social conduct in the above outlined way, which results in pragmatic philosophical considerations of the issues such as complexity, power, intuition, decision making, collaborative working, learning and communication, and the relationship between agency and structure in the local context. This represents a shift from a model-based, instrumental approach to researching . . . towards a praxis-based theory and research. The former produces universal theory which, while sound, is not always useful in the specific context of application. The latter focuses on the empirical reality . . . by taking into account different contexts . . . thus addressing complexity, non-linearity, values, multiple perspectives and social processes. . . ."

These and other approaches to management research do represent a move away from conventional research paradigms, even though, as we said above, they do include indicators of good thorough research. But there is an increasing realization of the need for new methods and new ideas of research, both because of the changing nature of the problems being researched and their underlying complexity, as we have discussed throughout this book, but also because of the increasing need for knowledge as it works in practice, in the context of application, rather than theory for its own sake – what has been termed "Mode II research" rather than conventional Mode I research (Starkey & Madan, 2001).

All of the above also implies a change in the relationship between the university academic and the "real" world of the practitioner. As we suggested in

Chapter 1, and have continued here, old ideas of the "academic" who studies and extends the subject and the "practitioner" who applies it are insufficient for Management Science. It is difficult to be a good practitioner without some element of research and reflection; on the other side, rather than academic research simply feeding into practice, historically and currently much of the best research has come about from the reverse process: "research" in the classic sense of real studies giving rise, sometimes serendipitously, to generalized theory and insights (Williams, 1999). What we need is a bringing-together of the roles of the "academic" and the "researcher". Schön (1983) concluded the need in general for a merging of these roles and a tighter partnership between research and practice institutions. Lallé's "actor-researcher" for example is neither of these – s/he fulfils both roles. Starkey and Madan (2001) therefore call for restructuring of academic institutions and the academic–practice interfaces to improve the partnership and promote and speed up knowledge flow between them.

> There should not be pure researchers or pure practitioners. The reflective nature of Management Science and the complexity of our domain of interest mean that "practitioners" reflect on their actions, and on a series of interventions, producing general insights; and "researchers" have to devise ways to embed themselves within practice to generate research findings. While this might require a change to how we think of research, this "Mode II" research promises to produce useful developments for our discipline.

13.4 The implications for teaching

The conclusions for academic research are mirrored in the conclusions for university teaching of Management Science. If our development as Management Scientists depends so heavily on reflection, then as well as teaching the various tools and techniques, our teaching has to develop students by allowing them to reflect on real situations (or at least simulacra of real situations). Reflection becomes the basis for much adult education. Boud, Keogh and Walker (1985), for example, explore what is meant by reflection in learning. They point, for example, to Mezirow (1981) (based on Habermas' work), who describes various aspects of what he calls "critical reflectivity": "affective reflectivity" describes reflecting on how we feel about a situation; perhaps more relevant, in the light of Chapter 12, "judgemental reflectivity" describes reflection on our value judgements; more relevant is "discriminant reflectivity", looking for causes and effects – reflecting on our practice to see what actually happens and the effectiveness of our perceptions and actions; perhaps particularly worth considering is "theoretical reflectivity", coming to the realization that our taken-for-granted assumptions about the complex world in which operate are not adequate to explain our experience satisfactorily. Boud, Keogh and Walker then explore how this meaning needs to be reflected in planning education.

Unlike straightforward teaching, the inculcation of Management Science by experiential methods requires the student to act and reflect on what s/he has done, to ensure his/her gradual improvement as an analyst – otherwise the exercise is pointless. People learn, through their experience, the rules and principles that will guide their behaviour in certain situations. A very simple model to represent this ability to learn through experience and reflection has been described by Kolb (1984) as a learning cycle with four stages (see Figure 13.1).

In the first stage of the cycle, concrete experiences, the student will use their previous experience as a starting point, trying out various ideas that they already have knowledge about. As they move on to the second stage, reflective observations, they will reflect on their actions noting their implications – they

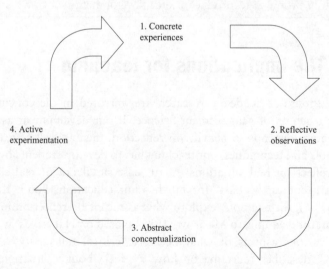

Figure 13.1 The Kolb learning cycle (taken from Kolb, 1984)

should "become an observer of their own thinking and acting" (Senge *et al.*, 1994). In the third stage, the student would conceptualize these observations into general abstract concepts for future use, and perhaps also research a wider knowledge base that could inform their understanding, which may allow growth in their area of expertise, perhaps bringing new methods and skills to light that would influence their approach. Finally, in the last stage, the student would use these new insights and skills to test their approach, allowing experimentation. They will continue round this learning cycle until a clear understanding is reached, reflecting as they go on the knowledge they may have gained and its use in different situations.

The Kolb learning cycle is well-known and used widely in management teaching (e.g. Reynolds, 1998). In particular, it has been used to demonstrate the usefulness of experiential learning techniques when learning about OR by Scott (1990), who also describes different types of technique of learning for different points in the cycle. That is, using his terms:

- *divergent* techniques in moving from concrete experiences to reflecting upon them (which promote creative, divergent thought: brain-storming is an example);
- *assimilation* structuring techniques (influence-diagrams, mind-mapping, hypothesis-forming etc.);
- *convergence* techniques as the student moves on to those areas in which to experiment, and;
- *accommodation* techniques to make use of the gained knowledge.

Williams and Dickson (2000) describe work within a well-known Master's course in Operational Research to strengthen this process of moving from concrete experiences to abstract conceptualization. They describe "experiential learning" sessions, and particularly an exercise as part of the students' three-month practical summer project, a requirement to write a "Reflections" section in their dissertation as an aid to allow the student to express his/her thoughts and experiences of working on the project to help to force his/her round steps 2 and 3 of the learning cycle. Students are asked to consider such issues as: the project context and client organization, the process of (possibly changing) problem definition, the relationship with the client or end user, the role of OR/MS in the project and the lessons learnt about OR methodology, difficulties in the execution of the project, things that could have been done or done differently, and so on. The particular importance of the three-month practical summer project – which forms part of most UK OR/MS MSc courses

– is that it allows the student to become embedded in a situation with all of the dynamic and behavioural complexity of a real organization, which it is difficult if not impossible to replicate in the classroom.

But there is a further, more difficult, aspect to OR/MS education. In order to enable lifelong development, we need to promote the discipline of reflection, to help students to reflect on their future interventions – particularly as intervention situations provided within a classroom situation or even in a student project have some degree of artificiality about them, and their reflections will be more valuable when based on interventions taken in their professional life. Thus, all of the aspects of this chapter have to form part of the learning process. The reflections provided within an OR/MS education should not been seen as there simply to provide the insights that come from reflecting on the experiences, but they should be seen as training in *how* to reflect and to help provide a process for self-reflection.

All this implies that academics who are not experienced in their craft – or who do not go outside to practice their craft – are not OR/MS academics, even if they come under that title. OR/MS is only OR/MS when motivated either to solve real problems, or to develop tools known to be needed to solve real problems. Teachers of OR/MS need to have experienced the complexities of the realities Management Scientists try to solve, and have wrestled with the need to be creative, to bring structure to a disorganized situation, and to have reflected and developed as an analyst from that reflection – to put it crudely, they should have under their belt experience of that for which they are preparing their students.

> Our development as Management Scientists depends heavily on reflection. Therefore, as well as teaching the various tools and techniques, our teaching has to develop students by allowing them to reflect on situations as close to real-life as possible. But also, in order to enable lifelong development, we need to help students to learn how to reflect on their future interventions.

The Final Note: The Future

In the last chapter, we came back to the same place as in Chapter 1 and thus in one sense our book has come full circle. So, what now about the future? Where is Management Science going?

We have made a variety of optimistic and pessimistic comments throughout this book. But our general outlook now has to be optimistic. Abdel-Malek *et al.*'s (1999) survey, which we quoted in Chapter 11, concluded that "the inferred feeling of the practising segment of the community is that OR is growing, has its problems, but is evolving and changing."

OR/MS clearly has leading successes. There are around 400 analysts in the UK central government (excluding the defence arena), badged under "Operational Research" (GORS, 2008), and OR analysts at the "Prime Minister's Delivery Unit" regularly brief the UK Prime Minister. There are more than that number of analysts in the government's defence laboratory (the Defence Science and Technology Laboratory, dstl, formed in 2001 after a large proportion of defence work – including a number of OR analysts – was split off into a new public–private partnership). Forder (2004) reports that OR "is undoubtedly a thriving element in the support that the defence science community provides to the UK Ministry of Defence. Its buoyancy in the face of reducing defence budgets over the past decade arises from a number of factors," including "the profound changes in the strategic environment, which have increased uncertainty in defence planning and widened the range of contingencies and issues to be examined." Similar developments – although with, of course, much smaller bodies of analysts – are in the civil world. The continuing success of work displayed in the US "Edelman" prize competition, the European "EURO Excellence in Practice" awards and the UK OR Society "Goodeve medal" competition shows that there is much excellent practice making a real difference to our world today.

But the *phrase* "Management Science" – or "Operational Research" – may be less visible than its success. Indeed, Pidd (2001), in his Presidential Address to the OR Society, to which we referred in Chapter 1, talked about "the paradox of contemporary OR. We are successful and yet almost invisible. There is great demand for the skills and approaches that we offer, but much of this work is not labelled as OR. The scenario identified as absorption by the OR Society's Commission on the Future Practice of OR, but thought by it to be unlikely [see Chapter 11], has crept up on many of us by stealth. Of course there are exceptions, including those OR groups . . . that continue to thrive and are clearly identifiable as OR. Yet most jobs requiring our skills and insights are not labelled as OR."

So, Management Science has found two roles. One lies within Operational Research or Management Science analysts who declare themselves to be as such. But the ability to comprehend and analyse the complex situations found within modern management is fundamental to being able to operate within management, and so Management Science – properly understood and properly practised – has become the foundation discipline underlying all other management disciplines. And this is even more true as the business world becomes more complex, and continuous new trends – such as e-business – arise and need to be understood and incorporated. I hope that this book has helped to explain the discipline and outline its main aspects. Good practising!

References

Abdel-Malek, L., Wolf, C., Johnson, F. and Spencer, T. (1999) OR practice: survey results and reflections of practising INFORMS members. *Journal of the Operational Research Society* **50**, 994–1003.

Ackermann, F., Eden, C. and Brown, I. (2005) *The Practice of Making Strategy: A Step-by-Step Guide*. London: Sage.

Ackermann, F., Eden, C. and Williams, T. (1997) Modelling for litigation: mixing qualitative and quantitative approaches. *Interfaces* **27**, 48–65.

Ackoff, R. (1967) Management misinformation systems. *Management Science* **14**, 147–156.

Ackoff, R. (1974) *Redesigning the Future: A Systems Approach to Societal Planning*. New York: John Wiley & Sons, Inc.

Ackoff, R. (1979a) The future of OR is past. *Journal of the Operational Research Society* **30**, 93–103.

Ackoff, R. (1979b) Resurrecting the future of Operational Research. *Journal of the Operational Research Society* **30**, 189–199.

Ackoff, R. and Emery, F. (1972) *On Purposeful Systems*. London: Tavistock Publications.

Adler, P. A. and Adler, P. (1987) *Membership Roles in Field Research*. Newbury Park, CA: Sage Publications.

Altschuler, S., Batavia, D., Bennett, J., Labe, R., Liao, B., Nigam, R. and Oh, J. (2002) Pricing analysis for Merrill Lynch integrated choice. *Interfaces* **32**, 5–19.

Alvesson, M. and Deetz, S. (2000) *Doing Critical Management Research*. London: Sage.

Anderson, J. (1987) An approach for confirmatory measurement and structural equation modeling of organizational properties. *Management Science* 33, 525–542.

Argyris, C., Putnam, R. and Smith, D. (1985) *Action Science*. San Francisco: Jossey-Bass.

Ashby, R. (1956) *An Introduction to Cybernetics*. London: Chapman and Hall.

Association for Logic Programming (2007) url: http://www.cs.kuleuven.be/~dtai/projects/ALP/ (accessed: 2007).

Atkinson, C. and Checkland, P. (1988) Extending the metaphor "System". *Human Relations* 41, 709–725.

Banxia (2006) *Decision Explorer*, url: http://www.banxia.com/demain.html (accessed: 2006).

Barabba, V. (1994) The role of models in managerial decision-making – never say the model says. In: Wallace, W. (ed.), *Ethics in Modelling*, pp. 145–160. Oxford, UK: Elsevier Science Ltd.

Barnes, J. (1984) Cognitive biases and their impact on strategic planning. *Strategic Management Journal* 5, 129–137.

Beam, C. (2004) ASP, The Art and Science of Practice: How I started an OR/MS consulting practice with a laptop, a phone, and a PhD. *Interfaces* 34, 4, 265–271.

Bedford, T. and Cooke, R. (2001) *Probabilistic Risk Analysis: Foundations and Methods*. Cambridge, UK: Cambridge University Press.

Beer, S. (1959) *Cybernetics and Management*. London: English Universities Press.

Beer, S. (1966) *Decision and Control*. London: John Wiley & Sons, Ltd.

Beer, S. (1985) *Diagnosing the System for Organisations*. London: John Wiley & Sons, Ltd.

Belbin, R. M. (1993) *Team Roles at Work*. Oxford, UK: Butterworth-Heinemann.

Belbin, R. M. (2008) Belbin Team Role Summary Descriptions, url: http://www.belbin.com/downloads/Belbin_Team_Role_Summary_Descriptions.pdf (accessed: 2008).

Bell, P. (1998) Strategic operational research. *Journal of the Operational Research Society* 49, 381–391.

Belton, V. and Stewart, T. (2001) *Multiple Criteria Decision Analysis: An Integrated Approach*. Amsterdam: Kluwer Academic Publishers.

Bennett, J. and Worthington, D. (1998) An example of good but partially successful OR engagement: improving outpatient clinic operations. *Interfaces* 28, 56–69.

Bennett, P. (1980) Hypergames: developing a model of conflict. *Futures* 12, 489–507.

Bennett, P. (1994) The changing face of OR practice in the UK: present indicators and possible futures. *International Transactions in Operational Research* 1, 197–208.

Bennett, P., Ackermann, F., Eden, C. and Williams, T. (1997) Analysing litigation and negotiation: a case study of combined methodology. In: Mingers, J. and Gill, A. (eds), *Multi-Methodology: The Theory and Practice of Combining Management Science Methodologies*. Chichester, UK: John Wiley & Sons, Ltd.

Bereiter, C. and Scardamalia, M. (1987) *The Psychology of Written Communication*. Hillsdale, NJ: Erlbaum.

Berger, P. and Luckmann, T. (1966) *The Social Construction of Reality*. New York: Doubleday.

Blackett, P. (1950) Operational Research. *Operational Research Quarterly* 1, 3–6.

Bornstein, C. and Rosenhead, J. (1990) The role of operational research in less developed countries: A critical approach. *European Journal of Operational Research* 49, 56–178.

Boud, D., Keogh, R. and Walker, D. (1985) Promoting reflection in learning: a model. In: Boud, D., Keogh, R. and Walker, D. (eds), *Reflection: Turning Experience into Learning*, pp. 18–40. New York: Kogan Page.

Bourdieu, P. (1990) *The Logic of Practice*. Cambridge, UK: Polity Press.

Brennan, M. and Trigeorgis, L. (2000) *Project Flexibility, Agency, and Competition: New Developments in the Theory and Application of Real Options*. Oxford, UK: Oxford University Press.

Brown, J. S. and Duguid, P. (1991) Organizational learning and communities-of-practice: toward a unified view of working, learning and innovation. *Organization Science* 2, 40–57.

Brucker, P. (2007) *Scheduling Algorithms*. Berlin: Springer-Verlag.

Bryant, J. (1988) Frameworks of inquiry: OR practice across the hard–soft divide. *Journal of the Operational Research Society* 49, 423–435.

Bryant, J. (2003) *The Six Dilemmas of Collaboration: Interorganisational Relationships as Drama*, Chichester, UK: John Wiley & Sons, Ltd.

Bryant, J. (2007) Drama theory: dispelling the myths. *Journal of the Operational Research Society* 58, 602–613.

Bryson J., Ackermann F., Eden, C. and Finn, C. (2004) *Visible Thinking: Unlocking Causal Mapping for Practical Business Results*. Chichester, UK: John Wiley & Sons, Ltd.

Buchanan, D. and Boddy, D. (1992) *The Expertise of the Change Agent: Public Performance and Backstage Activity*. Englewood Cliffs, NJ: Prentice Hall.

Burke, E. and Kendall, G. (2005) *Introductory Tutorials in Optimization and Decision Support Techniques*. Berlin: Springer-Verlag.

Burrell, G. (1989) Post modernism: threat or opportunity. In: Jackson, M., Keys, P. and Cropper, S. (eds), *Operational Research and the Social Sciences*. London: Plenum.

Busby, J. (1999) The effectiveness of collective retrospection as a mechanism of organizational learning. *The Journal of Applied Behavioral Science* 35, 109–129.

Butler, J. C., Chebeskov, A. N., Dyer, J. S., Edmunds, T. A., Jianmin, J. and Oussanov, V. I. (2005) The United States and Russia Evaluate Plutonium Disposition Options with Multiattribute Utility Theory. *Interfaces* 35, 88–101.

Buzan, T. (2003) *The Mind Map Book: Radiant Thinking – Major Evolution in Human Thought*. London: BBC Consumer Publishing (Books).

C+ Editors (2000) II Testing for creativity and related psychology concepts. *Creativity Plus* 2.

Calori, R. (2002) Essai: Real-time/real-space research: connecting action and reflection in organization studies. *Organization Studies* 23, 877–883.

Cavaleri, S. and Sterman, J. (1997) Towards evaluation of systems thinking interventions: a case study. *Systems Dynamics Review* 13, 171–186.

Chapman, C. and Ward, S. (2002) *Managing Project Risks and Uncertainty: A Constructively Simple Approach to Decision Making.* Chichester, UK: John Wiley & Sons, Ltd.

Checkland, P. (1975) The development of systems thinking by systems practice – a methodology from an action research programme. In: Trap, R. and Hanika, F. D. P. (eds), *Progress in Cybernetics and Systems Research*, Vol II. Washington: Hemisphere Publications.

Checkland, P. (1981) *Systems Thinking, Systems Practice.* Chichester, UK: John Wiley & Sons, Ltd.

Checkland, P. (1999) *Soft Systems Methodology: A 30-year Retrospective.* Chichester, UK: John Wiley & Sons, Ltd. Published with the reprinted *Systems Thinking, Systems Practice.*

Checkland, P. and Holwell, S. (1998) *Information, Systems and Information Systems.* Chichester, UK: John Wiley & Sons, Ltd.

Checkland, P. and Scholes, J. (1990) *Soft Systems Methodology in Action.* Chichester, UK: John Wiley & Sons, Ltd.

Cicmil, S. and Hodgson, D. (2006) New possibilities for project management theory: a critical engagement. PMI Research Conference, Newtown Square, PA: Project Management Institute.

Cicmil, S., Williams, T., Thomas, J. and Hodgson, D. (2006) Rethinking Project Management: Researching the Actuality of Projects. *International Journal of Project Management* 24, 675–686.

Clark, D. and Scott, J. (1995) Strategic-level MS/OR tool usage in the United Kingdom: an empirical survey. *Journal of the Operational Research Society* 46, 1041–1051.

Collins English Dictionary (1986) *Second edition*, London: William Collins Sons & Co. Ltd.

Collins, J. and Hussey, R. (2003) *Business Research: A Practical Guide for Undergraduate and Postgraduate Students.* Basingstoke, UK: Palgrave Macmillan.

Comte, A. (1853) *The Positive Philosophy of Auguste Comte.* London: Chapman.

CONDOR (1988) Forces, trends and opportunities in MS/OR. *Operations Research* 36, 619–637.

Connell, N., Klein, J. H. and Meyer, E. (2004) Narrative approaches to the transfer of organisational knowledge. *Knowledge Management Research and Practice* 2, 184–193.

Cooke, R. (1991) *Experts in Uncertainty: Opinion and Subjective Probability in Science.* New York: Oxford University Press Inc.

Cooper, R. and Burrell, C. (1989) Modernism, post-modernism and organisational analysis: an introduction. *Organizational Studies* **9**, 91–112.

Cooper, W., Seiford, L. and Tone, K. (2006) *Data Envelopment Analysis: A Comprehensive Text with Models, Applications, References and DEA-solver Software*. New York: Springer-Verlag.

Corbett, C. and van Wassenhove, L. (1993) The natural drift: what happened to operations research? *Operations Research* **41**, 625–639.

Cronbach, L. J. (1951) Coefficient alpha and the internal structure of tests. *Psychometrica* **16**, 297–334.

Cropper, S. (1990) The complexity of decision support practice. In: Eden, C. and Radford, J. (eds), *Tackling Strategic Problems*, pp. 29–39. London: Sage.

Csiksznetmihalyi, M. (1996) *Psychology of Discovery and Invention*. New York: Harper Collins.

Dando, M. and Sharp, R. (1978) Operational Research in the UK in 1977: the causes and consequences of a myth. *Journal of the Operational Research Society* **29**, 939–949.

Degraeve, Z. and Schrage, L. (1998) HOP: A software tool for production scheduling at Bridgestone/Firestone Off-The-Road. *European Journal of Operational Research* **110**, 188–198.

Del Rosairo, E. (1994) OR brews success for San Miguel. *OR/MS Today* **21**, 24–30.

Denzin, N. (1989) *The Research Act*. Englewood Cliffs, NJ: Prentice Hall.

Doyle, J. (1997) The cognitive psychology of systems thinking. *Systems Dynamics Review* **13**, 253–265.

Drucker, P. (1974) *Management: Tasks Responsibilities and Priorities*. London: Heinemann.

Easterby-Smith, M., Thorpe, R. and Lowe, A. (1991) *Management Research: An Introduction*. London: Sage.

Edelman (2006) Annual Edelman Trust Barometer. A special supplement to *PR Week* (also available on http://www.edelman.com/image/insights/content/FullSupplement. pdf).

Edelman (2007) Edelman Trust Barometer 2007 url: http://www.slideshare.net/ edelman.milan/edelman-trust-barometer-2007/ (accessed: 2008).

Eden, C. (1982) Problem construction and the influence of OR. *Interfaces* **12**, 50–60.

Eden, C. (1987) Problem-solving or problem-finishing. In: Jackson, J. and Keys, P. (eds), *New Directions in Management Science*. Aldershot, UK: Gower.

Eden, C. (1988) Cognitive mapping: a review. *European Journal of Operational Research* **36**, 1–13.

Eden, C. and Ackermann, F. (1992) Strategic development and implementation – the role of a group decision support system. In: Kinney, S., Bostrom, R. and Watson, R. (eds), *Computer Augmented Teamwork: A Guided Tour*, pp. 325–343. London: Sage.

Eden, C. and Ackermann, F. (1998) *Making Strategy: The Journey of Strategic Management*. London: Sage.

Eden, C. and Ackermann, F. (2001) SODA – The Principles. In: Rosenhead, J. and Mingers, J. (eds), *Rational Analysis in a Problematic World Revisited*, pp. 21–42. London: John Wiley & Sons, Ltd.

Eden, C. and Huxham, C. (2006) Researching organizations using action research. In: Clegg, S., Hardy, C., Nord, W. and Lawrence, T. (eds), *Handbook of Organisation Studies*, 2nd edn. Beverley Hills: Sage.

Eden, C. and Sims, D. (1979) On the nature of problems in consulting practice. *Omega: the International Journal of Management Science* 7, 119–127.

Edwards, W. (1977) How to use multiattribute utility measurement for social decision-making. *IEEE Transactions in Systems, Management and Cybernetics* 7, 326–340.

Edwards, W. and Barton, F. (1994) Smarts and smarter: Improved simple methods for multi-attribute utility measurement. *Organizational Behavior and Human Decision Processes* **60**, 306–325.

Eilon, S. (1980) The role of management science. *Journal of the Operational Research Society* 31, 17–28.

Eilon, S. (1998) To charge or not to charge? *Journal of the Operational Research Society* 49, 396–402.

Eisenhardt, K. (1990) Speed and strategic choice: how managers accelerate decision-making. *California Management Review* 32, 39–54.

Ellsberg, D. (1961) Risk, ambiguity and the Savage axioms. *Quarterly Journal of Economics* 75, 643–699.

EPSRC (2004) *Review of Research Status of Operational Research in the UK*. Swindon, UK: Engineering and Physical Science Research Council/Economic and Social Research Council.

Ericsson, K. and Simon, H. (1993) *Protocol Analysis: Verbal Reports as Data*, Cambridge, MA: MIT Press.

Espejo, R., Schuhmann, W., Schwaninger, M. and Bilello, U. (1996) *Organisational Transformation and Learning: A Cybernetic Approach to Management*. Chichester, UK: John Wiley & Sons, Ltd.

Euro (2005) EURO Excellence in Practice Award Laureates, url: www.euro-online.org/display.php?page=bap4& (accessed: 2005).

Evans, J. (1993) Creativity in MS/OR: the multiple dimensions of creativity. *Interfaces* 23, 80–83.

Fang, L., Hipel, K. and Kilgour, D. (1993) *Interactive Decision Making: The Graph Model for Conflict Resolution*. New York: John Wiley & Sons, Inc.

Feldman, M. S. and March, J. G. (1981) Information in organisations as signal and symbol. *Administrative Science Quarterly* 26, 171–186.

Fildes, R. and Ranyard, J. (1997) Success and survival of operational research groups: a review. *Journal of the Operational Research Society* 48, 336–360.

Fildes, R., Ranyard, J. and Crymble, W. (1999) The management of OR groups: results of a survey. *Journal of the Operational Research Society* 50, 563–580.

Finkelstein (2005a) Editorial: logical and philosophical aspects of measurement. *Measurement* **38**, 257–258.

Finkelstein (2005b) Problems of measurement in soft systems. *Measurement* **38**, 267–274.

Finlay, P. and Wilson, J. (1987) The paucity of model validation in Operational Research projects. *Journal of the Operational Research Society* **38**, 303–308.

Flood, R. (1990) *Liberating Systems Theory*. New York: Plenum.

Flood, R. (1995) Total Systems Intervention (TSI): a reconstitution. *Journal of the Operational Research Society* **46**, 174–191.

Flood, R. and Jackson, M. (1991) *Creative Problem Solving: Total Systems Intervention*. Chichester, UK: John Wiley & Sons, Ltd.

Flowers, J. (2000) Wearing your clients' shoes. *OR Insight* **3**, 15–21.

Forder, R. A. (2004) Operational Research in the UK Ministry of Defence: an overview. *Journal of the Operational Research Society* **55**, 319–332.

Forder, R. A. (2007) Getting to the top: Engaging senior decision-makers with OR. OR Society Conference, Edinburgh, September 2007 (on keynote address CD). Birmingham, UK: OR Society.

Forrester, J. W. (1961) *Industrial Dynamics*. Cambridge, MA: MIT Press.

Forrester, J. and Senge, P. (1980) Tests for building confidence in system dynamics models. *TIMS Studies in the Management Sciences* **14**, 209–228.

Foucault, M. (1980) *Power/Knowledge*. Brighton: Harvester.

Fournier, V. and Grey, C. (2000) At the critical moment: conditions and prospects for critical management studies. *Human Relations* **53**, 7–32.

Fox, J. (1994) On the necessity of probability: reasons to believe and grounds for doubt. In: Wright, G. and Ayton, P. (eds), *Subjective Probability*, pp. 75–104. Chichester, UK: John Wiley & Sons, Ltd.

Fraser, N. and Hipel, K. (1984) *Conflict Analysis: Models and Resolutions*. New York: North-Holland.

Friend, J. K. and Hickling, A. (1997) *Planning Under Pressure: The Strategic Choice Approach*. Oxford: Butterworth-Heinemann.

Furnham, A. (1999) *The Psychology of Behaviour at Work: The Individual in the Organisation*. Hove, UK: Psychology Press.

Gabriel, Y. (2000) *Storytelling in Organisations: Facts, Fictions and Fantasies*. Oxford, UK: Oxford University Press.

Gass, S. (1987) Managing the modelling process: a personal reflection. *European Journal of Operational Research* **31**, 1–8.

Gass, S. (1990) Model world: danger, beware the user as modeler. *Interfaces* **20**, 60–64.

Gass, S. (1994) On ethics in operational research. *Journal of the Operational Research Society* **45**, 965–966.

Gass, S. and Harris, C. M. (1996) *Encyclopedia of Operations Research and Management Science*. New York: Kluwer Academic Publishers.

Geoffrion, A. (1992) Forces, trends and opportunities in MS/OR. *Operations Research* **40**, 423–445.

Gigerenzer, G., Todd, P. M. and ABC Research Group (2000) *Simple Heuristics That Make Us Smart*. New York: Oxford University Press.

Gillespie, R. (1991) *Manufacturing Knowledge: A History of the Hawthorne Experiments*. Cambridge, UK: Cambridge University Press.

Goodeve, C. and Ridley, G. (1953) A survey of OR in Great Britain. *Operational Research Quarterly* **4**, 21–24.

GORS (2008) Government Operational Research Service: Analysis that matters url: http://www.operational-research.gov.uk/recruitment/ (accessed: 2008).

Greenfield, D. (1996) OR overhaul. *OR/MS Today* **23**, 12–14.

Gregory, W. (1994) Critical appreciation: thinking, speaking and acting critically. In: Brady, P. P. L. (ed.), *New System Thinking and Action for a New Century*, Vol II, pp. 1555–1574. Louisville, Kentucky: International Society for the System Sciences (quoted in Midgley, 1995).

Guinness, O. (1973) *Dust of Death*. Nottingham, UK: Inter-Varsity Press.

Guitouni, A. and Martel, J.-C. (1998) Tentative guidelines to help choosing an appropriate MCDA method. *European Journal of Operational Research* **109**, 501–521.

Habermas (1972) *Knowledge and Human Interests*. London: Heinemann Educational Books.

Habermas, J. (1984) *The Theory of Communicative Action*, Vols I and II. Cambridge, UK: Polity Press.

Haré, R. and Secord, P. (1976) *The Explanation of Social Behaviour*. Oxford: Blackwell.

Hartley, A. (1989) In search of rationality: the purposes behind the use of formal analysis in organizations. *Administrative Science Quarterly* **34**, 598–631.

Heiss, J. (1981) *The Social Psychology of Interaction*. Englewood Cliffs, NJ: Prentice Hall.

Hesse, H. (2000) *The Glass Bead Game*. London: Vintage. Translated by R. and C. Winston.

Hipel, K., Kilgour, D., Fang, L. and Peng, X. (1997) The decision support system GMCR in environmental conflict management. *Applied Mathematics and Computation* **83**, 117–152.

Hodgson, D. (2002) Disciplining the professional: the case of project management. *Journal of Management Studies* **39**, 803–821.

Hodgson, D. (2004) Project work: the legacy of bureaucratic control in the post-bureaucratic organization. *Organization* **11**, 81–100.

Hofstede, G. (2001) *Culture's Consequences: Comparing Values, Behaviors, Institutions and Organizations Across Nations*. Thousand Oaks, CA: Sage.

Holder, R. D. and Gittins, R. P. (1989) The effects of warship and replenishment ship attrition on war arsenal requirements. *Journal of the Operational Research Society* **40**, 167–175.

Horner, P. (1991) Eyes on the prize. *OR/MS Today* **18**, 34–38.

Howard, N. (1971) *Paradoxes of Rationality*, Cambridge, MA: MIT Press.

Howick, S., Eden, C., Ackermann, F. and Williams, T. (2008) Building confidence in models for multiple audiences: the modelling cascade. *European Journal of Operational Research* **186**, 1068–1083.

Hussey, D. (1995) Competitor analysis: a case history. In: Hussey, D. (ed.), *Rethinking Strategic Management*. Chichester, UK: John Wiley & Sons, Ltd.

Hussey, D. (1998) The entry phase. In: Sadler, P. (ed.) *Management Consultancy*. London: Kogan Page.

Huxham, C. (2003) Action research as a methodology for theory development. *Policy and Politics* **31**, 239–248.

IFORS (2008) IFORS: International Federation of Operational Research Societies, url: http://www.ifors.org/ (accessed: 2008).

INFORMS (2006) "What Operations Research is", url: http://www.scienceofbetter. org/what/index.htm (accessed: 2006).

Institute of Management Consultants (1994) *Code of Professional Conduct*. London: Institute of Management Consultants.

International Organization for Standardization (1995) *Guide to the Expression of Uncertainty in Measurement*. Geneva: (1993, amended 1995) (published by ISO in the name of BIPM, IEC, IFCC, IUPAC, IUPAP and OIML).

In't Veld, J. and Peeters, J. (1989) Keeping large projects under control: the importance of contract type selection. *Project Management* **7**, 3, 155–162.

Ireland, P., Case, R., Fallis, J., van Dyke, C., Kuehn, J. and Meketon, M. (2004) The Canadian Pacific Railway transforms operations by using models to develop its operating plans. *Interfaces* **34**, 5–14.

Isenberg, D. (1991) How senior managers think. In: Henry, J. (ed.), *Creative Management*. Milton Keynes, UK: Open University Press.

Jackson, M. (1987) New directions in management science. In: Jackson, J. and Keys, P. (eds), *New Directions in Management Science*. Aldershot, UK: Gower.

Jackson, M. (1991) *Systems Methodology for the Management Sciences*. New York: Plenum Press.

Jackson, M. (1997) Pluralism in system thinking and practice. In: Mingers, J. and Gill, A. (eds), *Multi-Methodology: The Theory and Practice of Combining Management Science Methodologies*, pp. 347–378. Chichester, UK: John Wiley & Sons, Ltd.

Jackson, M. and Keys, P. (1984) Towards a system of system methodologies. *Journal of the Operational Research Society* **35**, 473–486.

Janis, I. (1973) *Victims of Groupthink*. Boston: Houghton Mifflin.

Johnson, G. and Scholes, K. (1993) *Exploring Corporate Culture*. Hemel Hempstead: Prentice Hall.

Johnson, P. and Duberley, J. (2000) *Understanding Management Research: An Introduction to Epistemology*. London: Sage.

Kahneman, D., Slovic, P. and Tversky, A. (1986) *Judgement Under Uncertainty: Heuristics and Biases*. Cambridge, UK: Cambridge University Press.

Kant, I. (2003) *Critique of Pure Reason*. Translated by N. K. Smith, Introduction by H. Caygill. New York: Palgrave.

Kaplan, R. and Norton, D. (2005) The balanced scorecard: measures that drive performance. *Harvard Business Review* **83** (July), 172–180.

Kapp, K. M. (2008) PowerPoint: What is appropriate, when and how? url: http://breeze.bloomu.edu/powerpointtips/ (accessed: 2008).

Keeney, R. (1993) Creativity in MS/OR: value-focused thinking – creativity directed toward decision making. *Interfaces* **23**, 62–67.

Keeney, R. (1996) Value-focused thinking: identifying decision opportunities and creating alternatives. *European Journal of Operational Research* **92**, 537–549.

Keeney, R. and Winterfeldt, D. (1989) On the uses of expert judgement on complex technical problems. *IEEE Transactions of Engineering Management* **36**, 83–86.

Kelly, G. (1955) *The Psychology of Personal Constructs*. New York: Norton.

Keys, P. (2000) Creativity, design and style in MS/OR. *Omega: the International Journal of Management Science* **28**, 303–312.

Kirby, M. (2002) *Operational Research in War and Peace: The British Experience from the 1930s to 1970*. London: Imperial College Press.

Kirby, M. and Capey, R. (1998) The origin and diffusion of operational research in the UK. *Journal of the Operational Research Society* **49**, 307–326.

Kleijnen, J. (2001) Ethical issues in modeling: some reflections. *European Journal of Operational Research* **130**, 223–230.

Klein, J. H., Connell, N. A. D. and Meyer, E. (2007) Operational research as storytelling. *Journal of the Operational Research Society* **48**, 1535–1542.

Kleinrock, L. (1975) *Queuing Systems*, Vol 1. New York: John Wiley & Sons, Inc.

Kleinrock, L. (1976) *Queuing Systems*, Vol 2. New York: John Wiley & Sons, Inc.

Koch, T. (2000) We live in a city, not in a study. *OR/MS Today* **27**, 16–17.

Kolb, D. (1984) *Experiential Learning: Experience as the Source of Learning and Development*. New Jersey: Prentice Hall.

Kotiadis, K. and Mingers, J. (2006) Combining PSMs with hard OR methods: the philosophical and practical challenges. *Journal of the Operational Research Society* **57**, 856–867.

Kowalczyk, R. (2004) The effectiveness of high-dependency care. In: Pidd, M. (ed.), *Systems Modelling: Theory and Practice*. Chichester, UK: John Wiley & Sons, Ltd.

Krantz, D., Luce, R., Suppes, P. and Tversky, A. (1971–1990) *Foundations of Measurement*, Vols 1–3. New York: Academic Press.

Kriger, M. and Barnes, L. (1992) Organisational decision making as hierarchical levels of drama. *Journal of Management Studies* **29**, 439–452.

Lallé, B. (2003) The Management Science researcher between theory and practice. *Organization Studies* **24**, 1097–1114.

Lane, D. (2000) Diagramming conventions in system dynamics. *Journal of the Operational Research Society* **51**, 241–245.

Langley, A. (1989) In search of rationality: the purposes behind the use of formal analysis in organisations. *Administrative Science Quarterly* **34**, 598–631.

Lathrop, J. (1957) Letter to the Editor: A Proposal for Merging ORSA and TIMS. *Operations Research* **5**, 123–125.

Le Menestrel, M. and van Wassenhove, L. (2004) Ethics outside, within, or beyond OR models? *European Journal of Operational Research* **153**, 477–484.

Lehaney, B. and Hlupic, V. (1995) Simulation modelling for resource allocation and planning in the health sector. *Journal of the Royal Society of Health* **115**, 382–385.

Likert, R. (1932) A technique for the measurement of attitudes. *Archives of Psychology* **140**, 55.

Linacre, J. (2002) Understanding Rasch measurement: optimizing rating scale category effectiveness. *Journal of Applied Measurement* **3**, 85–106.

Lindblom, C. (1959) The science of muddling through. *Public Administration Review* **19**, 79–88.

Locke, R. (1981) *Management and Higher Education since 1940: The Influence of America and Japan on West Germany, Great Britain and France.* Cambridge, UK: Cambridge University Press.

Lynch, P. (1998) Professionalism and ethics. In: Sadler, P. (ed.), *Management Consultancy*, pp. 60–80. London: Kogan Page.

Machol, R. (1982) The ORSA Guidelines Report – a retrospective. *Interfaces* **12**, 20–28.

Makridakis, S., Wheelwright, S. and Hyndman, R. (1998) *Forecasting.* John Wiley & Sons, Inc. (Wiley International Edition).

Mari, L. (2005) The problem of foundations of measurement. *Measurement* **38**, 259–266.

Marsh, B., Williams, T. and Mathieson, G. (1990) The use of mixed Prolog/Fortran for battle simulation. *Journal of the Operational Research Society* **41**, 311–318.

Marsick, V., Gephart, M. and Huber, J. (2003) Action research: building the capacity for learning and change. *Human Resource Planning* **26**, 13–18.

Mason, R. (1994) Morality and models. In: Wallace, W. (ed.) *Ethics in Modelling.* pp. 183–194. Oxford, UK: Elsevier Science Ltd.

Maylor, H. (2003) *Project Management.* London: FT-Prentice Hall.

McMillan, E. (2004) *Complexity, Organizations and Change.* London: Routledge.

Merkhover, M. (1987) Quantifying judgemental uncertainty: methodology, experiences and insights. *IEEE Transactions in Systems, Management and Cybernetics* **17**, 741–752.

Mezirow, J. (1981) A critical theory of adult leading and education. *Adult Education* **32**, 3–24.

Michell, J. (2005) The logic of measurement: a realist overview. *Measurement* **398**, 285–294.

Midgley, G. (1995) The nature of critical self-reflection. *Journal of the Operational Research Society* **46**, 547–552.

Midgley, G. (1997) Mixing methods: developing systemic intervention. In: Mingers, J. and Gill, A. (eds), *Multi-Methodology: The Theory and Practice of Combining*

Management Science Methodologies, pp. 249–290. Chichester, UK: John Wiley & Sons, Ltd.

Midgley, G. and Ochoa-Arias, A. (2004) *Community Operational Research: OR and Systems Thinking for Community Development*. New York: Kluwer Academic.

Mingers, J. (1992) Recent developments in critical management science. *Journal of the Operational Research Society* **43**, 1–10.

Mingers, J. (1997) Multi-paradigm multimethodology. In: Mingers, J. and Gill, A. (eds), *Multi-Methodology: The Theory and Practice of Combining Management Science Methodologies*, pp. 1–22. Chichester, UK: John Wiley & Sons, Ltd.

Mingers, J. (2000) Variety is the spice of life: combining soft and hard OR/MS methods. *International Transactions in Operational Research* **7**, 673–691.

Mingers, J. (2003) A classification of the philosophical assumptions of management science methods. *Journal of the Operational Research Society* **54**, 559–570.

Mingers, J. and Brocklesby, J. (1997) Multimethodology: for mixing towards a framework methodologies. *Omega: the International Journal of Management Science* **25**, 489–509.

Mingers, J. and Gill, A. (1997) *Multi-Methodology: The Theory and Practice of Combining Management Science Methodologies*. Chichester, UK: John Wiley & Sons, Ltd.

Mintzberg, H. (1973) *The Nature of Managerial Work*. New York: Harper Row.

Miser, H. (1998) What we learned early in the US Air Force about establishing and maintaining operational research groups. *Journal of the Operational Research Society* **49**, 336–346.

Mitchell, G. (1983) *The Practice of Operational Research*. Chichester, UK: John Wiley & Sons, Ltd.

Mitchell, G. (ed.) (1986) Report of the Commission on the Future Practice of Operational Research. *Journal of the Operational Research Society* **37**, 829–886.

Morgan, M. and Henrion, M. (1990) *Uncertainty: A Guide to Dealing with Uncertainty in Quantitative Risk and Policy Analysis*. Cambridge, UK: Cambridge University Press.

Mulligan, J. and Barber, P. (2001) The client–consultant relationship. In: Sadler, P. (ed.), *Management Consultancy*, 2nd edn. pp. 83–102. London: Kogan Page.

Munro, I. (1997) An exploration of three emancipatory themes within OR and system thinking. *Journal of the Operational Research Society* **48**, 576–584.

Munro, I. and Mingers, J. (2002) The use of multimethodology in practice – results of a survey of practitioners. *Journal of the Operational Research Society* **53**, 369–378.

Nash, J. (1950) Equilibrium points in N-Person Games. *Proceedings of the National Academy of Sciences* **36**, 48–49.

National Statistics (2007) Retail Prices Index: annual index numbers of retail prices 1948–2006 (RPI) (RPIX), url: http://www.statistics.gov.uk/StatBase/tsdataset.asp?vlnk=7172&More=N&All=Y (accessed: 2007).

Nonaka, I. and Takeuchi, H. (1995) *The Knowledge-Creating Company: How Japanese Companies Create the Dynamics of Innovation*. Oxford, UK: Oxford University Press.

Noorderhaven, N. (1995) *Strategic Decision Making.* Wokingham, UK: Addison Wesley.

Nutt, P. (1993) The formulation processes and tactics used in organisational decision making. *Organization Science* 4, 226–251.

Nutt, P. (1998) Decision makers evaluate alternatives and the influence of complexity. *Management Science* 44, 1148–1166.

Oakes, M. (1986) *Statistical Inference: A Commentary for the Social and Behavioural Sciences.* Chichester, UK: John Wiley & Sons, Ltd.

Operational Research Society (1996) Professional Membership: The proposals outlined. *OR Newsletter* (Operational Research Society, Birmingham, UK) May 1996, 22–23.

Ormerod, R. (1997) Mixing methods in practice: a transformation-competence perspective. In: Mingers, J. and Gill, A. (eds), *Multi-Methodology: The Theory and Practice of Combining Management Science Methodologies,* pp. 29–58. Chichester, UK: John Wiley & Sons, Ltd.

ORSA (1971) Guidelines for the practice of Operations Research. *Operations Research* 19, 1123–1137.

Palisade (2007a) @Risk for Excel, url: http://www.palisade.com/risk/ (accessed: 2007).

Palisade (2007b) @Risk for Project, url: http://www.palisade-europe.com/riskproject/ (accessed: 2007).

Pappis, C. (1995) OR in Europe: Facts about EURO member societies. *European Journal of Operational Research* 87, 424–429.

Park, H. J., Kim, J., Yi, K. S., and Jun, K. (1996) Proceedings of the 1996 Conference of the International System Dynamics Society, Boston, MA: International System Dynamics Society.

Parkinson, C. (1957) *Parkinson's Law and Other Studies in Administration.* New York: Random House Inc.

Pettigrew, A. (1977) Strategy formulation as a political process. *International Studies in Management and Organisation* 7, 78–87.

Phillips, L. (1984) A theory of requisite decision models. *Acta Psychologica* 56, 29–48.

Phrontis (2008) url: http://www.phrontis.com/ge.htm (accessed: 2008).

Pidd, M. (1995) Pictures from an exhibition: Images of OR/MS. *European Journal of Operational Research* 81, 479–488.

Pidd, M. (2001) The futures of OR. *Journal of the Operational Research Society* 52, 1181–1190.

Pidd, M. (2003) *Tools for Thinking: Modelling in Management Science,* 2nd edn. Chichester, UK: John Wiley & Sons, Ltd.

Pidd, M. (2004) *Systems Modelling: Thinking and Practice.* Chichester, UK: John Wiley & Sons, Ltd.

Polanyi, M. (1962) *The Tacit Dimension.* New York: Doubleday.

Pollecoff, M. (1998) Consultancy marketing strategies and tactics. In: Sadler, P. (ed.), *Management Consultancy.* London: Kogan Page.

Popper, K. (1959) *The Logic of Scientific Discovery*. London: Hutchinson.

Pugh, P. (1987) *Where does the time go? A review of development time scales for aircraft and guided weapons. Development Time Scales: Their Estimation and Control*. London: Royal Aeronautical Society.

Putnam, W. (1999) Transforming social practice: an action science perspective. *Management Learning* 30, 177–187.

QSR International Pty Ltd (2007) url: http://www.qsrinternational.com/ (accessed: 2007).

Raiffa, H. (1982) *Policy Analysis: A Checklist of Concerns*. Laxenburg, Austria: International Institute for Applied Systems Analysis.

Raimond, P. and Eden, C. (1990) Making strategy work. *International Journal of Strategic Management* 23, 97–105.

Ranyard, J. (1995) Supporting real decisions: a review of OR practice in the UK. *European Journal of Operational Research* 87, 474–482.

Ranyard, J. and Fildes, R. (1998) Winners and losers: adding organisational value. *Journal of the Operational Research Society* 49, 355–368.

Ranyard, J., Fildes, R. and Crymble, W. (1997) Death of an OR Group. *Journal of the Operational Research Society* 48, 361–372.

Rassam, C. (1998) The management consultancy industry. In: Sadler, P. (ed.), *Management Consultancy*. London: Kogan Page.

Reed, M. (1985) *Redirections in Organizational Analysis*. London: Sage.

Reynolds, M. (1998) Reflection and critical reflection in management learning. *Management Learning* 29, 183–200.

Richardson, B., Joscelyn, K. and Saalberg, J. (1979) *Limitations on the Use of Mathematical Models in Transportation Policy Analysis*, Ann Arbor, MI: UMI Research Press.

Rivett, P. (1994) *The Craft of Decision Making*. Chichester, UK: John Wiley & Sons, Ltd.

Robinson, S. (2003) *Simulation: The Practice of Model Development and Use*. Chichester, UK: John Wiley & Sons, Ltd.

Roethlisberger, F. and Dickson, W. (1939) *Management and the Worker*. Cambridge, MA: Harvard University Press.

Rosenhead, J. (1989) Operational Research at the crossroads: Cecil Gordon and the development of post-war OR. *Journal of the Operational Research Society* 40, 3–28.

Rosenhead, J. (1990) The dog that didn't bark: the unrealised social agenda of Operational Research. In: Bradley, H. (ed.), *Operational Research '90* (papers from the Twelfth IFORS International Conference on Operational Research, Athens, Greece, June 1990), pp. 11–21. Oxford, UK: Pergamon Press.

Rosenhead, J. (1998) Success and survival – a comment. *Journal of the Operational Research Society* 49, 408–412.

Rosenhead, J. (2001) Robustness analysis: keeping your options open. In: Rosenhead, J. and Mingers, J. (eds), *Rational Analysis in a Problematic World Revisited*, pp. 181–208. Chichester, UK: John Wiley & Sons, Ltd.

Rosenhead, J. and Mingers, J. (2001) *Rational Analysis for a Problematic World Revisited: Problem Structuring Methods for Complexity, Uncertainty and Conflict.* Chichester, UK: John Wiley & Sons, Ltd.

Rosenhead, J. and Thunhurst, C. (1982) A materialist analysis of Operational Research. *Journal of the Operational Research Society* 33, 111–122.

Rosenthal, R. and Jacobson, K. (1968) *Pygmalian in the Classroom: Teacher Expectation and Pupils' Intellectual Development.* New York: Irvington Publishers.

Ross, S. (2006) *Introduction to Probability Models.* New York: Academic Press.

Roth, G. and Senge, P. (1996) From theory to practice: research territory, processes and structure at an organizational learning centre. *Journal of Organizational Change Management* 9, 92–106.

Saaty, T. (1980) *The Analytic Hierarchy Process: Planning, Priority Setting, Resource Allocation.* New York: McGraw-Hill.

Saaty, T. (1994) *Fundamentals of Decision Making and Priority Theory with the Analytic Hierarchy Process.* Pittsburgh: RWS Publications.

Saaty, T. (1998) Reflections and projections on creativity in operations research and management science: a pressing need for a shift in paradigm. *Operations Research* 46, 9–16.

Sachdeva, R., Williams, T. and Quigley, J. (2007) Mixing methodologies to enhance implementation of healthcare operational research. *Journal of the Operational Research Society* 58, 159–167.

Salt, J. D. (2007) The seven habits of highly defective simulation projects. OR Society Conference, Edinburgh, September 2007 (on keynote address CD). Birmingham, UK: OR Society.

Saunders, C. and Jones, J. (1990) Temporal sequences in information acquisition for decision making: a focus on sources and medium. *Academy of Management Review* 15, 29–46.

Schnelle, E. (1979) *The Metaplan-Method: Communication Tools for Planning and Learning Groups.* Hamburg: Quickborn.

Schön, D. (1983) *The Reflective Practitioner: How Professionals Think in Action.* London: Maurice Temple Smith.

Schutz, A. and Luckmann, T. (1974) *The Structures of the Life World.* London: Heinemann.

Schwarz, M. (2003) A multilevel analysis of the strategic decision process and the evolution of shared beliefs. In: Chakravarthy, B., Guneter, M.-S., Lorange, P. and Lechner, C. (eds), *Strategy Process: Shaping the Countours of the Field*, pp. 110–136. Oxford: Blackwell Publishing.

Scott, J. (1990) OR methodology and the learning cycle. *Omega: the International Journal of Management Science* 18, 551–553.

Segars, A. (1997) Assessing the unidimensionality of measurement: a paradigm and illustration within the context of information systems research. *Omega: the International Journal of Management Science* 25, 107–121.

Senge, P., Ross, R., Smith, B., Roberts, C. and Kleiner, A. (1994) *The Fifth Discipline Fieldbook*. New York: Doubleday.

Shafer, G. (1976) *A Mathematical Theory of Evidence*. Princeton, NJ: Princeton University Press.

Shafer, G. (1994) The subjective aspects of probability. In: Wright, G. and Ayton, P. (eds), *Subjective Probability*, pp. 53–73. Chichester, UK: John Wiley & Sons, Ltd.

Silverman, D. (1970) *The Theory of Organisations*. London: Heinemann.

Simon, H. (1972) Theories of bounded rationality. In: McGuire, C. and Radner, R. (eds), *Decision and Organization*. Amsterdam: North-Holland.

Simon, H. (1982) *Sciences of the Artificial*, 2nd edn. Cambridge, MA: MIT Press.

Simon, H. (1991) Bounded rationality and organizational learning. *Organization Science* 2, 125–134.

Simon, H. (2001) Creativity in the arts and the sciences. *The Kenyon Review* 23, 203–220.

Simon, P., Hillson, D. and Newland, K. (1997) *PRAM: Project Risk Analysis and Management Guide*. Norwich, UK: APM Group Ltd.

Smith, B. C., Leimkuhler, J. F. and Darrow, R. (1992) Yield management at American airlines. *Interfaces* 22, 8–31.

Society for Modelling and Simulation International (2007) url: http://www.scs.org/ (accessed: 2007).

Spencer, T. and Graves, S. C. (2005) 2004 Franz Edelmann award for achievement in Operations Research and the Management Sciences. *Interfaces* 35, 2–6.

Spielberger, C. (1983) *Manual for the State-Trait Anxiety Inventory (STAI)*. Palo Alto, CA: Consulting Psychologists Press.

Stacey, R. (2001) *Complex Responsive Processes in Organizations. Learning and Knowledge Creation*. London: Routledge.

Stacey, R. (2003) *Complexity and Group Processes. A Radically Social Understanding of Individuals*. Hove, UK: Brunner-Routledge.

Starkey, K. and Madan, P. (2001) Bridging the relevance gap: aligning stakeholders in the future of management research. *British Journal of Management* 12, S3–S26.

Sterman, J. (1988) System dynamics and microworlds for policymakers. *European Journal of Operational Research* 35, 301–320.

Sterman, J. (1989) Modelling of managerial behavior: misperceptions of feedback in a dynamic decision making experiment. *Management Science* 35, 321–339.

Sterman, J. (1991) Skeptic's guide to computer models. Westview Press (obtainable from http://sysdyn.clexchange.org/sdep/Roadmaps/RM9/D-4101-1.pdf).

Sterman, J. (2000) *Business Dynamics: Systems Thinking and Modeling for a Complex World*. Chicago: Irwin/McGraw-Hill.

Stradspan (2006) url: http://www.btinternet.com/~stradspan/ (accessed: 2006).

Swart, J. (2006) Intellectual capital: disentangling an enigmatic concept. *Journal of Intellectual Capital* 7, 136–169.

Taket, A. (1994) Undercover agency? – ethics, responsibility and the practice of OR. *Journal of the Operational Research Society* 45, 123–132.

Tomlinson, R. (1998) The six principles for effective OR – their relevance in the 90s. *Journal of the Operational Research Society* **49**, 403–407.

Tonkin, C. (2002) *Consulting Mastery: The Ability Myth – When Being Good is Not Enough*. Newtown, NSW, Australia: Aragon Gray Pty Ltd.

Torrance, E. (1974) *Torrance Tests of Creative Thinking*. Lexington, MA: Personal Press/Ginn.

Tufte, E. (1990) *Envisioning Information*. Cheshire, CT, USA: Graphics Press.

Tufte, E. (2001) *The Visual Display of Quantitative Information*. Cheshire, CT, USA: Graphics Press.

Ulrich, W. (1983) *Critical Heuristics of Social Planning: A New Approach to Practical Philosophy*. Bern: Haupt. (Reprinted by John Wiley & Sons, Ltd, 1994.)

Ulrich, W. (1987) Critical heuristics of social systems design. *European Journal of Operational Research* **31**, 276–283.

Ulrich, W. (2000) Reflective practice in the civil society: the contribution of critically systemic thinking. *Reflective Practice* **1**, 247–268.

van der Heijden, K. (2005) *Scenarios: The Art of Strategic Conversations*. Chichester, UK: John Wiley & Sons, Ltd.

van der Heijden, K., Bradfield, R., Burt, G., Cairns, G. and Wright, G. (2002) *The Sixth Sense: Accelerating Organisational Learning*. Chichester, UK: John Wiley & Sons, Ltd.

Ventana Systems Inc. (2006) url: http://www.vensim.com (accessed: 2006).

von Bulow, I. (1989) The bounding of a problem situation and the concept of a system's boundary in soft systems methodology. *Journal of Applied Systems Analysis* **16**, 35–41.

von Neumann, J. and Morgenstern, O. (1944) *Theory of Games and Economic Behavior*. New York: John Wiley & Sons, Inc.

Wagner, H., Rothkopf, H., Thomas, C. and Miser, H. (1989) The next decade of OR: comments on the CONDOR report. *Operations Research* **37**, 664–672.

Wahlström, B. (1994) Models, modelling and modellers: an application to risk analysis. *European Journal of Operational Research* **75**, 477–487.

Walker, A., Kershaw, C. and Nicholas, S. (2006) Crime in England and Wales 2005/2006. Home Office Statistical Bulletin HOSB 12/06. London: Home Office.

Ward, S. (1989) Arguments for constructively simple models. *Journal of the Operational Research Society* **40**, 141–153.

Waters, D. (2003) *Inventory Control and Management*. Chichester, UK: John Wiley & Sons, Ltd.

Weick, K. (1985) The significance of corporate culture. In: Frost, P., Moore, L., Louis, M., Lundberg, C. and Martin, J. (eds), *Organizational Culture*, pp. 381–389. Beverley Hills: Sage.

Willemain, T. (1994) Insights on modelling from a dozen experts. *Operations Research* **42**, 213–222.

Willemain, T. (1995) Model formulation: what experts think about and when. *Operations Research* **43**, 916–932.

Williams, H. P. (1990) Model Building in Mathematical Programming. Chichester, UK: John Wiley & Sons.

Williams, T. (1999) Viewpoint more on case study papers. Journal of the Operational Research Society 50, 95–99.

Williams, T. (2000) The risk of safety regulation changes in transport development projects. International Journal of Project Management 18, 23–31.

Williams, T. (2003) The contribution of mathematical modelling to the practice of project management. IMA Journal of Management Mathematics 14, 3–30.

Williams, T. (2005) Assessing and building on project management theory in the light of badly over-run projects. IEEE Transactions in Engineering Management 54, 497–508.

Williams, T. (2007) Post-Project Reviews to Gain Effective Lessons Learned. Newtown Square, PA: Project Management Institute.

Williams, T., Ackermann, F. and Eden, C. (2003) Structuring a disruption and delay claim. European Journal of Operational Research 148, 192–204.

Williams, T., Ackermann, F., Eden, C. and Howick, S. (2005) Learning from project failure. In: Love, P., Irani, Z. and Fong, P. (eds), Knowledge Management in Project Environments. Oxford, UK: Elsevier/Butterworth-Heinemann.

Williams, T. and Dickson, K. (2000) Teaching real-life OR to MSc students. Journal of the Operational Research Society 51, 1440–1448.

Williams, T., Gittins, R. and Burke, D. (1989) Replenishment at sea. Journal of the Operational Research Society 40, 881–887.

Wilson, R. (1934) A scientific routine for stock control. Harvard Business Review 13, 116–128.

Wilson, T. (1971) Critique of ordinal variables. Social Forces 49, 432–444.

Winston, W. (2004) Operations Research: Applications and Algorithms. Belmont, CA: Brooks/Cole-Thomson Learning.

Woolsey, R. and Hewitt, R. (2003) The Woolsey Papers. Marietta, GA: Lionheart Publishing.

Wright, G. and Ayton, P. (1994) Subjective Probability. Chichester, UK: John Wiley & Sons, Ltd.

Yin, R. (1994) Case Study Research: Design and Methods. Thousand Oaks, CA: Sage.

Zdep, S. and Irvine, S. (1970) A reverse Hawthorne effect in educational evaluation. Journal of School Psychology 8, 89–95.

Zimmermann, H.-J. (2001) Fuzzy Set Theory and its Applications. Norwell, MA: Kluwer Academic Publishers.

Index

Note: Page numbers in *italics* refer to Figures.